CRIES OF HEARTBREAK AND HOPE FROM THE THOUSANDS OF LETTERS TO MELISSA SANDS

"I cut off all my friends that might disapprove..."
—*San Jose, California*

"It's funny, I am very much a feminist and this relationship contradicts every belief I have. Here I am stuck in this affair with a married man..."
—*Nashville, Tennessee*

"I am a religious person and I know the wrong of what we are doing."
—*Buda, Texas*

"I wouldn't ask him to get a divorce. I've been there and I know how hard it is..."
—*Costa Mesa, California*

"It's not a dependence but a deep love for someone who's right in my life, no matter how wrong I know it is..."
—*North Miami Beach, Florida*

"My married man wouldn't hear of me dating anyone else. He said that would be it."
—*Boston, Massachusetts*

"I didn't want to end the affair. I hated what you were telling me in THE MISTRESS' SURVIVAL MANUAL. I sat and read the book until the truths would become so unbearable that I'd want to throw it out..."
—*Eugene, Oregon*

Berkley books by Melissa Sands

THE MAKING OF THE AMERICAN MISTRESS
THE MISTRESS' SURVIVAL MANUAL

MELISSA SANDS
The Making of the American Mistress

BERKLEY BOOKS, NEW YORK

THE MAKING OF THE
AMERICAN MISTRESS

A Berkley Book / published by arrangement with
the author

PRINTING HISTORY
Berkley edition / April 1981

All rights reserved.
Copyright © 1981 by Melissa Sands.
This book may not be reproduced in whole or in part,
by mimeograph or any other means, without permission.
For information address: Berkley Publishing Corporation,
200 Madison Avenue, New York, New York 10016.

ISBN: 0-425-04751-2

A BERKLEY BOOK® TM 757,375

PRINTED IN THE UNITED STATES OF AMERICA

Acknowledgments

I cannot adequately express my gratitude to the thousands of women who have written and participated in this study. I sincerely hope my efforts have helped in some measure.

Special thanks to Roslyn Targ for her steadfast faith in me and for always doing more than is necessary with regard to all our projects.

I want to thank Rena Wolner, my publisher, for her commitment to this important issue that touches the lives of so many women. I am sincerely grateful to Linda Healey, my editor, for her subtle suggestions and easy manner and acute judgments. Her assets make our professional relationship a pleasure.

I must not finish my thank yous without adding an enormous debt of gratitude to Michael, my husband. He is a first rate editor as well as my inspiration and in no small way responsible for all my work.

Dedication

You are not alone
You are not the only one
Really going nowhere
Cause you picked a married one,
>And you're waiting for that Someday
>You've been waiting more than one day
>With that married man on your mind.

He has just gone home
You are still the lonely one
Tried to talk it over
Once again he had to run,
>And you're so afraid of losing
>But just look what you've been choosing
>That married man on your mind.

It will take time but they'll see
There's more than a mistress in me
It will take time but they'll see
There's more than a mistress in me.

Where do you belong?
Not in this sorority,
Where did you go wrong?
Was it your priorities.
>He's the first thing in the morning
>And the last thing in the evening
>That married man on your mind.

It will take time but they'll see
There's more than a mistress in me.
It will take time but they'll see
There's more than a mistress in me.

By Michael and Melissa Sands

Table of Contents

An Introduction   1

PART I   THE SHAPING OF THE AMERICAN MISTRESS

1. Passion in the Paycheck:
   Work and the Mistress   9
2. Strange Bedfellow:
   Morality, Sex, and the Mistress   32
3. Opposites Attract:
   Feminism and the Mistress   51
4. A Complex vs. A Complex Phase:
   Psychology and the Mistress   65

PART II   THE PROFILE OF THE AMERICAN MISTRESS

5. Living Single, Loving Alone:
   The Single Mistress   81
6. Passionate License:
   The Married Mistress   100
7. Jaded Lady:
   The Divorcée as Mistress   120
8. The Young, the Old, and the Tradition   137
9. Title, Position, and Fringe Benefits:
   Career and the Mistress   154

PART III THE MARRIED MAN/THE MAN IN THE MIDDLE

10.	THE TRIANGLE PAPERS	173
11.	THE MOMENT OF TRUTH: MARRIAGE AND THE BEDROOM	189
12.	OF TRIANGLES AND TRAPEZOIDS	198

PART IV OLD WIVES' TALES

13.	THE CONTENDERS	225
14.	THE TRIANGLE CONSPIRACY	242

PART V THE CHILDREN OF AFFAIRS

15.	DO MISTRESSING AND MOTHERING MIX?	261
16.	SOMEDAY'S CHILD	265
17.	THE UNMAKING OF THE AMERICAN PARENT	279
	EPILOGUE	297
	APPENDIX—MISTRESSES ANONYMOUS QUESTIONNAIRE	299

Table of Tests

Will a Married Man Edit Your Résumé?	27
Has the Revolution Recruited You?	43
Are You a Feminist/Chauvinist?	62
The Mistress' Maze	94
The Passion Factor	112
To Divorce or Not to Divorce	116
Was There a Mistress in Your Marriage?	129
Are You Mistress Material?	133
Are You Cut Out to Be a Career Mistress?	165
The Confessions of Your Married Man	210
What Keeps Your Man Married?	215
The Right to Spite	218
Is There a Love Affair in Your Marriage?	236
How High Is Your Adultery Quotient?	255
Do Mistressing and Mothering Mix?	262

The Making of the American Mistress

AN INTRODUCTION

The Making of the American Mistress

I became a celebrity because I was a pariah. The particular brand of pariah? A mistress. I cannot introduce you to this book without telling you a little about my past. Because although this book is about the phenomenon of mistresses in America, it all really began right in my own backyard.

At the age of twenty-six, I was single, ambitious, independent, college-educated, fairly attractive, and madly in love with a married man. I was on a roller coaster, in a waiting game, on standby, and alone. The worst thing of all was that there was no one to discuss all this with, except a boardwalk fortune teller or another mistress. So I found several other mistresses and began a consciousness-raising group called Mistresses Anonymous. There we could meet and help one another.

One day I heard of a suicide where the victim was apparently distressed because of a married man. Mistressing for this young woman was a fatal experience! I decided that if she had known of our Mistresses Anonymous meetings, perhaps she would not have felt so desperate. So I told a local newspaper about Mistresses Anonymous. When the piece appeared in the newspaper and was syndicated, suddenly my telephone went wild.

Television producers, especially Patricia McMillen of the *Donahue Show*, told me that I should publicize my group. Apparently Mistresses Anonymous could reach thousands, and thousands could relate to it. Reluctantly I appeared on nationwide television and publicly admitted I was a mistress. I told the audience about Mistresses Anonymous. And in telling it all over and over on show after show, I became a celebrity.

I was a pariah. I was violating a taboo. Having an affair was a scandal. Secrecy was a rule I was breaking. I was illuminating the stigma of being a mistress, my stigma for all to see. Why??? I was beginning to realize that isolation was the worst thing for a mistress. In any triangle it is always the mistress who is the outcast. That is unfair, unhealthy for the mistress and for society in general.

In becoming a pariah I lost my job, but I found a new career. Not in writing, because I had always been writing, but in researching mistresses. You see, while I was talking about the experiences of the mistresses in Mistresses Anonymous, literally thousands of mistresses all across America were sitting down and writing to me about their own stories. In a few short weeks women from every state wanted to join Mistresses Anonymous. Not being able to clone myself and run all these groups, I sat down and wrote the Mistresses Anonymous program out in book form. The result was *The Mistress' Survival Manual* (Berkley Books, 1979), how to give up or marry that married man.

Since the very first time I appeared on television I have been deluged with mail from women who are hooked on married men. In hearing from and getting to know so many mistresses, I found I became committed to them and their struggle just as I was to my own mistress struggle. *The Mistress' Survival Manual* answered questions and yet at the same time it raised more. And it engendered a new deluge of corresponding mistresses, especially because I included a questionnaire for the mistress.

In *The Mistress' Survival Manual* I dealt with the life of a mistress and her future. But the fundamental question of *why* was there in my own mind, and in the mind of every woman who found herself building her life around a married man while he built his life around his family. Why did I—does anyone—become a mistress? Surely no one seeks the role of a pariah.

I recognized a need to address the question of why, especially when I realized just how many hundreds of thousands of mistresses there were. Mistresses need to understand what led them into the arms of a married man.

Society needs to know all it can about the making of the American mistress. Triangles are as indiscriminate as love and passion. As you encounter in the following pages the phenomenon of mistresses in America you will see friends, family members, and possibly your future or the future of your daughter or your mother.

It's odd to realize that no one before me has seriously looked at the mistress. After all, she is one-third of the adultery story in any marriage. Reams have been written about marital infidelity, and yet about the mistress virtually nothing has been known. Her side of the story has always been taboo.

I don't advocate mistressing per se, mainly because of the toll it often takes on the mistress herself. All morality aside, it is humanism that we need in considering the mistress. I advocate looking at her in the triangle context with understanding and curiosity. She is part of society—and a rather large part.

Throughout the pages of this book you will meet the mistresses themselves and hear what they have to say. You will see some stunning findings on how women become mistresses. You will also find controversy, because my hypotheses have proved to be true, and they falsify the stereotypes.

To give you a glimpse, in the first part I have focused on some forces that shape women into mistresses. Working has given women a new identity and a new salary. For many it has also lead to mistressing. The seventies have left us spinning in an age of moral relativity. The mistress and morality are strange bedfellows, but bedfellows, nevertheless, owing to the sexual revolution. The upper tiers of the feminist community have shunned mistresses. Perhaps they felt mistressing and feminism were incongruous. However, the opposite is true. Feminists make good mistresses. Finally we'll take on the psychological community. Is mistressing as complex as has been supposed? How has the psychological community failed the mistress?

In the second part, we will meet various segments of the mistress community themselves. There are the single mistresses, who live and love alone owing to their priorities. There are the married mistresses with one too many husbands in their lives. There are the divorcées who make excellent mistress material. You'll meet the teen queens of triangles and the grandmother mistress who crochets dreams of her married man like any other mistress. You will see how parents are rearing their children to become mistresses without being aware of the mistress tradition they are passing on. Is mistressing a career, a destiny? Where do Freudian paradigms stop and where does the reality of loving a married man begin?

In the third part, we will look at the married man in the middle. What is the nature of this beast? What is he looking for in an affair with his mistress? Is he hungrily seeking the sex he's missing at home? Or is there a new double standard emerging, one of confidentiality? Married men labor within trapezoids as well as within triangles. They are beset with two sets of needs, two magnets, and one terrifying sense of indecision. What really goes on in the mind of the married man, in the rendezvous, and with his mistress?

In the fourth part, we will give the wife her due. Is the wife the martyr she is usually cast to be? Is she a co-conspirator in her own triangle? Is there a battle of the ages between wife and mistress or is the nature of the war more like a conspiracy? Wives have power in a triangle, why is it that so few dare use it?

In the fifth and final part, we will look at the children of affairs. How is your affair affecting your child? Some children get lost in triangles; some children get forfeited in triangles. Some lose something very precious: their own fathers. Some children find life because of a union between the mistress and the married man. What does the concept of "Someday" do to "Someday's child"?

Each chapter will shed some light on the making of the American mistress. If you are not a mistress, it will broaden your grasp of the mistress' experience. If you are a mistress, it will perhaps shed some light on how you got there. There are lots of new tests for all three members of the triangle—the mistress, the wife, and the man in the middle. People who get themselves into affairs quickly acquire a "past." This book will give them a key to understanding that past, and perhaps unlock doors to a new future. Every woman who is now in love with a married man can be more than a mistress if she so desires. Knowledge and understanding are valuable to any mistress, and to society as a whole. We can never learn enough about human relationships!

Once as a mistress and a pariah I learned a new perspective. Talking about it on *Donahue* first got me banned in Springfield, Massachusetts. However, in the long run becoming a social outcast has given me the insight and ability to cast out myths, misconceptions, and misogyny tailored for mistresses. The making of the American mistress is not a tale about a sensuous breed of beauties. It is a documentary about women and men in the eighties. It is a subject that will touch each and every one of you in some way at some time in your lives. None of us are immune to love and passion, and triangles are often within the strains of that romance.

Divorce was once a taboo subject, too. Until society realized that silencing the issue only made it more grueling. Once the phenomenon was faced head-on, some of the mystique and the misfortune faded. The subject of the mistress and the triangle will follow the same course, I believe. Exposing the mistress mystique is better for everyone. Life can change American dreamers into pariahs overnight. I know because it happened to me.

PART ONE

The Shaping of the American Mistress

Part One

The Eclipse of the
American Heiress

CHAPTER 1

Passion in the Paycheck: Work and the Mistress

"I am a working woman. As I drive to work every morning I always get stuck waiting for the traffic light at DeMott Avenue. DeMott Avenue is exactly halfway between my home and my job. It's become a cutoff point for me. Before I reach DeMott Avenue I belong to my husband. Once I pass DeMott I belong to my boss. 'Belong' may sound old-fashioned to you, but that's how I feel. How can I claim to be old-fashioned when I'm juggling all these roles; working and raising kids, being a wife and a mistress? I have no answer. I'm as confused as you are. And now my confusion is even interfering with my boundary treaty at DeMott. DeMott Avenue isn't dividing my double life as neatly as it did three years ago, when all this started.

"I'll try to start at the beginning and be more clear. I can't expect you to understand my mumbo jumbo. My passion, guilt, etc., are like my staff. We have running silent dialogues all day long whether I'm reading a report or making rice pudding.

"I'm thirty-eight years old. I've been married thirteen years. I have two children ages eight and ten. My marriage has its problems, but they're typical in these times, I guess. I don't really want a divorce. I love my new job. I love my boss. The two are interchangeable, I've come to realize that. I love my husband, too. The only thing I'm not sure of is how I feel about myself. I'm not sure I like what I'm doing, but I can't stop now.

"What am I doing? I'm having an affair with my boss. It's not just a physical thing either. Sometimes I wish it was that easy to understand. At the beginning we decided to be mature and rational about the whole thing. I never bargained for all the irrational passions I've felt—not to mention the other emotions like guilt. Well, I've been working here for nearly four years. The instant the personnel director introduced me to my boss we saw the magnetic sparks light up the field around us. We both ignored the chemistry for awhile. But in time it got to be too much.

"We worked well together. Jerry, my boss, delegated more and more responsibility to me. He treated me like an equal. He was in charge of a company productivity study. The assignment was quite a feather in his cap. Being a part of it was a feather in mine. I had transcended the impossible secretarial limits. Jerry respected my talents and my capabilities. The productivity report was lauded on the executive level. Jerry officially commended me. In the commendation was the consummation of our affair. The next day I made that treaty with DeMott Avenue.

"My new job did wonders for me, if not for my marriage. My husband didn't really want a working wife. You know, all that 'my wife shouldn't have to work' stuff. Double-digit inflation raised his consciousness if ever so unwillingly. If my husband knew, he'd blame it on the job. He'd probably be right. I never thought of having an affair before I started working. Life was simpler then but not better.

"Now when I cross the DeMott Avenue boundary, I wonder how many times I've violated that old rule about not mixing business and pleasure. It seems like a century ago that I used to wait for that light with a clear head. Now the traffic light changes from red to green and I change from wife to mistress. Things were so black and white before red and green began trafficking my emotions.

"I live in a two-paycheck marriage. I'm torn between two men. Should I quit my job or quit my husband? I just don't know what to do."

This De Mott Avenue wife/mistress is one of approximately 42 million working women. Going to work dramatically changed her life. She seems confused about many of the changes. However, she was right on target making a connection between her new working status and her affair with a married man. Working is a significant factor in the making of the American mistress. Perhaps passion in the paycheck is the most significant factor.

In the mistress community working is standard: 85% of all mistresses turned out to be working women. Only 10% of the mistresses my research covered did not work outside the home. About 5% were students, some of them working and others not. Nearly 50% of all the mistresses told me that their affair with a married man started on the job.

The high correlation between the trend of women going to work outside the home and the trend of having an affair with a married man is not mere coincidence. Working has a tremendous impact. Working seems to be a definite catalyst for affairs. Working leads to the makings of thousands of mistresses at least. As working women aspire to new heights of success, they still carry the old weights of chemistry and biology. There is a new respect for women and their capabilities in the working world, and yet an old attraction for their womanhood. Working has provided new challenges for women and new conflicts, temptations, and responsibilities.

There are many ways in which working influences affairs and triangles. I'm going to let the mistresses themselves describe the catalytic elements. You will see the impact of work environments. You will see the pull of camaraderie. Whether a job is hectic or monotonous is irrelevant. Each type of job triggers chemical pressure. Not mixing business and pleasure is an old rule seemingly made to be broken, like so many other rules. What are the effects of an on-the-job training program in romance? Do orange blossoms and valentines affect the ladder of success? As feminism changes the face of the labor force, how are things different?

Danger—Yours, Mine, and Ours

Dale described her hometown as a boomtown, population 20,000 and growing as fast as any town in southeastern Wyoming. Dale was dissatisfied with the career she chose back in college, so she learned a new one. At thirty years of age Dale works as a security guard in a mine. Because of the danger implicit in the job, she has medical training. Unfortunately she was not trained for the dangers of married men.

"In our job the two security guards have to work together in case of emergency. It's the kind of job where you have to trust and respect each other because of the danger. We're trained as an emergency team using air packs in case there is an explosion or fire so the inherent danger increased the trust between us."

The "us" Dale is talking about is her partner at the mine, Jim. He is thirty-two years old and married.

"We worked shifts and at night we were isolated from other people so we got to know each other's souls rather well. However, there was a matter of chemistry as well. We were friends first. The sexual attraction grew gradually. He says he saw me as sexually attractive immediately, before I saw that quality in him. Although I was attracted to him from the first day, I knew he was married and I shied away from him until we began working together so closely. Working together, we tried not to read each other emotionally or touch each other. Our willpower wasn't strong enough when we worked together alone every day and at night."

Dale said that she didn't choose to date a married man at all. The way she put it was, "My feelings overran my brain and I thought I was in love."

Jim has been cooling it lately because he's afraid of the danger of being found out. Dale thinks he'll never get a divorce because he believes in the family plus he loves his children.

"I soon came to hate the sneaking around, the excuses why he couldn't see me, and I hated keeping up a façade at work. I wanted to hug him and kiss him whenever I saw him. I hated having to be careful about how and what we said at work. Luckily I have friends and I'm very busy doing some volunteer work. Too busy to become a hermit, which is good. I hunt, fish, and look for arrowheads and travel when I have a chance (five days off after graveyard shifts). I own a home and have a dog, but nothing keeps back all the hurt and disappointment that I can't have my lover all the time."

Currently Dale is looking for the strength to get out of this affair. It's difficult when they work together and she loves her job and doesn't want to give it up.

"I truly hope I can get out of this affair and I hope I have learned what not to do when it comes to married men."

Dale's affair was a type of mining disaster that no one ever trained her for. Now she has the training and will be more vigilant.

The theme of chemistry and biology was just as much a part of this story as geology. Had they not been a team in an isolated mining job, this affair between Dale and Jim probably never would have happened. Dale didn't strike me as a starry-eyed romantic; the work situation created the romantics.

Co-worker appeal and environmental influence doesn't necessarily need danger and isolation to explode into a triangle. Take Melanie's experience:

Stocks and Bonds

Melanie said she felt cheated because her married man was married when they met. "The best men are already taken."

Melanie was a stockbroker. Her married man was a stockbroker too. They worked in the same office. She was thirty-six years old and single. He was forty-one.

"He was the first man of any marital status I had met in four years who came from a background similar to mine, who appealed to me almost immediately, and who appeared to be sensitive and realistic."

For Melanie all those assumptions proved to be true as they got to know each other better every day at work. They lunched together daily, and Melanie became confidante and consoler. It seemed that his wife had left him several times. During one of those separations their affair began.

Melanie knew it was a risk, but after all, risks were her business. He was a wonderful man. His wife must have been crazy not to realize that. The affair, which has been going on for two years now, has its ups and downs.

"I care for him as much as I care for myself. I can relax and be myself with him. That was a true luxury, not worrying about putting up a front. But having finally met someone who 'on paper' seemed to be what I had decided was what I wanted I resented his marriage. I resented the fact that his wife was so ambivalent towards him. I like his older boy, but I dislike the baby, a product of a short-lived reconciliation that I knew about. He told his wife about us. Her reaction was, 'If you want him you can have him.' I wish it were that easy for me but it's not. He doesn't really want me. He says sincerely that he wants to get back with his wife."

Melanie knows her relationship is like an investment of sorts. She's gambling on her married man, realizing that she is the one for him and not his ambivalent wife. It is for her the gamble of a lifetime. But when she takes stock of her life and her accomplishments and her failures, it's a sound investment.

"I've grown enormously in this relationship. I will never regret the experience no matter how it turns out."

It's hard to say how it is going to turn out. At the end of every working day Melanie's and her married man's lives look like the floor of the New York Stock Exchange. All their dreams, mutual bonds, investments and hopes are in pieces like the debris after a hectic day of trading. They are each taking stock of their lives, but the future of their affair is as unpredictable as any form of security.

As feminism places women in more diversified jobs and higher up on the personnel ladders, co-worker attractions become more numerous than secretary-boss stereotypical affairs. However, that is not to say that boss appeal has lost any of its potency. Boss appeal was a factor in our introductory profile about the DeMott Avenue mistress. This next story expresses it more obviously.

Covering All the Angles

Paula joined the ranks of the working women after her divorce. She liked the change, actually. She did well as a salesperson and was in time promoted to store manager of a floor covering firm. She had known her boss, Mel, the owner of the company for a long time before the affair began.

"Our first encounter was not a real date. An out-of-town business trip with others from our office put us together in a different background after being around each other in a business capacity for several years. I was already in love with him, though. I just had no idea the attraction was two-way until the trip."

Mel had always apparently been a sort of inspiration for Paula.

"I admired the way he handled people. He could make anyone and everyone feel comfortable—from the stock personnel right on up. I tried to imitate his friendliness. But for a female sometimes that friendliness was misinterpreted, so it was touchy ground. Being divorced, I was leary of men. Our relationship didn't just happen as far as I was concerned. I had fantasized about seeing him outside the office, but I never dreamed my fantasy would come true. He was the owner of the company and I was just one of many managers. I didn't premeditate our affair, not in reality, but it couldn't have turned out better even if I had."

Mostly their affair consisted of meetings at work, stolen moments of conversation, and occasionally an evening together. Paula was twenty-eight and Mel was forty, and sometimes Paula wondered if she would have found him as attractive at a singles bar as she found him behind his desk.

"I've been seeing him for three years, three months, and still counting. I know it is going to end sometime because he has no intention of ever getting divorced. Ours is not a relationship with a future. We live in the present tense. But it provides me with a wonderful social life even if it is limited. I love my job even more now that I have my boss in this way. Socially he has introduced me to activities and made me more conscious of the 'upper' social side of life. I look forward to the few business trips we have with relish and delight. I have developed good relationships with people who associate with him and/or sympathize with our situation. Emotionally now I'm not as stable, unfortunately, but one can't have everything. I love the romance of having an affair. And having my boss as my lover has done a lot for my self-esteem. It's great to know someone of that stature enjoys my company enough to take the risks that he takes."

Paula is in a way meeting many needs all rolled into one. She is earning her living, building a career, satisfying her romance quota and her need for affection; mixing business and pleasure adequately for her own desires. She's covering all the angles with her triangle.

Paula intuitively touched upon the appeal of her boss when she wondered about his appeal without the office in the picture. In all likelihood she wouldn't find the man as attractive without the embellishments of power.

Bosses are not like ordinary men. A boss transcends his appeal as a man by virtue of his position and his power. Position and power are a part of his work role and part of his total personality from the perspective of the employee. Power has been an aphrodisiac since the beginning of time. Loving and being loved by a powerful man was a way for women to attain power themselves. In the past that was chiefly the way for women, this power by association. It was as if becoming a doctor's wife or a judge's wife was a career accomplishment. The same principle applies to becoming the boss's mistress. Of course nowadays this is far from the only road to achievement for women, but the trend still exists. Ego-gratification by association was a factor in Paula's affair. It is an ego-boost to be considered "worthy" by the president of the company. All feminist or intellectual judgments aside, boss appeal is still a potent factor in the making of mistresses.

Another good example of boss appeal came from a mistress who seemed aware of how it was affecting her relationship.

"I've never felt this way about a man before. I work for him. I think perhaps most of this may be due to my hero fixation that subconsciously I have had for him since the first year I went to work for him. He's much older than I. He's in charge of fifty people in the office and a lot of the company's most touchy problems. He was a challenge for me, I guess. But once I got into this [affair] I realized that I couldn't keep up, hold up, or get out." *(administrative assistant, St. Louis, Missouri)*

What is it that bridges the gap between the top-echelon management type and the classic clerical employee? What is it that intensifies the bonds between co-workers? Chemistry as a basic human drive is only one element in the answer. The working world provides a framework that fosters professional validation, camaraderie; new emerging trends. It also provides good old-fashioned temptation, distraction from boredom, and a convenient avenue for double living.

What is professional validation? Professional validation is the reflection a worker looks for in fellow employees or superiors that is saying, "Good work." Professional validation is nothing new for men, since they have long been accustomed to looking for a sense of accomplishment through their job. However, it is a new area for women. Women who work are often adding a new dimension to their lives. They are reaching for a new sense of accomplishment through work. They are trying to develop a working role and a working self-image. Much of our self-image develops from the reflections we see of ourselves in others. Working women look for a new competent view of themselves in their co-workers. Oftentimes their husbands, if they are married, are ambivalent about their wives' winning approval and a separate identity outside their marriage and home. If the woman is single or divorced, she has only her co-workers to look to for her sense of working competence. We are all attracted to someone who has a good image of us. In the working environment that means someone who sees us as doing a good job, using our capabilities, and developing our potential. In affairs between married men and mistresses, professional validation plays a significant role, sort of like a mutual admiration society.

Interpersonal and Highly Personal Relationships

Jan was one of the new breed of career women in the field of insurance. Her career blossomed through her twenties in spite of a bad marriage and a good divorce. Jan was a personnel manager in charge of training new employees. It was sort of a lower management position in comparison to the executives in the company, but it was management. Part of Jan's job was to be a liaison between the executives and their expectations and the new personnel and their goals. Her training program had to inculcate the company's expectations into the new employees. Jan traveled frequently and had standard meetings with top management to keep up with company developments.

In the recent past Jan had become friendly with one of the vice-presidents. He was especially impressed with a new group of employees, and traced their excellent attitudes and job performance to Jan's training program. He wrote an official letter on the fine job Jan was doing and had it read at an executive session. Afterward they went out to lunch. His professional esteem for Jan was sincere. When they encountered each other several months later out of town, they began dating. His being married seemed irrelevant.

"Our relationship began innocuously, with no pressure from either of us. It was on mutual ground because of our business association and camaraderie. Ken appreciated my business acumen and respected my independence and professionalism. I've found since my divorce that single men tend to exert a primarily sexual pressure, married men seem to appreciate a woman as a total entity, a total human being. I was attracted to Ken because we related on an equal basis to each other. Our work enhanced our friendship. Our affair, on the other hand, wouldn't necessarily enhance our file unless we were discreet."

Because Jan was involved and in love with a married man she became sensitive to interpersonal conflicts between working men and women. Interpersonal relationships could easily become highly personal relationships. Women should know how to juggle this possibility without jeopardizing their jobs. The face of each new training class had more of a gender mix every time. Business etiquette had to change to accommodate the new business population. Her training seminars had to update current company policy and address the new conflicts that change always brings with it.

"I spent a lot of time discussing the idea of having a special seminar on gender interpersonal etiquette and dangers. Women trainees needed to know how to be professional and businesslike at the same time without sacrificing femininity. And they had to be made aware of the potential of chemistry and the ramifications. Ken joked about how I was really cut out for this assignment. But seriously he thought my idea was ingenious, innovative, and worthwhile. It was his reassurance that finally made me sit down and develop the seminar outline for *Etiquette, Chemistry and Company Policy.* It got me a great raise, but the money wasn't nearly as important as the esteem I acquired. Ken was not exactly a mentor to me, but without his support I wouldn't be the career woman I am now. I only wish that mistress etiquette could be as flexible as business etiquette. There's so little room for advancement in that part of my life."

Jan's story shows how the pat on the back can progress into a more passionate embrace for a job well done. A paycheck with a raise in salary is even greater with a little passion thrown into it. Being a company liaison in more ways than one gave Jan unique opportunities, perceptions, and conflicts. The job was highly influential in her life and her self-image and her relationship. Professional validation was at the heart of Ken's appeal.

Not all jobs come equipped with challenges and interesting opportunities. Most people don't thrive on the excitement generated by their profession. Many people work because they have to pay the bills; they don't "love" their jobs. Jobs can be boring and monotonous year in and out, day in and out. And in the face of that monotony, some employees look for something to distract them from their desk. Boredom is a great catalyst for affairs.

More Than Civil Service

Helen didn't want a job any more than her husband wanted her to go to work. They needed the money and that was that. Bickering over money had taken a toll on their marriage. Going to work couldn't do more damage, or could it? Helen was a housewife and mother and hadn't cultivated any skills other than the ones she needed to master those two demanding roles. She got a job as a file clerk at City Hall. She became a mistress to a fellow worker after ten months of working around him. Why?

"He has changed my life in the short time I've known him. He has made it easier to get up in the morning and go to work, because I know I will be able to smile and say hi in the parking lot at nine o'clock. During the day I can sit at my desk and see his police car from my window and watch him come and go out occasionally on calls during the day. At night, if I have to work late and it is dark when I leave, he will turn on the light on top of his patrol car for a second to say goodbye to me. If I'm exceptionally bored during work, I can go downstairs by his desk and talk for a few seconds. Phone calls are taped in the Police Dept., so I can't talk really on the telephone. On days that I know he's off, I try to keep busy by shopping or whatever. His love for me makes me feel desireable again and brand new. What my husband doesn't know won't hurt him."

Helen's affair ended before her husband ever found out about it. It seemed that her man in uniform didn't value fidelity to his mistress any more than he valued it to his wife.

"I had heard rumors going around from the other secretaries that he had gotten another girl pregnant. I did not know him at the time, but it shook me up. Then there were jokes about the young girl in the coffee shop across the street. I caught him in the parking lot when I was in tears to discuss these rumors. He joked about it. I didn't see it being funny. It made me think we were a dirty joke, too. I stopped seeing him except through my window at work."

Bureaucratic jobs breed boredom. Municipal monotony is an epidemic that can infect workers from coast to coast. A chemical reaction sparks up the office routine. It makes the day's pace change from a drag to a soap opera. Affairs can be the way to beat the daily grind of the rat race. They are the ultimate distraction for the mistress who works.

Helen's affair was short-lived, less than a year. I have found that most affairs last three years, eight years, or eleven years. I'm not exactly sure why those durations keep reoccurring, but they do. Perhaps it's chance or some cycle of tolerance or appeal. Duration is still a frontier, so to speak, to me. However, a significant fact in the duration issue is the job. Not only does having a job provide the mistress with a setting, a motivation, an attraction, but sometimes the very schedule for the affair. Jobs are convenient for running the affair smoothly. Sometimes without the job there would not be time for the affair. Or place or person. Convenience is a strong catalyst.

"I began writing this letter to you on a Saturday night. Next to me I had a glass of wine and soft music playing on the stereo. Unfortunately, the only one I have had to talk to on Saturday nights is my cat. My two girlfriends have boyfriends (single), and somehow I just can't get into sitting in a bar alone trying to make conversation with some jerk who just wants to get into my drawers. I guess what I'm trying to say is that the man in my life is probably at home on Saturday nights with his wife and their six-month-old infant. This afternoon while shopping (you guessed it—for HIS present for Christmas!) I saw your book [*The Mistress' Survival Manual*]. I couldn't resist spending my much-needed $2 for it. I was moved by what you said. I knew I wasn't crazy because I fell in love with a married man. We worked together every day. Getting involved seemed as natural as going to work. There he was, there I was, and a bond sprang up between us of genuine affection and love. When that is where love springs up in this crazy world, that is where you have to grab it. I spend so much time at work, it's a plus being in love there." *(Forest Hills, New York)*

"Let me begin at the inception almost six years ago when my husband and I separated permanently. I needed a steady income, rather than relying upon my own creative and fascinating but financially unproductive enterprises. I got in touch with a former business acquaintance and through her recommendations I was interviewed and hired by her husband. She no longer worked in the office with him. Within a couple of months her husband began making overtures toward me. Although I am considered a fairly attractive woman at thirty-six, I was still totally naive in the vein of married people's games. While I was married and living with my husband, I never thought of straying, but now the situation was different. The whole affair managed to get off the ground I think, now that I look back, because I felt it would be wrong of me to let my son see me go out with other men. I also thought that it might be detrimental in terms of my husband's well-being and support payments—he was torn up over our divorce. So this arrangement seemed ideal and convenient, a clandestine affair on both of our parts for mutual satisfactions." *(Honolulu, Hawaii)*

"I was a frustrated housewife. I never really knew how frustrated I was till I began working. I had always wanted to work but in my day, women had kids. Well, I had mine and now they were all in school. I loved working. I got involved with one of the men in the office—don't ask me how. I'm learning new things about myself all the time. Rendezvous were the biggest problem. Who had time between working, household backwork, shopping, keeping in touch with the kid's activities, the kids, my husband and on and on. The job was the rendezvous with a few extra added hours here and there. If I wasn't working I would have had no excuses for my absences." *(Cambridge, Massachusetts)*

One cannot conclude point-blank that if not for the job there wouldn't have been any absences or romantic liaisons in this case, but the job sure made it convenient. In numerous cases the job weaves in and out of the lifestyle of the mistress. Working women are finding certain fulfillments that they never expected.

The Fulfilling Life of the Office "Wife"

The "office wife" is a term that has a somewhat archaic connotation. It is a term used to describe the lifetime-loyal, 100% efficient secretary usually married only to her job and figuratively speaking to her boss. Their working relationship is akin to a marriage in terms of commitment which is selfless and duration which is years. The office wife looks out for her boss's reputation, his productivity, and his well-being. She's the homemaker at the office, making it a place of peak efficiency and comfort. In the past, office wives were a stereotype of spinster career women. Although the connotation of office wife is passé, there are new versions springing up. Mary Jane is one of the new breed of office wives. She finds it very very fulfilling.

"I met my married man when I became his secretary in 1967. At the time I was in the process of getting a divorce. From the very beginning of our working relationship there was a strong attraction physically between us and we were both aware of it. However, I realized and he confirmed in a brief exchange on one occasion, that he had no intention of leaving his wife and kiddies and getting serious with me and I was smart enough at the time not to get involved. So for six and one-half years ours was a strictly business relationship, although we did have several lunches and talked a great deal about his family, my social life, and business affairs.

"Then he left the company and I stayed. Occasionally we had lunch and there was still that unspoken feeling that we could really make beautiful music together. During the time I worked for him and the time that I didn't I maintained a healthy social life and had a steady boyfriend most of the time. Then in 1977 I was looking for a better position and he was looking for a new secretary. We came to an agreement without too much trouble and I went to work for him again. The attraction was still there. After much thought and discussion and his promise that he would shortly be leaving his wife, I decided this time to give it a whirl. Due to the nature of his job he traveled extensively. He was in sales. I traveled with him naturally as his assistant. It was easy to meet whenever we so desired. Lunches and dinners were routine.

"At my age, now forty, having children is almost out of the question and I don't have any great desire to be a mother at this time in my life. Marriage has never been important to me at any time in my life and after being single for over ten years, I even wonder sometimes if I could be happy making all the compromises one has to make to live with someone else. I've never lived with a girlfriend even, because it seemed like such a hassle and taking care of a man is twice as much trouble.

"I knew what I was doing when I got into this. I knew I had a 50/50 chance of his leaving and not leaving, but I still wanted to go ahead and do it. I want to say our relationship is the best one I have ever had with any man so far and that's important to me—more important than a Saturday night date. Sometimes I feel absolutely spoiled.

"I have lots of friends and activities, and I'm rarely lonely. Since he travels so much and is one of those overachievers, I'm sure even if he and I were married I wouldn't see him more than I do now. Right now it's as important for me to work with him since that is as large a part of his life, as it is to be a wife. In fact I am a wife. In fact if I had a choice, I would rather be his assistant—I would see more of him. I'm sure I have the best of my man's time and personality and I am usually content with that."

Mary Jane is the new version of the office wife who has few complaints. For her it is a very fulfilling role. Her love affair with her married man has added to her working life. The effects upon her job and her lifestyle have been good ones for the most part. Convenience was like a lubricant to a good relationship for Mary Jane. Temptation was an escort. Temptation played an important part here as it does in so many affairs that explode on the job.

Temptation? The concept seems foreign in our discussion of behavior motivations. Affairs on the job are influenced by sociological developments like group dynamics, self-image strivings, and interpersonal loyalties. Passionate distractions on the job are a byproduct of situational factors. Where does a biblical, value-laden concept like temptation fit into all this? I'm making room for temptation not to be judgmental or particularly religious, but to prove a point which should clarify itself shortly.

"Working with him, we often had to go to building sites where new offices were being constructed. He had to supervise the workers and see that things were being done properly. We had to contract lighting, telephone service, things like that, so we were out of the office a lot. We talked a lot and grew close. One day he had many problems, and I wanted to talk. I just couldn't go home and neither could he. We just drove around. We parked and talked. We had never dated after office hours although we were tempted. We had already shown interest in each other in other ways, such as kissing and holding hands. I didn't choose to date him. We fell in love. We each had marital problems. We needed each other." *(Houston, Texas)*

The making of that mistress was influenced by the office environment or lack of it; co-worker attraction, perhaps boredom, convenience; but also willingness. Although she makes the case that she didn't choose to date him, she did choose. She allowed the bonds, the affectionate exchanges, etc. The temptation of their relationship was right there and this mistress and married man accepted it. Temptation is always there. Accepting it is human. The importance of realizing this is we must realize that we are responsible for our actions and our choices. Why? Because we will experience the consequences of our behavior whether we like the consequences or not. Actions always have consequences. Some of the effects are good, such as in the case of the office wife Mary Jane. Sometimes the consequences are bad. Learning to look at affairs as temptation is constructive because there will be effects. Mixing business and pleasure is known to be dangerous. That is the proletarian commandment. When you violate that adage, what can happen?

"Recently he moved over in a promotion that made him head of our office employing 3000 people... a grand promotion for him... a disaster for me. It was my hard work that made him look so good. Business had become a large facet of our affair. I was hurt that I was remaining static and he was being promoted. There was nothing I could do about it. There was a new secretary waiting for him in his new office. No matter how much he assured me he needed me to keep up my end of the operation to ensure it was being done well and to keep him informed, I felt I had been relegated back to the position of secretary. It's too late that I learned that I should have been interested in making my job performance look good and not making his performance look so good." *(Trenton, New Jersey)*

"Our affair got too hot to handle anymore. I couldn't take seeing him every day and hearing his wife's voice on the phone. It was driving me nuts. The only option I had was to quit. Before I got the strength to do that, I was fired." *(St. Louis, Missouri)*

"I told him once again that we had to end it. Much to my surprise he said okay. And he said he wouldn't hold it against me as far as my job went. First and foremost he wants me as an employee. He has stated that many times." *(Germantown, Ohio)*

"Everyone at work knows about it 'under the table.' No one above us in management comments but our colleagues do. Some criticize and joke—most ignore it, thank heaven." *(Gresham, Oregon)*

"We were both very civilized about the death of our affair. We were professional all the way, discreet to the last. But I still had to handle this feeling of oh I don't know guilt, sorrow, regret, every time I saw him in the elevator or at a trade meeting." *(medium city, Arkansas)*

"I had to leave the company. Everyone knew about us and it was downright embarrassing. I felt sorry for his next sales manager. I was going to be a tough act to follow. Mistresses make the best employees, you know. They work like dogs, and expect nothing in terms of raises or promotions. They do it just to get a kiss or an extra hour once in a while. They work late without a moment's notice and are only too glad to take on extra chores or responsibilities, because it may mean a little more time around their beloved. What a jackass I was!" *(Seattle, Washington)*

"I walk around the office now and marvel at the fact that he and I were once so intimate and now I don't even notice him. Isn't that odd? It's like that affair never happened at all although for the two years it did, it was a scandal." *(suburb, Chicago)*

Affairs aren't necessarily detrimental, but they more often than not create ramifications that the triangle players never bargained for in the initial pact with passion. Consequences are not something you think about on the way in, but only on the way out, with all the wisdom of hindsight. Loving a married man can be so overwhelming and consuming that the last thing you can do is work. Mistresses can make ideal employees if their married man is the boss, but if he isn't they can be the worst employees. Working definitely has an impact on the affair. And the affair certainly has an impact on working and your job performance.

Whether you work in a bustling office, a deserted mine, a dull factory, or a fascinating field, you can find yourself in a hotbed for an affair with a married man. If the situation doesn't get you, the chemistry can. If camaraderie doesn't distort your co-worker, the monotony might. 85% of mistresses are working women getting passion as well as work experience. By 1990 some 52 million women will be in the job market. How many of them will find passion more marketable than anything else? Working is highly significant in the making of the American mistress. However, no inanimate concept can take all the credit. The working woman who opts for mistresshood must not lose sight of credit. She must get credit for the work she is doing and take credit for taking passion home in her paycheck. She must not credit her married man with too much, nor credit herself with too little.

Being a working woman myself, I know how hectic life can get. Sometimes important concerns get lost. For the working women I have included the following test. It's a footnote on this chapter that can keep you one step ahead of impending trauma.

Will a Married Man Edit Your Résumé?

If you are involved with a married man on the job or through a business association, chances are he is capable of editing your résumé. If you are being drawn closer and closer to an affair with a married co-worker, will he in time affect your résumé?

From talking with working women about their affairs with married men, I have learned that hindsight is enlightening and instructive. The following test will help you develop hindsight upfront.

I want you to interview yourself; give yourself an update on your job performance. I want you to write a personnel report about how your personal affairs are affecting your work record. A married man is often a consuming, demanding, and distracting passion. It is easy to see his impact beneath the lines of any job productivity study, once you know where to look. If you are a mistress and a working woman, or thinking of mixing the two, what kind of résumé and personnel report will you be writing?

Directions: This is a multiple-choice test. Read the statements or questions and then choose one answer. Write your answer in the space provided. Not all answers will reflect your situation exactly, so you may have to choose the closest one. Then proceed to scoring and evaluation.

1. How is an affair in your job setting handled when your co-workers become aware of it?
   (a) it is seized upon with relish and gossiped about endlessly (b) it is virtually ignored (c) it is viewed as a definite black mark on the professional image of the people involved   1. _____
2. How much power does the married man

in question have with regard to your job? Does he control advancement for you or firing you?
(a) no (b) yes (c) possibly   2. _____

3. How would you assess your job objective right now?
(a) It's the last priority, getting through the day is the first right now (b) I am currently performing well and working toward promotion and raises (c) I'm uncertain with regard to my job; maybe I'll transfer; maybe I'm too concerned with making my married man look good on the job   3. _____

4. Your company has the following policy on affairs—
(a) My company prides itself on respecting individual rights to privacy (b) My company values discretion not morality (c) My company has an official policy of dismissal for inappropriate personal involvements between co-workers   4. _____

5. How would you characterize your married man's gossip quota?
(a) He gossips occasionally but I'm not sure if he would talk about us (b) He guards intimacy about his own life and about the affairs of everyone (c) He relishes a good gossip tidbit and enjoys disseminating it around the job   5. _____

6. As far as your job schedules go—
(a) Our schedules are flexible; we see each other more now since we acknowledged chemistry (b) Our job entails being together (c) Our paths rarely cross and are inflexible in that way   6. _____

7. How does your social life tend to influence you at work?
(a) I have learned to effectively compartmentalize my social, work, and emotional lives (b) My concerns come to

the job with me usually (c) My social
life dominates me, my job, everything   7. _____

8. How does your occupation mix with a
potential affair through the job?
(a) An affair would be highly dangerous
for me in my job; like teaching or the
ministry my behavior is supposed to be
impeccable (b) An affair wouldn't be
particularly relevant to my occupation
(c) A mix would be dangerous only if it
affected my job performance   8. _____

9. In case your affair ended without his
consent, would your married man's
capacity for spite or envy be—
(a) insignificant because he's the kind of
person to accept things gracefully (b)
dangerous because he would make things
difficult for you owing to his excessive
pride or jealousy (c) questionable
because you have never thought about it   9. _____

10. Is this particular job worth gambling
with as far as you are concerned?
(a) I don't really know anymore (b) No,
it was hard getting this job and it's an
important step for me (c) Yes, I can
always find opportunity in my field; my
skills are always needed   10. _____

Scoring:

In the column marked Answers, list all your answers from 1 to 10. Then find the point value for each of your answers in the table below. List the point value for each answer in the column marked points. Then total up your points and fill in the number in the space for Total. Then proceed to the evaluation.

Scoring Table

							Answers	Points
1.	(a)	5	(b)	1	(c)	10	1. _____	_____
2.	(a)	1	(b)	10	(c)	5	2. _____	_____
3.	(a)	10	(b)	1	(c)	5	3. _____	_____
4.	(a)	1	(b)	5	(c)	10	4. _____	_____

5.	(a) 5	(b) 1	(c) 10	5. _____	_____
6.	(a) 5	(b) 10	(c) 1	6. _____	_____
7.	(a) 1	(b) 5	(c) 10	7. _____	_____
8.	(a) 10	(b) 5	(c) 1	8. _____	_____
9.	(a) 1	(b) 10	(c) 5	9. _____	_____
10.	(a) 5	(b) 10	(c) 1	10. _____	_____

Total _____

Evaluation:

Your score can range anywhere from 10 to 100 points. Proceed to the category which includes your particular score. What is your personal personnel report saying?

A Progress Report: 10–30 points. If you scored low in this test, your job performance reads like a progress report. An affair doesn't have a high potential of adversely affecting your résumé. You are in control of your business sense, and your married man doesn't pose a constant distraction or a significant threat. Maybe that's because of his integrity or your maturity or the nature of your job. Your job setting isn't gossip-oriented nor is your company affair-conscious. Your disposition is logical and your work is efficient. Being a mistress doesn't have much to do with your working world. Your married man has little leverage to edit your résumé or affect your position. Be a bit wary though if your affair is in its initial stages. Sometimes married men acquire more and more power as time goes by. Don't let anything hamper your nice personnel Progress Report.

A Nonproductivity Report: 31–65 Points. If you scored in middle ground on this test, your job performance reads like a critique. The salient theme in your personnel report is a decline in your job productivity. It's not easy to determine why you've gone nonproductive, but if you are in the grips of a triangle it's probably that. Your married man is indeed editing your résumé; how much is up to you in the near future. There are a lot of uncertainties out there on the work front. For instance, what will he be like if you end the affair; would he affect your job security or advancement; would he distribute your intimate secrets to a gossipy audience? These are some questions worthy of your concern because they will affect your personnel report. You may think your affair isn't hazardous to your occupation, but your married man may be hazardous to your work image. Get a handle on your productivity now before your résumé is ruined permanently!

Handicap Report: Grounds for Dismissal: 66–100 Points.

The higher you scored on this test, the more your affair would jeopardize or is jeopardizing your job. Whatever job objectives you once had are lost in the sea of passion. You are very vulnerable to harm because your married man, presently or potentially, controls your job. He can fire you, keep you in a static position, or make things highly uncomfortable for you at work. He has a few qualities that are negative as far as your work reputation goes, too. He talks too much and displays too much pride and envy. Watch out in case you get on the wrong side of those qualities. Possibly your occupation or your company has strict spoken or unspoken rules about passion mixing at the job. You may think that love is fine and rosy now, but you may soon find out that your love can mark you with an indelible scar, snickering whispers, or worse, a pink slip. Look before you leap, and if you've already leaped try to make things as safe for yourself as possible. Hindsight now may salvage your personnel report.

In Conclusion:

The interview is over. Now you know if and how your married man can edit your résumé. Assessing your job performance every once in a while is good business sense. Your job productivity should be important to you because you can be sure it is important to your employer. Writing a personal personnel report is a way of employing hindsight upfront, where it can do the most good. Hindsight is a skill that should be cultivated before regret has a chance to slip in. Be the sole writer of your résumé, don't let anyone or anything do or undo your job! Your work record is a matter of success or unemployment. Passion in the paycheck can undo your salary altogether!

CHAPTER 2

Strange Bedfellows: Morality, Sex, and the Mistress

Does morality make the mistress or does the mistress make morality? That question sounds like an excerpt from a communiqué with a sphinx. Yet, seriously, it is a riddle that has kept surfacing throughout all my interviews and research with mistresses. Whenever we talked of sex, there it was. It's a little like that old stumper, "Which came first, the chicken or the egg?" Unlike the chicken and egg riddle, I really tried to fathom the mistress and the morality question.

I'm putting the question to you at the beginning of this chapter so you can mull it over and see how it weaves in and out of our discussion of sex and sexual mores. Later we'll get back to it in detail.

I very honestly can't write about the sexual activities of the mistress without making one point. Contrary to popular belief, mistresses are not privy to an undercover X-rated community sex manual. If they were I'd market it not only for the sake of my pocketbook but for the good of all humankind! I was a mistress and now I am an expert on mistresses and I assure you that is not the case.

You may think that I'm joking, but there are myriads of people who feel that the mistress has a magical sexual power. Mistresses are alleged to have sexual secrets, secrets that make them irresistible to the married man. Armed with this highly classified information, they weave a sexual spell that no wife can break even with the help of Marabel Morgan (Author of *The Total Woman*). The erotic adventurousness of the mistress is legendary. It is whispered that the mistress will do "things" that no respectable wife would dream of even in her wildest fantasies. And then there is the matter of skill. It is assumed that the mistress does nothing with her married man except perform sexual feats with him and upon him. Naturally all that practice makes her skill incomparable. Equipped with those secrets, that shamelessness, and those skills, the mistress is a unique breed of sexual animal.

That is a review of the myths about the mistress and her sex life. There is no mistress's sexual text. The mistress may not be superhuman, sexually speaking, but her "sex" does have a life sometimes quite different than those outside the realm of triangles.

In exploring the sexual activities of the mistress in America we are going to look at several aspects. We are going to hear from the mistresses about some of their particular pleasures and problems. Since affairs do exist in a clandestine atmosphere, does that cast a special eroticism? Sometimes the sexual responses of the mistress reflect the patterns of many women who aren't mistresses. Sometimes the patterns tend to hold true for only the mistress community. In our modern quest for sexual satisfaction, has guilt become extinct? Has the sexual revolution created some sort of mistress revolution? And then, finally, why do morality and mistresses make such strange bedfellows?

For those interested in my methodology, perhaps you might be curious as to how I obtained data on so personal a realm. My questionnaire has a number of pertinent questions and suggestions for the mistress to add more comments whenever she was so inclined. I asked specifically, "How rewarding was the sexual aspect of your relationship? More rewarding than with other lovers before him? Did your married man's infidelity (sleeping with his wife) inhibit you? Describe any aspects of your sex life that shed light upon this subject." These and some others you'll see in a few pages stimulated the feedback that provided the basis for this chapter.

One word of caution before we look at the sexual behavior and the sexual motivation of the mistress. This chapter deals with only the mistresses' actions and reactions. The married man's side of the relationship will be dealt with later in the section devoted to him.

What is the sexual reality for the mistress? Is there one sexual reality? Although, unlike the myth, there is no singular sexual reality; there are patterns and collective experiences that emerge. There is no single sketch that applies all across the triangular board for all mistresses, but there definitely are experiences that are characteristic.

For instance, *the Peak Affair*.

"My sex life was the most rewarding of my life. I had considered myself a frigid woman before him. My former husband and former encounters made me feel that I must be frigid. What a pleasure to finally find at thirty-eight I wasn't... and what a relief." *(suburban Chicago)*

"Sex with my married man was an experience I never had before. I learned that that's what it's supposed to be! He treated my body like it was a delicate, the most delicate thing in the world." *(Goldsboro, North Carolina)*

"With this man [married man] I never get enough love-making. I've never been that way with my husband, not even in the beginning. I never liked sex so much in my life." *(Dover, Delaware)*

"Although I'd had sex since 17½, since my freshman year of college, he was the first man I consistently had orgasms with. I waited ten years and got much, much more than I had ever dreamed it was possible to have in a sexual relationship." *(C. Beach, South Carolina)*

These descriptions all attest to some peak of sexual gratification that was reached with this married man. The Peak Affair makes every mistress who experiences it feel in a sense she was virginal, inexperienced, until the union with this married man. The mistresses in this grouping never knew the true joy or pleasure of sex totally until their affair. The Peak Affair has been reported by single, married, divorced, and virgin mistresses, although the former virgins admit that they have no mode of comparison. The Peak Affair is a zenith in terms of sexual satisfaction and fulfillment.

"I recall this one time my married man and I went to a motel and forgot to turn on the air conditioning for hours. By the time we realized it, we were entirely slippery from sweat, lust, and passion. It had taken so much planning and waiting for that day. But it was a real climactic memory for me." *(Island Park, New York)*

That last quotation suggests some of the underlying variables that influence the Peak Affair. The sexual relationship of the mistress and her married man usually exists in the limits

THE SHAPING OF THE AMERICAN MISTRESS 35

of time, space, availability, and romance. The mistress rarely gets to see her married man compared to the other responsibilities on his schedule, excluding work time if they work together. Therefore, their meetings have to be planned carefully and waited for longingly. The intrigue, the pathos, the repressed desire, all tend to explode in a burst of spontaneous passion when they are finally together. Naturally, under this clandestine set of variables, sexual experience is enhanced. However, just how much of the passion is programmed by the triangle is hard to pin down. I would only venture to say that it varies according to each set of triangular circumstances.

The clandestine aspect of affairs also creates what I call a Wartime Sensuality for the mistress.

"Sex wasn't that important at first but became increasingly so. Each time we made love I was afraid it would be the last. My sex life with him surpassed anything I have ever encountered. He has released any tensions and relaxed any inhibitions I had in the beginning. He has opened up a whole new world for me sexually. I can't bear the thought that it might end any day because of his wife." *(Uniontown, Pennsylvania)*

"Whenever we went into the bedroom it was as though we had been lovers for years. We've known each other for eleven years, but our sex didn't start for ten of those years. But, immediately we knew each other's needs and likes. There was none of that trial and error period. For the first time in my life I spent the whole day in bed, finding I was multiorgasmic. My ex-husband considered me frigid. We exist in a fantasy-like world. Our sex has no tomorrow so we make it count now." *(Dallas, Texas)*

Some mistresses enter into each sexual encounter with a Wartime Sensuality of sorts. This may be the last time we ever make love or this may be the only time we will have together for the next few months. Affairs have no security so each episode has to be savored. There may be no war out there, but being discovered could always mean death to the liaison. This Wartime Sensuality makes some sex lives appear to be passionate peaks.

The clandestine aura that is bred by triangles does create passion that enhances the experiences of the mistress. Simultaneously, however, the same aura creates mistrust, anxiety, competition, and jealousy. These influences make sexual experiences problematic and painful.

The Does He or Doesn't He Controversy

"I know I hold back sexually. I can't forget he's doing the same things with her, probably telling her the same things he's telling me. Whenever we make love it's a real problem." *(Orem, Utah)*

"Whenever we're together I get these flashes of him and his wife in bed together. It's like a nightmare that ruins my sexual climb. When I confess these images to him, he says they seldom do it. That doesn't help." *(Stockton, California)*

"Our sex is so special and I know he doesn't have that with her [his wife] now. At least he swears that they don't make love anymore, not since we met." *(Philadelphia, Pennsylvania)*

The Does He or Doesn't He Controversy is highly sensitive ground for the mistress. The married man's other sex life with his wife is labeled infidelity. That's a twist by definition. My spot on the questionnaire that probed his sexual activeness with his wife uncovered this controversy. The controversy is a source of anxiety, dishonesty, and gullibility. Many mistresses firmly and fanatically believe that their married man is "faithful" to them. They fear the other reality. Mistresses tend to believe that there are a lot more platonic marriages out there than there are.

At the root of this controversy is jealousy; sexual jealousy is the cruelest kind for many. And this dragon that haunts the mistress cannot ever be totally killed by the married man. His wedding ring is always reflected somewhere on the armor.

"I can hardly stand to talk about or write about him making love with his wife, I can't stand it!! My only consolation is that it's not that often. Sex with him is *one* of the reasons I can't end the relationship. He has to be the most tender, loving, giving man alive. I can't stand the thought of sharing this, him!!!" *(Hartford, Connecticut)*

"He and his wife were sharing the same bed. The thought of him in the same bed with her was troubling. As time went by, that feeling turned into torture. It inhibited me terribly at times. Sometimes it made me all the more determined to make things better with us." *(Akron, Ohio)*

Jealousy speaks for itself. In doing so the last quotation suggests another battle with which the mistress had to deal. It is the *How Do I Rate With His Wife* problem. That competition is inevitable for some and a drawback.

"I wondered if I was better in bed than his wife. It inhibited me in the respect that perhaps she [his wife] was better than me." *(Salt Lake City, Utah)*

"I know that I was better than his wife because he always told me I was. I don't know if he was telling me the truth. I know I always tried extra hard sexually, because I knew I was competing with someone [his wife]." *(Atlanta, Georgia)*

The mistress has this legacy of competition with which to contend. It goes along with the triangle territory. Some married men are more lucid than others about how a mistress measures up to a wife, sexually speaking. Their comments will come later in the chapter that explores the conjugal bed and how it influences affairs. Whether or not the mistress is familiar with her rating, she is definitely familiar with the insecurities of being compared. The competition takes its toll on sexual enjoyment.

"My married man was oh so gentle, tender, so eager to please. He never once made me feel dirty about what we were doing." *(Gladstone, Missouri)*

Doing something that is "dirty," being used, these kinds of concerns bring us to another ramification of the secret aspect of affairs—*Guilt, the Mistress' Eternal Companion*. Now, whether or not the mistress is afflicted with guilt varies.

"I could never let myself be free sexually. I couldn't be myself. I couldn't let go because I couldn't forget that he was married. I felt guilty." *(Nashville, Indiana)*

"I never felt guilty. Why should I? His wife never cared what he wanted. She refused to have oral sex with him. She insisted on the same routine every time. All she cared about was herself so why should I feel guilty for making him happy." *(Seminole, Florida)*

"I have tried many times to end the affair, because of guilt. I am a religious person. I know my heart would be broken if my dear husband had become so involved. I have brought guilt, unhappiness and frustration into my life. It's always with me." *(Racine, Wisconsin)*

Regardless of feeling guilty or guiltless, every mistress makes some remark on guilt. I never mentioned the word "guilt" in any of my questions. Yet the word was rampant in the answers. Guilt seems to be an inevitable concept. Each mistress meets up with it sooner or later. While some defy it, others find guilt hampers their sexual freedom.

If the triangle titillates sexual experience and also tinges it with anxiety, why tolerate it? Why tolerate a sexual relationship that is a double-edged sword? The overwhelming reason seems to be love.

"Our lovemaking was so special because our love is so special." *(Camden, New Jersey)*

That simple statement says it for many. I found that many mistresses entangled the concepts of sex and love. Their affairs were characterized as friendships or love relationships of which sex was an integral part.

It has long been assumed by everyone that sex is the main reason for the relationship between the mistress and the married man. I asked, "What do you think is the main reason for your relationship—sex, friendship, business, or any other?" I made it a point not to mention love in the question. I made it a point to mention sex, first. The answer that far outnumbered all others was friendship. This consensus on friendship was not limited to questionnaires either. Friendship was the fundamental foundation cited incessantly by mistresses whether in conversation or in writing. It was stated outright and woven in with sexually related answers.

"Of course the sex is important. It's always important when you love someone." *(Washington, D.C.)*

It was often brought to my attention that sex was a part of any adult relationship. That certainly is true today. Somehow people forget that when it comes to the mistress/married man relationship. Their affair is presumed to be all sex and nothing else. Therefore, the salient point should be made that sex is not the essence of the mistress' relationship with her married man. There is a physical side but there are other sides too.

I know there is a sound reason why people choose to believe that the mistress' hold on the married man is purely sexual. It is less threatening. Characterizing an affair as a one-night stand is easier to take. Characterizing a mistress as a nymphomaniac diminishes her character, her worth, and her threat. It is much easier for a wife to admit to herself that her husband had sex with another woman than to admit that he is in a caring total relationship with another woman.

Chemistry is certainly not to be ignored for its initial impact or its role, but it should not be overestimated either. Mistresses are women in relationships of long standing, not one-night stands. The sexual behaviors and motivations for sex are reported from ongoing affairs, not flings.

The mistress' inclination to combine or confuse, depending on your perspective, the aspects of love and sex is like many women. Physical and emotional needs are inextricably meshed for the female oftentimes. Is it our upbringing or our gender; is it our immaturity or our maturity? The answer could be debated eternally. I point it up to further affirm that mistresses are like most women, not any stereotypical sex machine.

The entire probing of the sexual behavior, needs, and pleasures of the mistress testifies to the proven facts that females do have a sexual need and drive. That may seem redundant in the post-Hite Report era. However, this information came from women of the last generation, too. It seems that long before *The Hite Report*, some women didn't need written validation for their sensuality.

Although a majority do mesh the physical and emotional aspects of sex and love, there was a segment of women who had explicitly sexual relationships. Those who unabashedly admitted that sex was the main reason for their relationships tended to be married women or newly divorced ones.

"After my separation from my husband, sex just disappeared. I found my married man to fill that gap. I was used

to frequent sex. I missed the frequency I had had in marriage."
(a rural area)

Sometimes mistresses were in the initial stages of an affair. Sexual activity seemed uppermost in their minds. Sometimes the sexual relationship had gone on for years.

The next profile is representative of an affair in existence basically to satisfy sexual need.

Evelyn is a production supervisor at a large automobile corporation, a foreperson. She has been married for ten years and is twenty-eight years old. Her affair is in its fifth year. Her married man is thirty-two years old and works under her as a relief production operator.

"I had been having pain during intercourse with my husband. The first time I was with my married man I told him about it. He gave me oral sex to make sure I would climax. Then we had intercourse. There was no pain.

"The next time I had my period so he didn't want to have oral sex. I would have enjoyed being touched but he didn't, except for a little foreplay. After intercourse and only his orgasm, I told him that I was disappointed. If he wanted to be my lover I needed him to be concerned with my orgasms too. I had too many times with my husband when he was not concerned and I grew to resent it. The next day he apologized and said that he had thought about what I said and that he understood. I was so relieved. I had been so afraid that I made that demand too soon. I was afraid that he would think I was too demanding. After we cleared the air, he was and has been the best lover any woman could hope for.

"Now for the first time in years I enjoy sex. Lots of times I feel high. I used to be so afraid my husband would have an affair because things were not right between us sexually. Now look who's having the affair. Sex isn't a good enough reason to divorce my husband. I plan to continue with my lover and hope for the best."

Evelyn's story emphasizes the female need for sex. It suggests sexual starvation as well. The fear of being demanding points up typical fears regarding sexual behavior, too. Evelyn was nearly apologetic for explaining technique, and timid about her sexual rights. However, fear and timidity aside, she was seeking sexual fulfillment. Apparently Evelyn could explain things better to a co-worker than she could to her own husband. Sex is frightening, awesome, sensitive, and necessary.

It is time we eliminated the gender-fixed labels with regard to sexual needs. Men are not all out for sex. Women are not their sexual victims, victims of the male appetite. Mistresses are not all being used. Sex may be more embellished with emotion for women, but not in all cases. Sex-as-motive for a relationship with a married man for the married mistress is often wrapped up with passion. We will explore that in depth in another part of the book. For Evelyn, having an affair was better than getting a divorce. That is a moral judgment. So now we reach the subject of morality, the question that riddled us from the beginning—does morality make the mistress or does the mistress make morality?

Everyone knows that going out with a married man is wrong. He is someone else's husband. Yet despite that seemingly clear statement, there are thousands of women in America in love with married men. Why? What was the motivation of the mistress? I asked her, "Why did you choose to date a married man?"

"I liked him." *(Kansas City, Missouri)*

"We were friends." *(San Francisco, California)*

"I was newly divorced and was not interested or ready for a heavy relationship. His unavailability appealed to me. He was safe." *(Mentor, Ohio)*

"I had a very strong attraction to him from the day I just saw him. I had never felt so strongly attracted to anyone. The chemistry was unbelievable. I wanted to know more about him." *(Rushville, Nebraska)*

"I was lonely." *(Shawnee, Kansas)*

"We worked together." *(Brooklyn, New York)*

"It didn't matter that he was married, so was I. I thought he was attractive years before we got to know each other." *(Fort Branch, Indiana)*

Over and over I read the same answers. They all seemed to have a candid air about them. The answers were usually remarkably brief. There were some parts of the questionnaire that lent themselves to long essay responses. This was not one of them. There was an absence of the philosophical here. Rather, the motives were all basic. Recurring time and again were friendship, chemistry, loneliness, safety; expressed in different ways but saying the same thing. The reasons cited were simple. Yet the morality riddle wasn't simplified at all by these pragmatic answers. Because in some ways the mistress is influenced by social mores; in others she herself designs a personal moral code.

Exploring both angles, first, how does morality make the mistress? Our modern moral climate has tended to increase the mistress population. Look around you at society in the seventies. Changes are abundant. Divorce is now commonplace. Sexual codes of behavior have become much more liberal. Virginity at the time of marriage is on the decline. Living together is on the increase. Extramarital, premarital, and postmarital sexual activity is a fact of life for marrieds, singles, and divorceés respectively.

The media are continuously advertising and dramatizing the changes in American mores in magazine articles, motion pictures, and television programs. Every day we are confronted with another tale of teen pregnancy, sex and the single parent, another affair in another marriage; the list is endless.

Dating a married man may indeed be wrong, but it is another strand in the fabric of our eclectic mores. Our moral climate is full of alternative lifestyles and institutions in crisis. It is sometimes said we live in an era of moral relativity. Mistresshood thrives in such a state of cloudy affairs.

One of the best ways to fathom reality in the moral sense is to focus on the word ethics. Because, out of all the possible choices out there and all the possible codes of behavior, we each develop a code of sexual ethics.

The following test grapples with the issue of ethics. If you are a mistress, it will shed light on the making of you personally as an American mistress. If you haven't been involved in an affair as of yet, what is your likelihood?

Has the Revolution Recruited You?

Have you ever looked for the sexual revolution? Have you wondered whether or not it has passed you by? Are you passée or have you been passed over somehow? Your life doesn't have that wild orgiastic flavor that you read about. In fact sometimes you can't even relate to those articles in *Cosmopolitan*. Maybe you have felt that the sexual revolution skipped your generation. Maybe you have assumed that today's teenagers are the only ones liberated enough to live it up. Why didn't the sexual revolution recruit you—or did it!

I assure you that there has been a sexual revolution. Perhaps it isn't as dramatic as the media depict it, but it has happened. The revolution that our sexuality has undergone is one of ethics, I think, rather than simply behavior. What are your sexual ethics? We all have a set of ethics that govern our sexual behavior; let's look at yours. Then we'll be able to determine if the sexual revolution has affected you, and how.

Directions: Read all the statements below. After reading each one decide whether you think it is True or False. Then write True or False in the space provided at the end of each statement. After responding to all the statements, proceed to the scoring and evaluation, and what it means.

1. My faith in marriage has been destroyed by the high divorce rate.

   True or False? _____

2. Marital status should not be a factor in deciding whether to date someone or not.

   True or False? _____

3. After marriage, fidelity depends on one's needs and the circumstances.

   True or False? _____

4. Monogamy is an impossible ideal.

   True or False? _____

5. Words like "cheating" and "adultery" are too harsh to describe extramarital indiscretions.
                    True or False? _____

6. Sexual needs make their own moral code.
                    True or False? _____

7. Sometimes an affair is a better alternative than a divorce.
                    True or False? _____

8. Virginity is an outmoded burden.
                    True or False? _____

9. Love is not the only rationale for good sex.
                    True or False? _____

10. Women have the same right to cheat on their spouses as men.
                    True or False? _____

Scoring:
False answers are worth 5 points. True answers are worth 10 points. Go back and give yourself points for each answer. Then total up the points. Check your score with the valuation paragraphs that follow to see where you fit into the sexual revolution.

Evaluation:
 50–65 Points: The Tory. If your score fell in this range, your sexual ethics have been affected little by the sexual revolution. Like the Tories, the British colonists who opposed the American Revolution, you have opposed the sexual revolution. You probably think fidelity is worth pursuing regardless of circumstances. In your view monogamy isn't an impossible dream, nor is virginity an outdated practice. A marriage that needs an affair to survive isn't worth saving. Your conservative stances makes you seem almost old-fashioned in this day and age. Yet, you need your rigid moral code to ensure romance, honesty, and security. Your values are true and you are not apt to be confused by new situations. A Tory loyalist, you are loyal to yourself and your mate regardless of temptation.
 70–85 Points: The Cadet. If your score fell in this range,

your sexual ethics are beginning to change. Like a cadet you are learning new revolutionary strategies. You are in a period of transition and could become a full-fledged member of the vanguard. You don't see sex as black and white. There is a whole world of gray there. Sometimes sexual needs do produce a morality of their own. Sometimes an affair is better than uprooting everything and divorcing. Good sex is not always a function of love. Physical attraction is a reality. Women have sexual drives that have to be met and can't always be met in the traditional conjugal framework. Your answers were laced with some true and some false. This means that your sexual ethics vary from situation to situation. Experience seems to be your teacher and you have learned a few lessons from the sexual revolution.

90–100 Points: The Vanguard. If your score fell in this range, you are in the vanguard, leading the sexual revolution. Your sexual ethics are quite liberal, a sign of the times. Since you choose so many true answers, it seems that you don't believe in absolutes. Your values have been affected by modern society. For instance, the high divorce rate has eroded your faith in marriage. You're not geared for expecting "happily ever afters." Marital status isn't important in evaluating a lover. If you enjoy each other and satisfy needs that's enough. Sexual needs do produce a moral code of their own and that's fine. The traditional standards like virginity, monogamy; these are ideals and unpractical. Fidelity is difficult to enforce and whether or not you would adhere to it depends upon your marriage at the time. Your ethics have been formulated by the sexual revolution to a high degree. You are out there in front, one of the liberal vanguard.

In Conclusion:
The sexual revolution didn't arrive with orgies and aberrations; it arrived subtly. Your behavior didn't suddenly take on outlandish new practices, but your ethics did change, making new behaviors acceptable. Affairs are a byproduct of the sexual revolution. Your attitudes towards affairs and all the ramifications of affairs show how the sexual revolution has affected you. The higher your score the more you have been affected, the more your attitudes about marriage and sex have changed. And even if your closets aren't full of spare lovers, even if *Playgirl* isn't in your library, you may still have been a recruit in the sexual revolution!

The preceding test individualizes the subject of mores. It narrows down the morality maze to how it applies to you. In the final analysis we do develop our own morality. Along those lines, so does the mistress.

How does the mistress make morality? In sociological jargon the mistress internalizes changes or new societal norms. The mistress lets her personal experiences, in other words, influence her moral judgments. What are some practical applications of all this?

"I was resigned to being a mistress for the rest of my life until reading your book, *The Mistress' Survival Manual*. Since I had two divorces behind me (for a total of twenty-one years of marriage), I figured I was a bummer at marriage. I was resigned to believe that I was a failure at it. So this love [with a married man] was safe. This love wouldn't hurt me (or so I thought then)." *(Hoffman Estates, Illinois)*

"I wouldn't ask him to get a divorce. I've been there and know how hard it is. His marriage has been bad for six years, but his future is his. For his sake, being a mistress is all I can be for now." *(Costa Mesa, California)*

"Not only the young and middle age get involved with a married man. I did, much to my regret, and I am seventy years young. I am a widow four years and at times very lonely, as are most of the hundreds of widows in the large complex where I live. This hasn't solved my loss or my loneliness, which I'm sure is the only explanation for becoming involved with a married man." *(Florida)*

"My husband isn't enough. Our [my married man's and my] sex life is so fantastic. He can last five times as long as my husband, and I have him four or five times a week. Whereas my husband only makes love to me once a month." *(Rhode Island)*

"I was a virgin until I was forty. That was long enough. I felt like a freak anyway. Being a mistress certainly wasn't worse. And I fell in love." *(Cleveland, Ohio)*

This has been labeled the "Me Generation" by Tom Wolfe. That label very much applies to the mistress and the making of her own morality. Divorced mistresses may not trust marriage any longer because the institution reneged on its "till death do us part" guarantee. Widows find that their needs outlive their husbands. Married women may find fidelity impossible. Career women may find celibacy unhealthy. Marital statuses become less important than personal needs.

Just as sex tends to be all wrapped up in love, so is morality. Sometimes a wedding band doesn't stop neighbors or co-workers or friends from falling in love. Once they have fallen, former codes of behavior become impossible and love conquers all. Included in that conquest are the conventions surrounding marriage. Love negates the unwritten commandment Do Not Love Someone Else's Husband; and the written one Thou Shalt Not Covet Thy Neighbor's Wife.

Another element to include in this morality dilemma is the practical considerations.

"He's [my married man] got six kids, a nagging wife, and two jobs. He can't afford a divorce. He needs me. How can I walk out on him when he's got all that against him." *(New York City)*

"His wife told him if he leaves her, he'll never see his kids. She can do it, I've seen it happen to my brother. He can't have us both any other way but this." *(Des Moines, Iowa)*

"Sometimes I get depressed because I feel trapped in my marriage. But I'm scared. I have no job, no skills. How could I support myself and my kids if I left my husband? My married man doesn't want a divorce so I'd be stuck there too." *(Reno, Nevada)*

The mundane factors and injustices of life can't be discounted. Some married men aren't financially suited for the divorce game. Some married mistresses can't survive alone according to their calculations. Some fathers don't want to lose their children. Some wives don't appreciate their husbands. Some husbands don't appreciate their wives. Lack of appreciation isn't good enough grounds to dismantle a family or destroy a lifestyle. You may or may not agree with any of these statements. However, these concerns all have something to do with the mistresses loving married men and their justifying their love and adjusting morality.

Although fidelity loses out in many moral calculations by married mistresses, it triumphs for most of them. Even the married women who defy fidelity to their husband give it to their married man with the exceptional conjugal duty.

"I couldn't go out with anyone else. I feel it would be like cheating." *(Boise, Idaho)*

"He's the only man in my life, save my husband. These are the only two men I've ever been with. I would never take another lover. I wouldn't do that to him." *(Culver City, California)*

Fidelity to the married man established itself as a norm. Mistresses as a group may be unconventional in choosing the affair, but they are very conventional in their behaviors. The majority are faithful to their married man, in spite of his dual sexual role. They are old-fashioned in their dedication to the value of fidelity. Exclusivity is the rule not the exception. Most married men would tolerate no less. Mistresses don't want to incur the married man's wrath, jealousy, or hurt him. They don't want to feel the guilt that "cheating" is bound to bring. Within the community of mistresses faithfulness is the predominant value; cheating is wrong.

I asked, "Did you date; have sexual relations with other men?" "How did your married man feel about your dating or having sexual relations?" "How did you feel about this?"

The answers here established fidelity as a norm.

"He [married man] wouldn't hear of me dating anyone, much less anything else. He said that would be it. Besides, I couldn't do it. I love him. I know I'd feel cheap and guilty anyway." *(suburb, Boston)*

The morality that the mistress makes has standards like fidelity as well as having a tendency to make exceptions. Her morality is not just one long list of circumstantial dodges. Her morality is rather a combination of life's lessons, old-fashioned values, and even religion.

Exactly how religion fits into the riddle of the mistress and morality is difficult to say. But it's in there.

"I am a religious person and know the wrong of what we are doing. Do unto others as you would be done by. That is in my thoughts all the time." *(Buda, Texas)*

"I teach religion and I sing with the choir in church on Sunday. God help me but I met my married man in church. He is the organist." *(McKeesport, Pennsylvania)*

"I was raised Roman Catholic but I do not go to church on Sunday or practice my religion much. But I do pray a rosary every night." *(New Orleans, Louisiana)*

"I have found it increasingly more difficult to continue going to church, etc., as I feel like a hypocrite. I continue to go and am active in church activities with my husband as my dad is the minister." *(Portland, Oregon)*

"I agonized much over the fact that I am a Christian and had fallen from grace. Being a Missouri Synod Lutheran and having good scriptural knowledge left me with no excuses. I was always fighting it yet giving in to it, over and over, until I thought I was going to lose my mind." *(Missouri)*

"I still go to Mass every Sunday morning and I receive the body and blood of Christ too. I don't care about anything except that I know God loves me and understands. Sometimes we don't have a choice and God knows all things, including that." *(Savannah, Georgia)*

Religion is a part of the lives of some mistresses and it is missing from the lives of others. Moral codes do have something to do with religious affiliation and membership, but I'm unclear as to what where the mistress community is concerned.

There is currently a dispute over whether or not we are in a religious revival or in a religious decline. The religious experiences of the mistresses reflected both points of view. There were atheists as well as born-agains. Some kept up with the practicing of religious rituals. Others admitted they had lapsed as far as into agnosticism. To satisfy curiosity regarding the mistress and her religious affiliation, here is a breakdown of approximate religious data.

In response to my "What religion, if any, are you?" approximately 20% were nonreligious. Either they left the space blank or described themselves as agnostic or atheist. Or they wrote "Does not apply." 10% labeled themselves Jewish. 33% said they were raised as Roman Catholics. The largest approximate grouping, 50%, were Protestants. That Christian category includes answers of Protestant, Baptist, Methodist, Lutheran, Episcopalian, and the like. A few Mormons answered in the survey but they seemed to be statistically insignificant, except in proving that all religious types can become mistresses.

In exploring the sexual questions and the sexual answers of the mistresses some absolutes surfaced. The mistress is a mirror, often reflecting the sexual diversity of females in total. She has problems and pleasures in her behavior patterns like all women. However, her mistress membership makes those problems and pleasures somewhat different, even while the emotions remain the same. The clandestine shadow of the mistress does cast a unique shade, in fact several. Guilt is certainly alive and well, if not triumphant. The mistress is also a mirror reflecting the moral trends of society at large. There is a mistress revolution of sorts facilitated by moral relativity. The mistress revolution has followed the sexual revolution. It is unfair to judge the mistress as immoral, since most mistresses do have a moral set of ethics. The mistress community reflects sexuality, morality, even religion, like any other human grouping.

Stereotyping the mistress is standard. Judging her is status quo. Understanding her, on the other hand, is statistically a rarity. Morality and the mistress with all the sexual and ethical ramifications is indeed complicated. As the mistress ventures out from behind the scarlet "A", she becomes less enigmatic. Her morality is certainly not bizarre, nor is her sexual behavior. Yet the scarlet A was at times easier to understand. With new information and perspective the mistress can be understood. In answer to the question does morality make the mistress or does the mistress make morality, the sphinx and I agree the answer is yes!

CHAPTER 3

Opposites Attract: Feminism and the Mistress

Feminism is, for some, an enigma. Contrary to popular opinion feminists make good mistresses. Isn't that a conflict of interests? A feminist-oriented person is assertive. She has a raised consciousness. A male chauvinist is clearly the opposite of a feminist. And yet many feminist thinking mistresses have tinges of male chauvinism running through their veins. They must. Even the most self-sufficient, independent mistresses. Because if you are a feminist, how did you wind up catering to a married man? If you are bright, successful, and straightforward, how come you are so addicted to the subservience of a triangle?

Perhaps we should spend some time probing this enigma of mistressing and feminism and its dichotomy. At first glance feminism and mistressing do seem to be at opposite ends of some pole. And yet in this case opposites attract. Feminists make good mistresses. Many mistresses claim to be liberated women.

In this chapter we are going to hear how mistresses answered my question, "Did you consider yourself liberated, in what way?" As the mistresses and I try to define what "liberated" suggests, you will begin to understand the confusing dichotomy that emerges. You will begin to see that feminist tendencies harmonize in the making of the American mistress. After all, mistresses are only a cross section of females, females gripped in triangles. As such, you will see old role stereotypes for women adding up to the making of mistresses.

There are some fringes of the radical feminist movement that condemn mistresses and ostracize this segment from the movement's wing. This extremism is really sexism and it increases the struggle for the mistresses. It can really all be discussed in relation to the issue of power. Feminism, mistressing, sexism, all are bids for power or powerlessness. Each in its own way makes thousands of American women choose and pursue mistressing.

Being liberated can refer to a variety of areas in the life of a woman. Mistresses labeled themselves liberated often, and feminist often, too.

"Yes, I consider myself liberated. I attended Wellesley College, where women learn to think of themselves as men's equals in all ways. I never considered that I needed a man to help me establish my identity. I always took for granted that I would have a career, and considered marriage and children vague distant prospects. I am still pursuing the same career goals as actively as I did before I met my married man. I am both geographically and financially independent." *(Virginia Beach, Virginia)*

"I am liberated in some ways. I am extremely strong-willed. My goals in life are totally career-oriented at this stage, although the career I seek is traditionally for women. I'm not shy when it comes to meeting men and feel more at ease among men than women." *(West Acton, Massachusetts)*

"I feel that a career is important to a woman and that being a housewife is not her only option although I believe that nothing is wrong with a woman who chooses this. I also feel that women are as capable or more capable in many jobs that are dominated by men. It depends on the individual and not on their sex. I, myself, do not have big career plans, but I do enjoy working and feel that I would be bored at home fulltime." *(Troy, New York)*

"I am liberated in some ways. I believe in equal pay for equal work. I believe in equal responsibilities, opportunities, and equal pleasure along with hardships in any type of man/woman relationship. I am a union production worker and that in itself makes me liberated by profession." *(Ann Arbor, Michigan)*

"In all honesty I am very liberated in my job, but in my personal life I would have to say no." *(Washington, D.C.)*

THE SHAPING OF THE AMERICAN MISTRESS

"I am definitely a feminist. I am an earnest supporter of the Equal Rights Amendment. I am capable of standing on my own two feet and will not be a 'squaw' for any man." *(St. Louis, Missouri)*

"Occupationally I am liberated. Emotionally, I'm almost liberated. I used to cater to men and be almost subservient because that was the way I was raised. I also did not have much self-esteem and thought I had to be meek and mild to get my way and get people to like me. Since living and working on my own for ten years now, I began to change and fight back the way I was brought up. I think I'm finally on my way to being liberated because I like myself more and the way I run my life. Plus I'm not scared of people anymore." *(Manteca, California)*

"Yes I am a liberated woman. I know what I want and I go after it. I want to become a mechanical engineer. There aren't a lot of women in the field and I feel that I will be a good one. At last I found a man who knew of my abilities in the industrial field and wasn't intimidated. I felt confident of my future and happy in this relationship although it, too, is unconventional." *(Nashville, Tennessee)*

"It's funny, I am very much a feminist and this relationship contradicts every belief I have. All my goals, and values, are pure *Ms.* magazine, but still I'm stuck in this affair with a married man and I know that doesn't make sense." *(Westland, Missouri)*

These quotes are typical. They attest to the fact that in this day and age many mistresses are liberated in certain areas of life. And yet there remains an ambivalence when it comes to affairs of the heart.

Most mistresses described liberation in terms of careers, professions, or working. We have already seen that the majority of mistresses are working women ranging quite widely on the economic ladder. Most mistresses suggest that they are financially independent or self-sufficient or contributing to the family income. So in terms of money and the work ethic, mistresses tend to be liberated en masse.

As you may recall from the previous chapter, sexually speaking mistresses tend to be liberated by the sexual revolution that has seeped into American culture. However, there is a definite difference in their liberated attitude when the subject turns from sex to love. That is exactly where the ambivalence surfaces.

You see, the feminist-thinking working woman is independent, aware of her appetites, and free to pursue her goals. She depends on a man less than the traditional woman. She does not need a man for financial support, for an identity, or to fill her daylight hours. Her job or family fill these needs. Therefore, a feminist-oriented woman has characteristics that go surprisingly well with mistresshood.

After all, a married man has neither support nor security to offer. His identity and loyalty are already spoken for. Yet he has emotional gratification, sexual pleasure, friendship to offer. He has these to offer with no strings attached. An independent woman has no need of strings. She has her own life-support system already constructed. In the case of the mistress a little financial and sexual independence goes a long way—often right into the arms of a married man.

It is in the arms of that married man that many a mistress becomes confused about her feminist, liberated orientation. Obviously the life of a mistress does not lend itself to assertiveness, demands, or being in control of the love affair. So here, the active woman suddenly turns passive and becomes subtly disconcerted by the conflict of philosophies.

"I feel constantly on guard about my own instincts and feelings. There are many strong things in my life that give me one perspective: I am involved in my work, tending toward workaholism like my married man; in feminist groups and workshops on feminist issues. I lead a group on Women and Depression and believe me this affair has made me an expert. I have never referred to myself as a mistress, but I feel the effects of my second-class status in relation to this man. Mistresshood puts me in an entirely foreign perspective. I do not want to make demands on him that will push him further from me. I would make demands though if I felt they would be granted. More than one friend has told me this relationship is not in character for me, but right now I am just not close to understanding it or me." *(Jackson, Michigan)*

"I have a lot of feelings about being a mistress, most of them negative. I keep searching for reasons to continue in this affair with my married man to justify my subservient act. It's not a dependence but a deep love for someone who's right in my life, no matter how wrong I know it is in every rational way." *(North Miami Beach, Florida)*

"I consider myself liberated. I'm pursuing the career I want. I feel independent concerning my choices and my lifestyle. I'm raising a child while being a student and an employee. Since meeting my married man I feel less liberated. I guess I was sublimating my emotional needs there for a while, with mothering, studying, etc. I was denying myself a man's love rather than trying to integrate it into the rest of my life. This married man's love however, is not in step with my new lifestyle. The choices and freedom are missing. I thought I was making progress as a woman, now I'm not so sure." *(Tustin, Georgia)*

Remaining a mistress demands compromise with any feminist philosophy. A mistress must stand by ready at all times for the married man's rendezvous call. A mistress must bow to his schedule, his needs, and his responsibilities. A mistress must cope with the guilt that she is not being "sisterly" in courting a man who belongs to another woman. A mistress must be passive, usually dependent, concilliatory, and self-sacrificing. Those are simply the rules of most triangles. Triangles have boundaries, limits, and acceptable behaviors. The mistress' role is well defined in its "powerlessness" and its subservience. Her stance on waiting for him, on being loyal and faithful while he isn't, and on making no demands, and on giving without gauging how much one is getting is unliberated to say the least.

Mistresses need to be liberated financially, sexually, and occupationally. Mistresses need to be unliberated emotionally and socially. That is the dichotomy. That conflict is sensed by many women in the triangle. Hence the ambivalence, whether it is well defined or vaguely suggested.

Are mistresses unique in their ambivalence about feminism and love? Why does their liberation take them so far from nine to five and take them so far backward when the timeclock is punched out? How can so many women be so schizophrenic about their feminism? Why doesn't their liberated stance carry over into affairs of the heart?

It seems that feminism has made great strides on the outside, but progress is slower on the inside. Outwardly it is easier to show aggressive behavior. By that I mean going after a job, or to a bank and demanding credit. However, behavior concerning identity and roles is still scary ground for many women, mistresses included. Many women fear becoming "unfeminine."

Let me add here that these trends hold true for all women. It is useful sometimes to view mistresses as a microcosm of the female population. However, for mistresses these trends hold ominous ramifications.

What do we mean by "unfeminine"? In personal relationships women still genuflect to the male. Challenging his authority, his love, his wisdom, is often still construed by mistresses to be "unfeminine." You know what they say about women who make demands—they wear the pants in the relationship. That cliché says it all: all the prejudice against self-assertion, all the unflattering imagery, all the fear of becoming the castrating shrew. Our long-believed-in role stereotypes encourage women to be passive in their relationships, to let the men come first, to let the men run things. Bucking this rule can cause a woman to lose part of her traditional womanliness. Trying to juggle the new feminism and the old role of femininity is no easy matter.

"I am liberated in the sense that I have come to have the courage to do what is best for me first. As far as Women's Lib, it doesn't apply to me. Perhaps loneliness has caused me to feel that I need to be fulfilled and to be delineated by what a man feels for me and by the things I do for him." *(Oak Lawn, Illinois)*

"I consider myself liberated in some actions. I do believe in equal rights but I also think a man should have the authority." *(Minneapolis, Minnesota)*

"I like to pull my own weight so to speak, as far as my own finances and speaking my own mind. I believe in equality somewhat—like equal pay for equal work. I don't like being put down or ignored because I am female. Yet still because

I am female, I still like having doors opened for me." *(Allen Park, Michigan)*

"In some ways I am liberated; as far as equal rights are concerned. But I consider myself very feminine." *(Huntington, West Virginia)*

"I am as liberated as our present culture allows a woman to be, without losing her feminine identity." *(Salt Lake City, Utah)*

"I am economically liberated as a woman. I support myself and my own home, but socially I am in favor of the old values of home, family, fidelity, and the husband being the head of the household." *(Baltimore, Maryland)*

"I do want my married man, but if I rush things or push him I'm afraid that he'll be turned off. He likes the side of me that's sweet and understanding and pretty. I'm unsure he'd still like the person who argues and stands up for herself." *(Peekskill, New York)*

You can see clearly how feminism is acceptable in the job market, at the voting booth, or at the bank. However, in the bedroom or anywhere inside the man/woman cocoon "femininity" prevails. In a nutshell that means passivity, the normative social role that has been handed down for women.

There is another traditional concept that influences the making of the mistress. This concept is not confined exclusively to the female gender, but proportionately more women still subscribe to it. This concept is romanticism.

Romanticism is a powerful potion. It conquers all of our senses with the sound of violins, the smell of musk, the taste of a kiss, the longing looks exchanged by lovers and the language of an embrace. It even conquers our sixth sense, reason. Reason is no match for romance. The passion and pathos of unrequited love is one of the eternal themes upon which soap operas and pulp novels thrive. If you doubt the priority of this in our culture, just look at how many women soap opera addicts exist or look at the sales figures of the romantic writers like Kathleen Woodiwiss or Rosemary Rogers. Women consume the theme of romance. In droves they pursue passion, and for many that means pursuing a triangle.

An unfortunate part of romanticism is the Bitter/Sweet Tradition. By that I mean we expect pain as a natural part of passion. When a love affair goes sour or causes pain, rather than abandon it we are taught that this is an integral part, the bittersweet price. The Bitter/Sweet Tradition makes longing, regret, sentimentality, daydreaming, etc., acceptable patterns to pursue. These romantic behaviors are seen as normal by women. Therefore, it is easy for mistresses to swallow their pain, loneliness, anxiety, right along with the ecstasy. It is typical behavior to lose sight of reason in the triangle. It is standard for the mistress to ignore her well-being and quite consistent with the Bittersweet Tradition and the romantic stereotype we have ingrained into the female culture.

Men can and do fall prey to romanticism and pathos too. However, it is rarely as damaging to men en masse. Why? Men still retain power in most relationships. Women shy away from the domineering role in relationships because that power is seen as detrimental to femininity.

Passive behavior and romantic moods are lovely at times. However, for the mistress these role stereotypes can be emotionally no less than suicidal. Romantic, passive roles encourage the mistress to wait, dream, and hope that "someday" she and her married man will somehow ride off into the sunset. If not, then to savor and prolong the passion nevertheless, for 'tis better to have loved and lost, etc.

"I know I must stop thinking about him. But the thoughts are the only thing I have in my life. I try to tell myself I should appreciate the fact that for a time in my forty-seven years I had something that few people ever find. What are the chances that I will ever find anything like this again? Isn't it awful I only had a short time with him! Was it better to have found it and lost it . . . or never to have known it at all? If you have a magic word to make me forget his love, his warmth, his passion, his intimacy, I will repeat it over and over. I hope he's having the same problems forgetting me, but men aren't like that, are they?" *(Rockville, Maryland)*

Men are not conditioned in this same way. For the mistress this role means sentencing herself to years of unrequited love, misery, and unhappy mooning. Cherishing romance and her feminine identity as she has learned these means giving the man all the options, power, and rights to making decisions. This is faulty because many married men don't have a clear vision of where they are going; they are in the middle.

Mistresses must learn the fine points of liberation. They must learn that prejudices about what's "feminine" and what's not, are just as wrong as prejudices about "women's work." Being a doormat, perfumed and smiling, isn't feminine. It is foolish. Rose-colored glasses and starry eyes may be romantic, but they are also foolhardy. Stereotypes rarely serve women well. If you have learned that lesson in the job market, take it and apply it in your relationships.

It is this basic confusion, caused by role stereotypes and fear of being unfeminine that produces the dichotomy of feminism and the mistress. It explains why a liberated woman can cater to and moon over a married man who is virtually never available. It explains how intelligent accomplished women give up years of their life to tortuous triangles in the name of love, without giving up or getting out.

I sincerely hope this explanation gets through to some feminists who have ostracized the mistress community. In my travels I have been confronted by feminist-women who dismiss mistresses as laughable reactionaries, by feminists who deny help to "unsisterly, husband-stealing" mistresses. This extremism in judgment and sentence is not feminism to me. It is sexism.

I was a mistress. I have always been a feminist. I found my dilemma neither laughable nor reactionary. I find this epidemic dilemma among women in need of attention and sympathy. I am for equality right down the line. I don't feel mistresses should be denied help or respect because they are involved with another woman's husband. There is always another side to the story. I think sympathy, help, knowledge, and understanding should be extended to all women, regardless of which angle they cohabit on the triangle. I hope the women's movement will be more generous in dealing with the mistress issue and in extending more help. Feminism cannot be selective without becoming sexist.

I believe in equality for mistresses and equality for wives. I have spoken out against sexism in roles, jobs, affairs, parenthood, and now feminism. Equality should not be a cause limited in scope to one gender nor should feminism be limited to some women and not others. I know mistresses are in many ways liberated and I hope I can inspire them to become more so and to create a world of equality.

"I decided to write to you after seeing you on the evening news. I am a wife and a mistress. I feel empathy for women in your position and wish there were some way we could all help each other. There is a definite need for women to bolster each other. I feel the biggest problem in these triangles is not the marriage or the married man, but us. I need and we need for women to be more understanding and supportive of each other." *(Baltimore, Maryland)*

"I like to think of it all as people's liberation. I believe no one should be locked into behavior patterns and fates by their gender." *(Whiting, Indiana)*

"Contact with women's groups has always helped me in the past. I find women's groups are devoted to pertinent issues and have served me well. I find a lack of women's groups on this subject. I read stuff only about wives and feminist publications never touch the subject of the mistress." *(Bodfish, California)*

Many mistresses are feminists. I trust the feminist movement will embrace the mistress as wholeheartedly as any other woman with a problem. Mistresses are already discriminated against by society. Discrimination by their sisters, too, only produces more mistresses and makes the years of mistressing longer. Sexism among women further polarizes the wife and the mistress, intensifying their competition and the perpetuation of the triangle. The only way to raise the consciousness of people in triangles is to broaden the understanding of all three—the wife, the mistress and the married man.

Mistress-hating among women results from thinking that mistresses have the power to steal husbands. Mistresses have no such power. Women who take this stance render themselves powerless as wives. Wives have no such powerlessness. The issues of feminism, sexism, male chauvinism, and mistresshood all vie for power or trade on powerlessness. Mistresses often exude powerlessness. Wives, too, plead powerlessness. Sexists condone it or actively promote it. Male chauvinists thrive on women's powerlessness.

Powerlessness is the crux of all the issues in the triangle.

It is something we all should speak out against. Powerlessness, timidity, fear of rejection and therefore inaction are women's enemies, not just mistresses' or wives' enemies alone. Powerlessness is the theme of triangles. It should be the one target of all feminists and of feminism. Mistresses must fight for the power over their affairs, all affairs in the world and in the heart. Wives must do no less. The obstacle is not so much each other as it is this conviction of powerlessness.

When I say power to the mistress, wives shudder. They shouldn't. Feminism is a quest for power over one's own life, no one else's. Mistresses in droves have learned the lessons of liberation. Their collective strides in philosophy and job action are laudable. Those lessons must be applied to love.

"I have broken up my affair and have proven that I am truly self-sufficient. I do not need my man to survive. But before this break I was very dependent on him for everything that I could possibly get, except financial help. Believe it or not, I supported not only him but his wife and their two children. I was told she was unable to work because of a back injury.

"I didn't want to end the affair at first. I hated what you were telling me in *The Mistress' Survival Manual*. I sat and read the book and could not put it down until the truths would become so unbearable that I'd want to throw it out. After I'd get over the trauma I'd be right back reading. The breakup has been difficult but not as bad as the constant waiting for him to call or come by. Thanks for opening my mind, my eyes and my heart." *(Eugene, Oregon)*

Often the essence of mistresshood is powerlessness. Learning about power is embracing feminism. All women should digest that lesson and step up on the feminist ladder. That lesson would unmake many triangles.

Until that lesson is fully grasped, feminists make good mistresses. Opposites attract. Feminists will make good mistresses as long as independence lives side by side with romantic dependence. As long as the Bitter/Sweet Tradition still figures in our cultural fantasies. The dichotomy will go on as long as feminism and femininity mean two different things.

In the realm of science opposites attract. I hope that same rule will apply one day to triangles. Then the opposite forces of power and powerlessness will attract. Then the enigma of feminism and the mistress will disappear.

If you are a mistress, now is the time for you to apply that lesson to yourself.

Are You a Feminist/Chauvinist

A "feminist/chauvinist" is a term I have coined to personify the dichotomy that lives within so many American mistresses. Does feminist blood run through your veins, veins that are also running with that old male chauvinsim? Is there sexism in you? Take the following test and see."

Directions: This test is made of statements and questions. After each you must choose one answer—either "always," "sometimes," or "never." Circle your answer. Then proceed to the scoring and evaluation.

1. When my married man and I discuss the future, we dwell on his obstacles, his kids, his financial drawbacks, and his timing schedule.
   always
   sometimes
   never

2. When my married man and I are going through a crisis, my job performance suffers.
   always
   sometimes
   never

3. If I had a sudden unexpected financial problem, I would ask my married man for money.
   always
   sometimes
   never

4. I spend hours assessing his odds for divorce, debating the issue with my girlfriends, and inadvertently probing him.
   always
   sometimes
   never

5. When his actions cause me heartache and pain, I hold back so as not to add to his pressures.
   always
   sometimes
   never

6. Since my married man my marriage or my views on marriage have changed.
   always
   sometimes
   never

7. I'm more inclined to worry and wonder about his situation, than to campaign for the Equal Rights Amendment at my local level.   always
sometimes
never

8. When he strongly objects to one of my friendships, I find myself eliminating that person from my life.   always
sometimes
never

9. My married man has become my best source of advice and approval.   always
sometimes
never

10. Rather than using my free time in hobbies and interests, I tend to use it waiting for him and hoping for his unexpected arrival.   always
sometimes
never

Scoring:
Each "always" answer is worth 10 points. Each "sometimes" answer is worth 5 points. Each "never" answer is worth 1 point. Write the number of points each is worth next to each circled answer. Next read what your score means.

Total your score.

Evaluation:

10–30 Points: The Feminist. If you scored in this range, your feminism is more than lip service. You are retaining your independence in thought. Your married man is not your sole source of advice, counsel, and approval. He isn't influencing all your views on marriage, your job performance, or your friendships. Although you are sympathetic to his problems and obstacles, you are sympathetic about your own, too. You don't hold back your pain or heartache, your pressures count equally. Feminism has made you self-sufficient and independent and you don't rely on a man for everything. And being that liberated makes you good mistress material because the married man can't be depended upon. Since you are strongly assertive, chances are that you will be strong enough to survive mistresshood when you find it stifling your feminist health.

31–70 Points: The Feminist-Chauvinist. If you scored in this range your feminism is divided. On the one hand some of your ideas and actions are very liberated. You may assert yourself to a degree. Sometimes you complain about your frustrations. Sometimes you dwell on his dilemma and odds, but not always. Sometimes your married man is your best friend and adviser and sometimes you don't take his advice. But at other times you may spend countless hours waiting for him to call or to come over. You worry more about things rather than take action. Too many "sometimes" answers is a difficult score to evaluate. You may be at a turning point headed for subservience. Or you may be holding your own and only accommodating occasionally. The key word for you is assertive. If your feminism is too divided, you may lose sight of it. Mistresses have a way of losing their identities. They have a tendency to become absorbed by the pathos of the married man. Right now you're in the middle. Be careful.

71–100 Points: The Unfeminist: If you scored in this range, you may be a feminist on the outside, but inside you are strictly unfeminist. Even though you may be well educated, well read, well tuned to all the feminist strides, your heart is reactionary. You may be the first woman banking executive or the first woman state trooper, but you are the last woman you think about. You are obsessed with his state of mind, not yours. You rely on his schedule, his timing, his assessment of the world, not your own. You would rather suffer silently than burden him with your pain. You take care of your household, your career, your finances, your children, and you take care of your frustrations too. You may be liberated and assertive in every episode of your life until you are in the presence of your married man. Then all you can think of is him. Sometimes the more independent we are the better mistresses we can be. The problem is that you can short-change yourself. Feminist strides should not stop when you leave the office or get out of bed. Your consciousness should be there in every conversation and thought of your married man. Unfeminism leads to unhappiness.

In Conclusion:
This test was really a one of degree—how much of your assertiveness gets translated into your behavior. Not your behavior at the office but that which governs the heart.

CHAPTER 4

A Complex vs. a Complex Phase: Psychology and the Mistress

The psychological community has somehow failed the mistress. I don't believe that their failure was deliberate or malicious. However, therapists for the most part have ignored the mistress, stereotyped her dilemma, or failed to grasp the unique problem of the mistress community.

This radical indictment of the psychological community is not only my personal judgment. Although I must confess that I have never been comfortable with the standard perception and analysis of the mistress. The indictment came to me piecemeal, in different comments and different experiences from individual mistresses throughout America.

"I feel I need some kind of help but first I have to understand how I got into this situation. I have discussed this in psychiatric therapy but never found any effective solutions because the problem was never dealt with specifically, only as part of an overall personality problem. I have come to the conclusion that only people with problems like this can help because they've been through it and understand." *(Seattle, Washington)*

"I spent several months in counseling but I quit. I kept talking about how not to pick up the phone or make it through the weekend alone and the counselor kept rehashing my childhood and how this trauma or that conflict was still influencing me. Now I am no dummy—I am an executive—but that counseling was too abstract." *(New York City)*

"I had been to a marriage counselor but discontinued it. He really offered no help, confidence, or reassurance as you have. He made me feel that this was a life-long sentence. I bought your book as soon as I heard about it and found the help I was looking for." *(St. Louis, Missouri)*

"I was glad to hear you disagree with a male psychologist on *Good Morning America*. I am certain that you and I and other mistresses know far better than a man what happened to us. I am a counseling psychologist, with a doctor's degree, and I believe that women are much better able to help themselves than a man can help us. No matter how well intentioned the men are, they are conditioned by society to think of themselves, and it is difficult if not impossible for them to empathize or grasp fully our situations." *(Newport Beach, California)*

"My area of specialty is human sexuality, particularly marital enrichment. From time to time I have encountered couples who are experiencing marital concerns where there is a mistress involved. I meet the needs of the couple in therapy. It leaves the mistress without attention. I'm sure my feelings about this ignorance of the mistress are shared." *(Springfield, Massachusetts)*

"I recently had a talk with a psychologist, trying to figure out why I let myself get in these situations. I feel cheap and hurt all the time and yet I can't break loose. The psychologist put me on a waiting list. This was at the county mental health clinic. I live in a small town and I work at the library. I'm going crazy waiting for my married man and now I'm going crazy on the waiting list for help." *(small town, West Virginia)*

That is a cross-section of criticisms from mistresses. It was the inadequacies, injustices, and misconceptions suggested here that led me down the path to explore the mistress and the field of psychology.

In this chapter we are going to outline the standard psychological perception, analysis, and profile of the mistress. Then I am going to compare that information with some of my relevant data on the mistress population. Is mistressing a complex? Or is mistressing a phase? Is it a psychological problem or a sociological development? Is Freud helpful or harmful? Does mistressing have psychological benefits for some? Is mistressing a pathology or a pull toward passion? The mistress syndrome is indeed a very complicated dilemma. It is unique and widespread.

THE SHAPING OF THE AMERICAN MISTRESS

The view that psychotherapy isn't perfect but hazardous is not new. The view that psychology is male-oriented is not new. The viewpoint that you will see here is new. It is an extension of some radical viewpoints. Even more important, it is a revelation of new data, new solutions, and new knowledge about the mistress community. Hopefully those in the psychological community will remain openminded and learn how to grasp and help a growing phenomenon—the mistress.

Exactly how does the psychological community perceive the mistress in America? To arrive at an answer I polled a number of prominent psychiatrists and psychologists. Very few responded to my questionnaire. That underlines the point that the mistress is ignored and low priority.

Several admirable and compassionate experts did respond. While I am not in agreement with most of their contributions, I sincerely applaud their cooperation on so unconventional a study. According to classic psychological opinion, the mistress is seen as a woman with a personality problem. The personality problems of the mistress vary.

"From interviews with women who have such relationships, I'd think first of the low-ego type, who doesn't believe she's worth a man of her own; next, of the fearful type, fearful of domination, who 'choses' a partner she's not likely to become married to; and the 'femme fatale' type, who feeds her ego by conquest of men she has to lure into an extramarital affair, i.e., she takes them away from their own wives; she's competitive. *(Morton Hunt, author of* The Affair *and other books on marriage, divorce, and intimate relations)*

"In addition to the above feelings of unworthiness, many 'mistresses' are still engaged in a vicarious Oedipal rivalry with their own mothers for the affection of their fathers. Part of the rationale for the affair is revenge on the mother, and the moments spent with the married man are perceived as being taken at the expense of the wife-mother. This may account for why so many 'mistresses' seem satisfied with so little in their relationships—the basic feeling is, 'I shouldn't even be getting away with this—how dare I ask for more?' Their mothers tend to be unaffectionate, rejecting types, so the girl turns more to her father for sources of affection; the mothers' possessiveness only adds to her rejection of the girl, who ultimately gives up direct competition for the more vicarious sort." *(Dr. Anthony*

Pietropinto, Medical Director of the Mental Health Program at Lutheran Medical Center, Brooklyn, N.Y., and co-author of Beyond the Male Myth *and* Husbands and Wives *with Jacqueline Simmenauer.)*

According to these evaluations of the "mistress personality," most opinion also implies that this is destiny. In other words, this fate is apt to be repeated in past as well as future behavior.

"It is quite probable that the 'classic' mistress will have a history of married men and a future of the same, if she is bound to her lifestyle by feelings of unworthiness, fear of commitment, and unresolved Oedipal rivalry." *(Dr. Pietropinto)*

The age factor was not cited in either of these opinions. However, it is usually assumed that the mistress is a young woman involved with an older man. That generic combination further enhances the Oedipal typology.

Permit me to summarize the psychological viewpoint on the mistress reflected here and by most in the community of therapists. The mistress is a woman with a personality problem, be it low self-esteem, fear of commitment, Oedipal hangovers, and/or masochism. Please make note that these are all in psychological terms. In other words we could say that these psychological problems in the mistress personality make up the mistress complex. The mistress complex, accordingly, is rooted in childhood. It is a complex that will in all likelihood dominate the woman's behavior and destine her to the mistress lifestyle forever unless she seeks out qualified help.

These are the educated conclusions and analyses. They are not mine. There are a meager few, women to be exact, who have taken a step back and questioned the analysis of the mistress and the validity of psychotherapy. I have done so with the urgings of many mistresses looking for help and finding none in conventional psychological typologies. Before I offer my opinions and my data step by step, I'd like to present a profile which will help explain my arguments.

Phases of the Moon

Nora felt drawn toward her married man as if the moon were controlling her the way it controlled the tides. In spite of her maturity for age thirty-two; her achievements in business, which were considerable; her marriage, which was stable; she could feel the magneticism eclipsing her rationality.

"The married man in my life was one of my clients. We had never openly explored our mutual attraction, but we both knew it was there. Then we were heading for a time when we would be working closely together. The sexual tension became irresistible for me and him. Our sex lives at home were routine. We, almost involuntarily it seems now, entered into an agreement whereby we would exchange sexual intimacy without it affecting our marriages."

Nora had never been unfaithful before. There had been temptation and her sexual activity at home was more infrequent than she would have liked, but she always abstained from affairs. Why this sudden change of policy? Nora didn't know. Maybe it was a full moon.

"I was naive to think that a major change in my sex life would not affect my husband's and my relationship. I had no idea of what I was getting into. The sexual intimacy led to emotional intimacy. Emotional intimacy led to emotional dependence. Then I felt unstable all the time, like my feet weren't on the ground. Fortunately my business didn't suffer. I was never that far into mooning for this man."

Nora's feet weren't on the ground because she was living in the clouds, wrapped in the newness of fresh passion and frozen in fantasy. It took awhile for the illusion to sour, but affairs go in cycles like all else in nature.

"I felt very uncomfortable with all this. I tried to alter my marriage, first by asking for sexual freedom. Then by separation. My married man was mostly unavailable and made me feel like a yo-yo on a string. I knew my attitude and need for him was my problem, but I found only conflicts in my emotions and no resolutions.

"I told my husband about it all and why I think it happened. We are now in the process of working things out, our sex lives and our emotional lives as well. The future is still nebulous, but now whatever becomes of my marriage will be my free individual choice. I still love the married man, but will never see him again. Nor will I try an affair again."

Sometimes the cycles we live are like those in nature. New moon, old moon; new love, old love. Full moons have strange effects as do human passions. Turning tides are like turning passions, strong and yet subject to ultimate control. Nora's four-year experience with mistressing was very much like the phases of the moon.

Nora's case and many others like it refute the tenets that traditionally are held with regard to the mistress situation. My research suggests that Nora and thousands of other mistresses do not have personality problems. I believe there is no such thing as a mistress complex which fits *all* women who get themselves involved with married men. Nora's experience was a phase in her life, albeit a complex one.

It seems to me that most psychiatrists and psychotherapists forget the impact of sociological developments on the loves of mistresses. They talk exclusively of Oedipal rivalries, Freudian destinies and masochistic deficiencies in self-esteem.

First a word about the Oedipal fixation. The stereotypical mistress/married man couple had a huge age gap between them. This older man fixation supposedly grew out of the Electra tendencies of the mistress. Statistically I found no such typology. I researched the age span between the mistress and the married man. Nearly 40% of the mistress/married man couples had an age span of one to five years between them. Thirty % had an age span of six to ten years between them. Less than 20% had an age span of eleven to fifteen years between them. 9% had an age span of sixteen to twenty years between them. Less than 5% had a twenty-plus age span between them. And you must remember that the mistress population is varied in age. We will give an age breakdown later. Suffice to say here that mistresses come in all ages. Most get involved with a relative peer. Age spans become less significant as the mistress enters the later decades. There is no statistical evidence that mistresses are young Electra-oriented women, seeking out a father image in an older man.

In defining the mistress as a woman with a personality problem rooted in childhood, therapists assume habitual involvement with married men. In other words the mistress complex would manifest itself repeatedly throughout the life of the mistress. I researched mistresshood with pattern as a variable and found no such destiny. Married men, one after another, do not happen to most women in triangles. Mistresshood is not habitual. It is addictive. There is a difference. Most mistresses get hooked once; once is enough. The ones that encounter more married men are influenced by sociological factors as you will see further on.

The fear of domination, or, as I have called it, "the spinster syndrome," is another attempt at psychological explanation of a mistress' behavior. This theory suggests that a mistress seeks out a married man to avoid committing herself as in a marriage. I found this, too, to be an overgeneralization. Why? Marital statuses are varied. Singles are the largest proportion, but marrieds, divorcées, and widows account for approximately 60% of the mistress population. Each status segment has a vulnerability to the lifestyle, as you will see in detail as we focus on each. Again sociological considerations often make the mistress.

By sociological developments, I mean situations: roles, pressures, and needs in the life of the woman who becomes a mistress. For example, for a divorcée fear of remarriage; sexual tension of the job; sexual liberation. These are what is called "situational factors." They are different in the life of each mistress, yet very influential.

"I am working toward a career which demands a great deal of advanced training but allows a very stable financial life in the long run. I enjoy being free of the obligations that most women my age have, husband and children. While I ponder my decision not to have children (whether I marry or not), I never doubt my devotion to career as a wise choice for me. My married man was the first man I had met who fully understood, even applauded, my profession plans. I admired him. He was clearly an intelligent person who was comfortable with me as I choose to be. For me being a mistress fit." *(Johnson City, Tennessee)*

"I am twice widowed and now have a live-in lover for three years on and off, who is married. My marriages haven't been made in heaven but they suited my life well. One of my husbands for twelve years was much younger than I, but he was a good father to my infant son. My infant son needed a father more than I needed a grand passion. Another of my husbands was an alcoholic, but I stood by him too. As you can see I am a woman of contradictions, romantic and practical; serious and with a sense of humor. I am a sensualist, too, who in her later years of womanhood has found out what a wonderful body and soul she has and all because of a married man. He gave me what neither husband did and I want to throw bouquets at being a mistress. This is one situation that is giving me the best."
(New Hampshire)

These two examples are of women who found married men convenient and consistent in their situations. Throughout the pages of this book you will see situational factors at work again and again in the making of the American mistress. Situational factors, be they working, morality, sexuality, or liberation, create far more triangles than Freudian stereotypes.

Is there a typical mistress personality profile? Many in the psychological community say yes and continue with the esteem deficiency, etc. And of course the masochism. I have given a great deal of thought to the questions both of self-esteem and masochism and what kind of woman becomes a mistress. There are other ways of looking at these personality elements. Apparently other mistresses, too, have silently pondered all this.

"I have thought a great deal about this matter, and I truly do not think we are lacking in self-esteem. We are merely victims of our humanity. When a man comes to us with a tragic tale, we feel compassion and that's how we get into trouble. I am a psychologist and work at a university. I fell for a man on the job who was in such need as this—compassion, etc. He really played on my sympathies. When I finally broke off with this married man, I lost my job and my research grants, friends, and most of my professional reputation. We females are the compassionate ones. The man rarely is. We end up losing. Men take mistresses and expect them to wait around, because often that is what the wife does. Perhaps we have more self-esteem than the woman who is the wife to a man like this, because we think more of ourselves than to become locked into a permanent position of 'waiting' through marriage." *(San Jose, California)*

Thought-provoking, I think. Why is it that the entire question of self-esteem is always leveled at the mistress? The wife who is locked in the triangle for years, just as is the mistress, surely should be quizzed too about her lack of self-esteem or masochistic tendencies. A wife suffers pain, lies, and humiliation and yet the self-esteem issue is never extended to her angle in the triangle.

As for what kind of woman becomes a mistress, how about this? A woman who is compassionate, who listens more than she talks, who is more giving than selfish, who is altruistic. Why do we never hear these characteristics?

Now sometimes these characteristics can get out of hand and cease to be virtues. With mistresses that is often true. Yet my point is this—we always hear the profile of the mistress in neurotic psychiatric terms. The same vocabulary of the personality complex is always applied to the mistress. There is never any word about humanism, naiveté, or normality. This mistress complex as defined by the psychological community is an overgeneralization. It is a stereotype written with Greek tragedy and Christian predestination and irrelevant to the real profiles and lives of many mistresses. Mistresshood is not a pathology. It is, for most women who get involved with married men, a phase. Rather than a destiny, it is an experience limited in time.

Saying that mistressing is a phase is not to say it is simple. Mistresshood is indeed complicated, dangerous, and intense. I will try to summarize what the mistress phase is and how best to deal with it.

The mistress experience is like no other. While each mistress' tale is different, the mistresses themselves tend to share identical emotions and experiences. I'm going to focus on three aspects of mistressing that are central to understanding the mistress experience. These are isolation, complexity, and totality.

Loving a married man demands secrecy. As time goes on, that secrecy becomes more difficult to handle and maintain. Mistress/married man relationships occur in seclusion; they exist in private and total privacy, hidden from the outside world by his other life. This isolation breeds communication, intimacy, and romance. It also breeds loneliness, frustration, and anxiety. Mistresses tend to eliminate friends who are potential critics or tattlers, and to stay at home alone in the hope of hearing from the busy, often unavailable married man.

"I cut off all my friends that might disapprove. I did not feel worthy of my religious friends. My married friends were a no-no because they were wives. I refused to go anywhere for fear of missing a call or a visit. That left me alone and I soon became dishonest, lying to get off from work when I felt upset. I became an emotional wreck, often crying when he was away and high as a kite when he was with me." *(San Jose, California)*

Those extremes of feelings bring us to the next characteristic of mistressing, its complexity. Mistressing is pain, but it is pleasure too. It is highs and lows. It is agony and ecstasy. The life of a mistress is a roller coaster, either peaks or pits. It is pure passion and intensity. The experience is seen as a lifesaver for many, full of wonderful benefits. The misery is the bittersweet price.

"Jed has changed my life. I am now on my own. I used to drink a lot and now I hardly ever do. I read some books I would never have touched. I've lost twenty-five pounds. Jed wants me to get a better job and I'm looking. He fills me with pride and encouragement. As for my emotional state, I really don't know. But he has done a lot for me." *(small town, Washington)*

"My married man made me realize that I was capable of loving again very deeply. I had been living an empty, cold existence, surviving from one day to the next barely. Now I am back in the business of living making a new life for myself. All this is because of his love. My emotional status is another matter. For the first time in my life I've found the love of a lifetime. Unfortunately I also found long depressions when he's gone and panic at not being able to have him forever. It's that roller coaster you talk about." *(Camden, New Jersey)*

"I will never be sorry because he made me into a whole total woman. I am aware of myself and of the birds singing as never before. He brought out things in me that were repressed. I never felt so glad to be a woman. I hate the times away from him, the nights alone are hell. I can't bear the thoughts of the good times he has with his wife. I want desperately to forget him sometimes, but then he's here and we're back in the business of bliss again." *(Farmington, New York)*

The high points are so exquisite that a mistress yearns for more. The low points are so depressing that it becomes impossible to imagine life without him, which is equated to this depression on a constant basis. That is where the addiction comes in. Many mistresses tell me time and again, "I can't live like this anymore; but I can't live without him." Life becomes a quest for more time with the married man, for a deeper commitment, a more hopeful future. And so the melodrama takes shape. Will he or won't he commit himself?

Mistresses find themselves starring in a soap opera, where every day holds dramatic possibilities and every conversation holds profound clues. Will he divorce his wife? Will she become pregnant? Will I get fired if someone on the job gossips? Will he get fired? Will divorce leave him penniless? Will he forfeit his children? The suspense is enough to keep any mistress addicted to tomorrow's episode. The panic and the promise are enervating, excruciating, and captivating.

In all this melodrama the mistress loses sight of herself as a person outside the triangle. She loses her identity as anything but a lady-in-waiting. The married man holds all the cards to the future. He has all the answers, to all the questions. The addiction is complete when the mistress gives the married man all this power and keeps all the hope for herself. He becomes the first thing she thinks about at dawn and the last thing she thinks about at night. The mistress' identity revolves completely around the married man. She's hooked waiting for another high, waiting for Someday, or waiting for a way out. Powerlessness is the key word for her. Passion is the theme. Destiny is the plot, and not much of one because destiny often means nothing happens.

The triangle for the mistress tends to become a total obsession. The passions are consuming. One of the main elements consumed is reason. Rationality gives way to the torrent of passion. Women have been reared to place a premium on romance. Mistresses exemplify that lesson. Mistresses are in what you might call "Triangle Warp." Their life takes on a different time scale, a different schedule, a different time zone—dominated by the married man.

The mistress is not "sick" psychologically. Situational factors lead many women into affairs. Passions and preoccupations keep them there. Then there is the "Investment Clause." The Investment Clause is not only reserved for mistresses. Many women use it, but the mistress is a classic case. It says, "I've invested so much emotion in this relationship and so much time. How can I give it up after all I've put in?" This investment-type thinking makes it harder to walk away from the triangle, just as it can make it hard to nullify a marriage or a long engagement. So the mistress has passion, life's lessons, and common thinking-patterns all keeping her in her triangle.

The mistress dilemma is not a personality problem. It is a temporary question of lost identity. You cannot reach a mistress through Freudian analogies or lectures. You must slowly change her focus from the married man back to what is best for her. Most mistresses want a resolution but find resolving their mistresshood hard. The mistress must realize she has the resolving power. She must learn to tap her power, exert her rights, and manage her destiny.

I can't list treatment in a paragraph. In *The Mistress Survival Manual* I have developed a program to help a mistress understand her behavior and sort out her future. It is a process in which she regains her identity and the control of her life. She learns to see traps like the Investment Clause. It is based on conscious decisions and options, not unconscious Freudian legacies. Mistresses labor under ordinary problems of love and unique problems of mistressing. But the combination is not psychotic. My program is simple and it works, as many mistresses have told me.

Can passion be so potent a force in ruling the mistress? Is my say-so backed up by anyone in the psychological community? There is a new study by Dorothy Tennov, PhD, a practicing behavioral consultant and professor at the University of Bridgeport, called *Love and Limerence: The Experience of Being in Love*. Dr. Tennov distinguishes between love and romantic madness, which she calls "limerence," and gives us a new understanding of the appeal and strength of infatuation. I recommend this book to any mistress looking for a normal explanation for her romantic behavior.

About the mistress and personality types, Dr. Tennov said, "My whole philosophy is that we've done ridiculous things with personality types. People are individuals. Typologies add up to insults and are not very fruitful."

THE SHAPING OF THE AMERICAN MISTRESS

I would like to go a step further. The psychological community has not only ignored and overgeneralized the mistress experience, they have done damage to women with their intellectual simplistic paradigms. Reading their analyses of depressing destinies and uncontrollable fixations can only make a mistress feel more helpless about herself and her future.

"I always felt that I had been a terrible person for being a mistress. I read a few things in the library that made me feel even worse. I guess I never thought there were other women out there like me. Until I heard what you had to say, I always felt ashamed and afraid that there was nothing I could do for myself." *(Ann Arbor, Michigan)*

By defining the mistress as a woman with a personality problem, the psychological community is labeling these mistresses as "sick." That lowers self-esteem further. It tends to make a woman feel worse about herself. Mistresses gain guilt from wives and doom from psychiatrists. It has a spiraling, downward effect on their self-image. They continue in the tortures of the triangle because they feel even more helpless and more convinced they deserve this misery. Psychotherapists concentrate on the subconscious world, which is beyond the mistress' control. What mistresses need is direction on conscious behaviors, not concentration on the fact that their actions are beyond their grasp. Many mistresses get themselves into affairs and are capable of getting themselves out of the affairs. Guidance to self-help is needed, not self-damaging philosophies.

The field of psychology has been dominated by male thinking. That hasn't helped with the understanding of the mistress' situation. However, women, too, have been guilty of dismissing the mistress experience with generalizations.

"I'll be glad to share with you whatever contributes to the improvement of conditions for mistresses. I am very much annoyed by many of the recently published studies and books by women on women that put us in a bad light, books that emphasize our weaknesses or that focus on our condition without showing what environmental pressures put us into bad circumstances. I do not like being constantly characterized as 'wanting to fail' or 'having math anxiety' or being 'emotionally inferior as a mistress.' I believe that we need to build up our image and to gain strength, not accept defeat because of this or that." *(Orlando, Florida)*

Standard psychological stereotyping doesn't initially make a mistress, but it does figure in the making of the mistress. Many women continue in their hopeless affairs because they believe it is a destiny or a syndrome beyond their control. Reading Freud can be an ominous, intimidating experience. For many it can do more harm than good to apply psychotherapeutic explanations to the mistress experience.

The psychological community must learn to outgrow the myths about femmes fatales and masochistic Electras, just as larger society must outgrow the myths about black negligees and caviar. They must learn to deal with the mistress as she is—an ordinary woman with a problem, yes, but not a psychological problem destined to plague her eternally. The mistress is no more "sick" than the husband or the wife in a triangle. Each has a dilemma. The mistress' dilemma will not be helped so long as despair permeates her definition in Freudian imagery. Most mistresses don't need years of therapy. Sometimes all they need is some self-analysis in front of a mirror or a calendar.

Mistresses don't need the burden of a "mistress complex." The complicated phase that a triangle brings is enough of a burden. The psychological community must reassess their beliefs, look at my research, and mobilize their resources in a new direction. Kids in the sixties were vulnerable to drugs. Women in the seventies and eighties are vulnerable to married men. Mistressinq isn't a pathology. It is a social phenomenon; ordinary and yet extraordinary, a complex phase not a complex.

PART TWO

The Profile of the American Mistress

CHAPTER 5

Living Single, Loving Alone: The Single Mistress

What is it like living single and loving a married man? Who are the single mistresses? What do they do with their time and with their married man? How do they feel about things like marriage, freedom, and their futures? Are their married men taking them to some destination of their own design or are they preventing them from getting there?

We've looked at forces that contributed to the making of the American mistress, now it's time to look at those forces in action. We're going to look at slices of life for some of the mistresses whom I have met.

The first category is the single mistress, because her grouping is the largest in the mistress community. 40% of women who get involved with married men are single. In all likelihood that suggests an image, some cross between the cover girl on a fashion magazine and a black widow spider. Because of that prejudice, I'm going to introduce you to a cross-section of mistresses. They share a single status and some other variables, but they are quite diverse in other ways.

The profiles will illustrate along the way what makes singles prone to becoming mistresses or what makes them choose mistresshood. If you are a mistress, you will learn something about how you got there. If you are not a mistress, you'll learn about it the easy way.

Promises and Secrets

Charmaine is full of the promise of life. At twenty-four years old she is bursting with life's possibilities and simultaneously bursting with a secret. I'd better let her get it out before she explodes.

"Thank you, thank you. I am so damn grateful to have someone to tell this to. Why do people have such a need to tell all about themselves? I'm afraid I'll die and no one will ever know what's so vital to me. This may be the most important thing that has happened in my life, him.

"Yes, he's a fine human being and I want everyone to know how fine. I want to shout about his photography awards and how I've never felt so good. I was beginning to think that what I wanted was sheer illusion and could never truly exist, much less happen to me."

Charmaine is working as a secretary now just to make ends meet. Her love and her hope is all wrapped up in the theater and John. She's torn between acting and designing sets, and she's quite good at both. She and John met while working on a local stage production. They started to carpool. They both saved energy and expended it. John, thirty-one, and Charmaine seemed full of energy and incapable of running dry.

"His being married didn't bother me in the beginning. I was nowhere near ready to get married, so I can wait it out with his being married. Now we're overjoyed to drive somewhere after rehearsal, talk things over, talk theater, and hold hands. We make love like a couple of kids in the backseat, 'cause right now that's the best we can do."

Charmaine measures the passage of time by opening nights and cast parties. To be more exact, she and John have been going together for two years plus. No one knows because no one would understand.

John doesn't have any children by his wife. She, his wife, has one from a former marriage. John loves the child, being a father, and wants to have more children. John's wife doesn't want any more.

"I'm hoping that his wife's refusal to have his child will drive them apart. Aren't I hideous? But then again, the promise of his child is a wonderful thing for me to think about. His wife's wrong. Wrong for him anyway."

Charmaine feels her life is just blossoming. Her career in the theater is germinating. Love is blooming. Her identity is strengthening. Only her future with John is a promise that might never be any more than a secret.

"Because of John I have experienced the beauty of caring and intimacy that I knew was out there somewhere. I won't be afraid to be what I am and work for my theatrical aspirations. I will always know I'm special. I will always be pretty. I will never settle for less in a man, or less from myself, or less from life."

Because John likes her and all she hopes to be, Charmaine says she likes herself more. The only thing she doesn't like is being a mistress. Over and over to me Charmaine's life says promises and secrets. And although her future seems fertile, and her past furtive, it is the present that she explodes with. She has told me a secret promise, "I will never never date a married man again.

"I haven't the foggiest if John will divorce; it's a wish I promise to make come true."

Charmaine promised herself and me that her secret will someday see the light of life. In a way it has.
What you should note about the profile of Charmaine is her youthful present orientation, the isolation that is involved in having an affair, and her tendency to delay commitments like marriage and children. They all have something to do with being single, but not always.

The Chain of Command

Bobbi was a soldier, not figuratively but literally. She was in the army. She loved the military life. What might seem like a restricted way of life to some people was to Bobbi a life filled with opportunity.

"The army has given me a home. To me it is a structure. Right now because of my age, twenty-eight, I have a lot of decisions to make. For instance I've narrowed down where I'd like to live and settle down. I have decided I definitely want to continue my education. The army will help me to do that."

The army provided Bobbi with another opportunity—that of becoming a mistress. These days that is the source of confusion. It has also made Bobbi's time of decisions one of indecision.

"I met Tex because we both work in the same building. He's in the military too. Actually we were just passing each other. I worked the day shift, he the night shift. He was locking up one morning as I was coming to work. That was the first time we spoke to each other."

Although Bobbi remembers that first conversation perfectly, quite a bit has occurred in her life since then. And in Tex's life too.

"Tex had been married for six years, but not happily. They had been high school sweethearts and you know how bad those matches can be. His wife hates being married to a military officer. She hates the army, the transfers, the living arrangements, everything. Since he and I are both in the military by choice, we share that way of life and that thinking, do you know what I mean? We complement each other. And there's no hassle because he is not in my chain of command."

When Bobbi talks about her chain of command she is referring to her hierarchy of bosses in the army. She's in a chain of command, all right. She is in chains to Tex. Who will give the ultimate commands for their future? Right now they are both drawing up strategy plans for the future, individually and together.

"Tex left his wife. They have one child, whom he really misses. Tex wants custody so I'm going through a lot of changes about the whole subject of kids. I thought I never wanted children. But now I might wind up as a stepmother and maybe even have one of our own. Tex's wife is fighting the divorce tooth and claw. They had a lousy marriage and so it's logical I guess that they are going to have a lousy divorce too."

Military life has certainly given both Bobbi and Tex stamina. All that training seems to be helping them cope with the stresses of changing their lifestyles. Being in the army may mean taking orders some of the time, but both Bobbi and Tex seem bent on designing their own orders for their own lives. They seem to be on the right track. We are all in some chain of command. Bobbi's got it all organized or at least she's on her way. She's more than a military person and more than a mistress. In her chain of command she gives orders and takes them.

"Loving a married man is hard, even when things are looking up for the future. Sometimes I think it's because our lifestyle has these imposed restrictions."

Bobbi is referring to the army. But what lifestyle has no restrictions? For a mistress, she's doing fine.

Sometimes our values change, as in Bobbi's case. Sometimes our values betray us. It's a nasty lesson in irony, but it happens.

Independence ... Prize or Price

Deidre is lying in her bed alone only hours after having her first abortion, at age thirty-five.

"On top of the experience being brutal and devastating, I really wanted that baby. Just how much I never admitted to myself. I endure this because I wasn't smart enough to avoid falling in love with a married man."

It's ironic that Deidre should say she wasn't smart. Actually she belongs to a club whose members are in the top IQ stratum of America. Certainly her brains have served her well in the business world after a magna cum laude graduation from Radcliffe. And she had a reason, surely, at the beginning of her affair.

Deidre met Paul at a convention. They shared the same business; at first the same intentions not to get strings attached to each other. They strung each other along periodically for seven years, until this present crisis that Deidre strung out.

"I knew I had a good thing with Paul. The chemistry was wonderful. I had never been to bed with anyone before. I was always shy, alienated, and too busy with studies or, afterwards, working. The relationship was safe, satisfying. I liked my independence. It was like a prize I had won."

That particular quotation is how Deidre felt the first couple of years into the affair. She had always been different. She had been smarter than most, intellectually; more successful than most, speaking of women in high management. Being a mistress was another role that was different.

Deidre's mind was always drawn to the logic of things. When logic was absent she knew instinctively that things in her life weren't right. This love affair was going nowhere. Then her pregnancy really did it.

"Being pregnant with Paul's child was horrible. I had so many new feelings, of maternalism, filial feelings, positive feelings. Then I had all these negative feelings because he was married. It was too illogical so I chose abortion."

Deidre was having postpregnancy depression because now the abortion, which seemed logical, didn't solve her conflicts. Still not being able to desert logic, she got to the heart of her problem. This list was responsible, for "I'm not going to see Paul anymore, because I love myself more than this."

Here is her list that prompted that decision.

Things I like about being a mistress/	*Things I dislike about being a mistress*
romance	insecurity
illusion	despair
spontaneity	anxiety
ecstasy	pain
intimacy	loneliness
intrigue	disappointment
fun	isolation
erotic	guilt
freedom	shame
	embarrassment
	frustration
	depression
	fear

unhappiness
confusion
suffering
addiction
despondency
pressure
compromise
loss
distance
tension
stress
panic
hostility
dishonesty

In the wake of the list Deidre wrote me that,

"I've made my final decision to leave the man I love. I see now that I must. I'm sick to my stomach because of this list and the abortion and the fear that I could go on for years like that woman who was a mistress for forty years in your book. I think my personal little hell here was created by my independence. It's a price that I've paid."

First Deidre said "prize" about her independence. Then she said "price." Indeed she paid an expensive price for a prize that looked awful in a logical list. So how did someone so smart get into so stupid a dilemma? Hindsight provided the logic for Deidre. It goes to prove that mistresses can be very smart and not so smart. Thirty-five is not too old to learn.

Deidre's story points up the relationship that exists between being independent and becoming a mistress. The next story points up another relationship. A different kind of independence cast in carefree, kicks, and fun.

Playing with Fire

Ramona was a pyromaniac—romantically speaking that is. Love to her had to have a touch of arson, that fire. Her self-ignition started the summer before she met her married man.

"I had always been plump and worn glasses. That summer I came out of my shell—I was down to a size eight and got new contact lenses. I never knew I could be desirable till then. I began going out with numerous guys and going to bed with them—just for that feeling. I didn't want anything more than the fun of dancing and making love. I guess I read too much of *Cosmopolitan* and *The Sensuous Woman*"

Ramona met Larry the first time when he did some repairs on her car. Then she began running into him on Saturday nights at clubs. It was a small town and a small world.

"Larry told me he liked to socialize. I felt sorry for his wife. Then the more I saw him the more we talked, and teased. There was something dangerous about us. It was fire between us. His being married made it exciting, I guess."

The internal combustion got to be too hot to avoid, so they consummated their affair. The consummation provided what has turned out to be so far an eternal fire.

"Married men make love to you differently. A single guy feels he can make it with anyone so he comes to your bed and does it without a second thought. A married man makes love to you with feeling."

Ramona admitted that she got a kick out of the intrigue of loving a married man. However, the inconvenience was a problem. She lived with her parents and that wouldn't do. So she rented an apartment with a fireplace. But the fires all came from her and Larry.

Did Ramona know she was playing with fire?
"Well, I do hate the waiting. I'm holding on till Thanksgiving because we can spend a whole night together when he goes 'hunting.' For me it's worth it. He's fun and it's free. There's nothing else that makes me feel so exciting."

Loving a married man gave Ramona just the right amount of passion and pain. It kept her always burning—and for a romantic arsonist that's perfect!

Operator ?!

All the while I got to know Katherine, I kept thinking it would be poetic justice if she were a telephone operator. She wasn't. She was a nurse. If anyone was the operator it was her married man. Even he was understandable, if not altogether likable.

As a nurse, Katherine was constantly surrounded by life and death. However, the matters of life and death that were most crucial to her came over the telephone. All day, every day, she waited for the telephone. Twenty years of being a mistress and most of it revolved around the telephone.

"I've spent two decades of my life, from thirty-three to fifty-four, waiting to be paged on the hospital intercom. I've even dubbed it my tyranny of the telephone."

Katherine's married man was a doctor, a surgeon, a man with a problematic alcoholic wife and an aging mistress. Managing all that apparently was a handful.

"Steven and I didn't meet often at all. Maybe once every three weeks. But every day he'd call. He'd be erotic over the phone. He'd be romantic and jealous. He'd tell me all about his wife's escapades and his embarrassments."

Katherine lived her life on duty, off duty, years in and out. In most respects her life was dull, except for that telephone.

"He's with me twenty-four hours a day, even when we're apart." That seemed to be what kept her going all those years.

"There was never anyone else before my married man. He's enough for me."

Katherine didn't have very exciting expectations. Throughout her courtship she told me that "everyone I worked with hated him so badly for the way he treated me, you know, never getting a divorce and marrying me. Naturally I defended him and made excuses for him. I needed him. He was my everything. I could not live without him. Bullshit—he was my only thing."

What Katherine had was really more of a phone pal than anything else, but it was that or being totally alone. To some women having someone who doesn't always give is better than having no one to even disappoint you. Somehow life, marriage, children, all passed her by while she nursed life and death and that telephone.

Steven wasn't all bad. His wife was an emotional invalid and had attempted suicide twice. It seemed that "her father took it upon himself to tell her that the problems in their marriage were not between them, but because of the other woman in Steven's life."

At least I thought that the good doctor wasn't too bad until the end of Katherine's story.

"Keep in mind I'm fifty-four and he's sixty-three, and we've been together for twenty years. Out of the clear blue sky he has told me he has become infatuated with someone from his past. We weren't having trouble. We were getting along fine as usual. The other woman is his age, married and divorced three times and an alcoholic. I can't understand his leaving one alcoholic for another and more problems. He is not one. He also said it might just be a fling."

What's even worse than what he said to her was the fact that he said it all over the phone. After twenty years he just said goodbye and hung up.

Katherine's profile had something to do with low horizons and downright loneliness. Single living ages into "spinsterhood" for some. The stigma is nothing compared to the being alone all of the time. For this type of single woman a married man is better than no man.

In fact all the slices of mistress life presented here demonstrate variables shared by single women who become mistresses. And while none of the women here characteristically go out looking for a married man, they do exert a choice by accepting one. A passive choice or a choice by default, but still a choice. It can all be summed up in the word priorities. Whether you are talking about the career woman or the independence buff, the socialite or a woman who sees herself as a hopeless "spinster," you are talking about priorities. Mistresses are not choosing marriage and family. They may be hoping, but that is not the same thing. They are choosing their work, or their immediate pleasure, or compromise for the man they love. If it is not a choice of priorities, it is the absence of them.

Mistresses are usually aware of their priorities. They are also aware of the traditional life elements that are passing them by.

"Sometimes I wanted him to get a divorce, but I'm in a career and really don't want marriage the majority of the time." *(Midwest, thirty-five)*

"I always knew I was trading off. I was putting years of energy into my job, while most women put that energy into looking for a husband. I wasn't contented but I compromised with someone else's husband." *(Decatur, Georgia, forty-one)*

"He gave me the freedom that I needed to work at my career. A husband might not have done that. As well as the chance to know a very fine individual." *(Utah, twenty-three)*

Among single women there is a definite trend now to view work as a life goal. Most single women work and many take that work seriously. Single women who feel this way are well suited to married men, at least from that career standpoint. Married men can offer companionship and affection and yet not make demands that would jeopardize the career climb. However, when career is the priority it does entail sacrifices in the more traditional areas.

How do the mistresses feel about marriage? As they approach the end of the childbearing span, how do they feel about children?

"I don't want marriage now. So his marriage is not my concern. What scares me is what will happen when I am ready to get married?" *(Arizona, twenty-three)*

"I guess I've never gotten married because I never really worked at it. I never looked for a husband. Man-hunting, all that trapping stuff, was beneath me. I don't really know what to do about it now." *(Peekskill, New York, thirty-eight)*

"I always wanted to get married. It just didn't happen for me. I wasn't one of the lucky ones." *(Howard County, Maryland, fifty five)*

For a mistress the concept of children is often twofold. There are the children whom the mistress and her married man could have. There are the children he already has. Oftentimes she has feelings about both.

"I do want children. I'm thirty-two, time is running out. I'm jealous about his children. I feel jealousy. I want them to be 'ours.'" *(Washington, D.C.)*

"How do I feel about children, don't remind me. I've been a mistress for thirteen years and now I'm too old to have children. How could I have let that happen!" *(small town, Maine, forty)*

I never really wanted children. Then I fell in love with him and now I look at every baby I see with longing. I don't know if it is my age, I'm thirty-one, or love. I just can't wait any longer for his divorce. He says he needs more time. I don't have more time to give." *(suburb, Boston, Massachusetts, thirty-one)*

"I'm too young to think about children yet. I've seen his. I've even babysat for them. I love them." *(New Haven, Connecticut, twenty-one)*

"Yes I've met his children. They were sick and he brought them to our office, but they did not know who I was. Loving, Mother from afar. I wanted my own but I knew that he would never allow it so I just compensated by pretending that his were mine." *(Benton, Arkansas, thirty-one)*

The passage of not going through parenthood can become quite a conflict for the mistress. Especially because the married man's children are so much a part of her life, whether she ever sees them or not. You can catch up with marriage, but after a fixed span of time you can't catch up with motherhood, not firsthand anyway. It's a priority that some mistresses ignore until it's too late. It is a matter of biology, and chemistry often eclipses it. I point it out here in this chapter and for the single mistress to alert her. If you want to be a parent, realize it before it is too late.

Not all mistresses are young and have their whole life ahead of them. But whether you are thirty, forty, or fifty, you still do have a future. How does the single mistress feel about the future? Being single, after all, means that the future is her domain and her design. How is the single mistress planning her future?

I found that the single mistress, and she is not alone in this, is not actively concerned with her future. Her future is not seen as her responsibility. Her future is often "Will he get a divorce?" Her future life plan is "on hold" or progressing only in so far as he is moving or not moving toward D-day, or divorce day.

Sometimes the entire concept of the future is avoided. Being a mistress regardless of status usually means not looking ahead or behind but just at the moment.

"I am at the end of my rope with him. I am still attractive, educated, have many interests, but emotionally I cannot handle being a mistress any longer. He keeps promising divorce, but how long should I give him? One year, five? He's had four already. David says that January will be the month for divorce. So now January will be the beginning of my future." *(Huntington, West Virginia)*

"I don't know about my future. He's changed my life, though. I spend more time alone, waiting for him to call or come over. I moved to another town so I could live alone and see him more; therefore I changed jobs. My emotional life is low, low. But generally I am an optimist." *(New York City)*

See the theme running through here? The married man is credited for the changes that have occurred. He is given the power to make the changes in the future of the mistress' life as well as his own. Looking at the married man to get the answers for the future is fallacious. He has no answers for himself, much less for the mistress, as we will see later in the book.

Comments about the future are often limited to one word,

sometimes optimist, sometimes pessimist. It takes more than one word to make a future. The future is too one-dimensional for the mistress, if she admits the concept at all. It is as a concept one of her biggest problems.

This future issue is most salient for the single mistress. Where is she going? Wherever she winds up, it will be her own doing.

"I wasn't going anywhere but crazy until your book made me write that essay on where I'll be five years from now. I had never thought that far ahead. I was writing a fairy tale according to the scoring. Now I've started meeting with a few other mistresses in our own little Mistresses Anonymous." *(small town, Southwest)*

"Loving my married man became my whole life and I was shocked how I changed to accommodate him. I took that test, *A New Man, A New Neurosis* and *Which Came First*—plans or married man. He changed me and all my goals. Now I'm finally starting to look again at my future." *(Memphis, Tennessee)*

Living single and loving a married man is the most common combination for mistresses. 40% have a lifestyle that includes priorities that tend to facilitate the affair with the married man. Goals like careers, independence, thinking only of today, not expecting the best of life, delaying commitments—these are some of the variables. Goals are very important for singles. They determine what you get out of life and what you miss getting. They can reveal to you how you got to where you are right now.

If you are a single mistress and didn't see yourself in any of the profiles, you will get to know more about yourself from analyzing what I call *The Mistress' Maze*. If you are not a mistress, knowing more about your goals can't hurt.

The Mistress' Maze

Are you familiar with mazes? A maze is a kind of puzzle, the kind that is a network of intricate paths. The object of the maze is to find your way through the labyrinth from beginning to end. Sometimes the life of the mistress becomes very much like a maze.

Has it ever puzzled you—how you got so involved with someone else's husband? You weren't looking for a married man. You weren't planning on falling in love with a married man. You never thought in a million years it could or would happen to you. Somehow it did. The question is how. Chances are you've given all this a great deal of thought, but you wind up confused in a maze of questions.

This test is designed to help you sort out the reasons why you in particular got involved with a married man. It is to be hoped that it will help you navigate through your mistress' maze.

Directions: Read all of the following statements carefully and choose from the multiple choices the best answer for you. Fill in your answer at the end in the space provided. Then proceed to the scoring and evaluation.

1. Marriage
   (a) doesn't just happen; you have to plan for it (b) is in the cards or it isn't (c) can distract you from your ambitions   1. _____
2. Housewife—
   (a) domestic technician (b) bore (c) companion   2. _____
3. A woman's childbearing span
   (a) seems to be getting longer but I haven't given it much thought (b) is still a fixed reality (c) is getting longer as we get older and more knowledgeable   3. _____
4. A sense of achievement is
   (a) more of a male preoccupation than a female concern (b) a goal that raising a child can satisfy (c) a drive that certain people feel more than others regardless of gender   4. _____
5. My goals
   (a) shift (b) are rigid (c) are flexible   5. _____
6. Satisfaction is
   (a) sharing my time with someone I love

(b) having a good time (c) getting things done   6. _____

7. Security
   (a) can be acquired through mutual trust
   (b) can't be assured because life has no guarantees (c) is best acquired if you depend on yourself for it   7. _____

8. A husband of one's own
   (a) would be nice to have but it doesn't always happen to everyone (b) is a goal everyone can achieve; for every woman there's a man waiting (c) can make you happy as well as miserable   8. _____

9. People have children because
   (a) they want to bear the fruit of their love (b) they have sex; the motive is simple, natural and that basic (c) they want to create, mold, and somehow ensure their mark on the world.   9. _____

10. Feminism
    (a) has helped me expand my occupational horizons (b) is useful to me sometimes and other times it's not (c) can go too far and become sexism   10. _____

11. Romantic love
    (a) can be very nonproductive (b) if cultivated properly can last a lifetime (c) is the most exciting thing in life   11. _____

12. The work you do is best described as
    (a) your occupation (b) your career (c) your job   12. _____

13. Love
    (a) comes and goes and passes some of us by (b) has many faces including parental love, platonic love, and romantic love (c) should be prized, grasped, and stolen if necessary   13. _____

14. A man's place
    (a) I'm not sure where it is anymore (b) is equal to a woman's place in whatever situation (c) is next to a woman.   14. _____

15. Success is
    (a) something that usually takes years of

dedication and hard work (b) achieved
when two people work together and
satisfy each others' needs (c) different
things to different people   15. _____

Scoring:
Each answer is worth a certain number of points. List your answer in the space provided. Then list the number of points as indicated in the table in the column labeled Points. Add up your points and read the Evaluation to see what your score means.

							Answer	Points
1.	(a)	5	(b)	1	(c)	10	1. _____	_____
2.	(a)	10	(b)	1	(c)	5	2. _____	_____
3.	(a)	1	(b)	5	(c)	10	3. _____	_____
4.	(a)	1	(b)	5	(c)	10	4. _____	_____
5.	(a)	1	(b)	10	(c)	5	5. _____	_____
6.	(a)	5	(b)	1	(c)	10	6. _____	_____
7.	(a)	5	(b)	1	(c)	10	7. _____	_____
8.	(a)	10	(b)	5	(c)	1	8. _____	_____
9.	(a)	5	(b)	1	(c)	10	9. _____	_____
10.	(a)	10	(b)	1	(c)	5	10. _____	_____
11.	(a)	10	(b)	5	(c)	1	11. _____	_____
12.	(a)	5	(b)	10	(c)	1	12. _____	_____
13.	(a)	10	(b)	5	(c)	1	13. _____	_____
14.	(a)	1	(b)	10	(c)	5	14. _____	_____
15.	(a)	10	(b)	5	(c)	1	15. _____	_____
							Total	_____

Evaluation:
15–60 Points: The Jigsaw Puzzle. If your score fell in this range, your life is like a jigsaw puzzle. You are fixed neither on a specific mating plan nor on a career. You are very much present-oriented. You live for today. Planning isn't one of your preoccupations. Marriage you think, may or may not be in the cards. And besides, husbands can make you miserable as well as happy. Your goals shift. Your definitions of things like security and success indicate that these things are hard to pin down. There are no absolutes out there in your view. Feminism is useful and at times useless. A man's place or the span of a woman's childbearing years—you don't have rigid, definite theories about these. You tend to take life a day at a time just

the way you take your job. In a nutshell, you have no clear priorities. Priorities are just not your priority.

With such a jigsaw puzzle philosophy of life, that married man just happened. Since no career worries made him seem disadvantageous, since you weren't husband hunting anyway, he fit in at the moment. You probably didn't take him seriously at first. He was just another slice of life. The danger, though, is that with your jigsaw lifestyle that married man can become your first and only priority.

65–100 Points: The Family Album. If your score fell in this range, you would like to see your life as in the pages of the family album. Marriage should be a planned goal according to you, and family living is your priority. You value sharing and planning things with your man. A housewife to you is a companion. A man's place is next to a woman. Children are the fruit of love between two adults. And love should be cultivated to last and last. Aside from romantic love there are parental, filial, and platonic affections. Security, success, their definitions are intertwined with family cooperation and productivity. Concerns like feminism and your occupations have their place, but not above your relationship. You are designed to be the star, the wife, the mother in a family album.

Therefore, loving a married man must be frustrating for you. You are right when you throw up your hands and wonder how such a traditional girl like you got wrapped up in the arms of someone else's husband. It was in all likelihood his respectability, his warmth, his parental knack that attracted you in the first place. Now you want him to be your husband and the father of your children. Unless he's inclined to become part of your family album; your priorities are definitely going to make you an unhappy mistress!

105–150 Points: The Résumé. If your score fell in this range, your life tends to read like a résumé. You are basically career oriented. Yes, you see your work as a career which is a lifelong commitment. Marriage isn't out of the picture entirely, but you are leery of it getting in the way of your rigid goals. Achievement is one of your drives and you feel that it's natural. You are quite liberated and value equal treatment of the sexes. You are independent and feel that is the best insurance for security. You can't bank on finding the right man so you feel it's better to develop your skills and work toward success. Your work isn't all drudgery because work can give one a sense of accomplishment. There may be room for childbearing, as the span gets longer according to new knowledge in the field. You give yourself lots of options, but your main priority is career.

Since your ambitions don't give you a great deal of energy or time for social life, your married man fitted into the résumé easily. You probably met him through work and you two probably share great professional camaraderie and respect. Since his other life makes demands on him, he is not likely to make demands on you. That arrangement seems just what you were looking for at the start. You must be careful, though, because loving a married man can interfere with your work, upset your priorities, and ruin that résumé!

In Conclusion:
Your choice of a married man was, strangely, a byproduct of your priorities or lack of them. Getting a clear idea of what your goals are can help you learn how you wound up a mistress and how that married man will affect the fruition of your goals. A mistress often feels imprisoned in a maze. However, you got yourself into that labyrinthine network and you can navigate it if you are careful and aware. A maze always has a way in and a way out. Your mistress maze is no different.

The single mistress is very important to me because I was once one. And the population is so huge. And the single woman's life and her entire future are at stake. Living single and loving a married man is sweet and sour. Life can be spiced up by a married man and he can fit well into your scheme of things. However, life goals can be spliced and that's what being single is when you are in love with a married man. It's living single and loving alone.

CHAPTER 6

Passionate License: The Married Mistress

One out of every four mistresses is a married woman. She is a woman who is torn between her husband and someone else's husband. She has a marriage license that supposedly means fidelity. She has a love outside her marriage that drives her to use some sort of passionate license. She is both a wife and a mistress at the same time.

We have all been conditioned to polarize the members of the triangle. There is the shameless, seductive mistress. Opposite her is the poor, martyred wife. The wife is seen as a victim of her husband's infidelity and his mistress' lust. However, in light of the real statistics, that polarization is inaccurate. The victimized wife and the victimizing mistress are stereotypes that shatter as the truth comes out. Twenty-five percent of the mistresses are themselves wives. There are no simple victims and villains in triangles.

The making of the married mistress in America is not simple. The married mistress is a player in two triangles, not one. The impact of her affair on marriage, family, divorce, children, and future is doubled. Usually that means double trouble. In the making of the married mistress there are some simple ingredients, but their impact and effect are traumatic.

Passion is a theme that you will find runs through many of the experiences of the married mistresses. In this chapter we are going to see what happens to the life of the wife when she becomes a mistress. Her marriage license and her passionate license create quite a love story. Who are the married mistresses? Why does it happen? What makes some wives honestly feel that fidelity is in some way cheating them? Marriage itself does play a significant role in the making of the married mistress. As the marriage vows are altered by the presence of one too many married men, what happens? Since the wife who is also a mistress is often a mother, how does motherhood further complicate matters? Can the wife who is the "infidel" handle an affair better than the wife whose husband is the unfaithful partner? And lastly when does an affair signal that it is time for a divorce? How can we ever distinguish between love and passion?

Before I present the first profile, I'd like to list a few related statistics. These are for you dedicated skeptics. In many of my audience-participation television appearances throughout the heartland of America, voices often rise up in disbelief that women, especially married women, are unfaithful to their husbands. These people think that men have such a monopoly on extramarital relationships. So for you...

Fact #1: By age forty, 40% of married women will have an affair. (Kinsey projection. Agreed-upon estimate by all researchers in the field.)

Fact #2: By age twenty-four, 24% of married wives will have an affair. (Playboy Foundation statistic, 1972)

Fact #3: The typical adulterer is in her mid-thirties, middle class, married about thirteen years, with at least one child. (Dr. Frederick Humphrey's reported findings as President of the American Association of Marriage and Family Counselors)

Note that these facts describe adultery for married women and not the mistress phenomenon per se. However, in the light of the high incidence of married women straying from their husbands, the size of the mistress population is easier to understand. Adultery leads to long-term affairs, oftentimes with married men.

I can honestly say that the number of married women in love with married men, other than their husbands, was surprising to me. Therefore, I was extra careful in assessing the numbers and especially interested in how it happened.

Patterns emerged with regard to the married mistress. Here are a few typical stories that reflect those patterns:

Loving Neighborly

Linda lives in a small town in Wyoming. There is no one who could be more surprised that Linda is having an affair with a married man than Linda herself. Linda is a full-time housewife, mother, wife, and a part-time lover. Here is how Linda explains it.

"I am married to a wonderful man and have been for twenty-four years. We have five daughters and three sons. The youngest is twelve, the oldest twenty-three. Eleven years ago a young couple with two small children bought the home next door to ours. We became fast friends and enjoyed doing things together, the usual like cookouts, parties, and vacations. I was not aware of it, but have been informed since that my neighbor fell in love with me the day we met. But it took eight years for me to feel the same about him. Now we are lovers and my life has become a horror show. I want to love my husband, but I feel I have stopped. I would never want to hurt my lover or his wife. I'm filled with guilt and he is too, but still we cling to each other. The problem I face is unique because I will be constantly faced with seeing him all the time because we will always be neighbors. If only I never had to look into his eyes again, I think I could do it. I could work on my marriage and try to recapture what I had before I met him."

At the outset Linda sounds calm, very suburban, and even contented in her marriage. Yet underneath she is consumed with this affair and how it is changing her self-image, her life, and her happiness. She seems to want it to end, but can't make the break from her lover.

Linda sounds like she had a full life before her married man's entrance. Eight children, a wonderful husband, a home and yet she now says, "I know it's love with my married man because he is my whole life." This is Linda's first dalliance with infidelity, and if she ever gets out of this three-and-a-half-year triangle, it will be her last.

Falling in love with a neighbor or someone in the immediate community is very common for the married mistress. These are basically the people with whom she comes in contact, especially if she doesn't work outside the home. Linda felt falling in love with a neighbor created a unique problem because she can't get away from him without moving. But loving neighborly is not unique; it's just the married mistress' way of having an affair and still keeping it in her own backyard.

Another pattern that emerged with the married mistress created an even stickier situation. This married man will be impossible to get away from because he is in the family.

Brotherly Love

Sueann and her married man have been in-laws for fourteen years. They have been lovers for five. Sueann's married man is her brother-in-law, her husband's brother. Sueann lives on a ranch in Oklahoma. Her married man does the repair work on the farm machinery. Sueann is thirty-one and her married man is thirty-nine.

"I'm not what you would call beautiful, I'm overweight and have reddish-dyed hair. I'm not the mistress type. My brother-in-law had wanted to date me for years and I wanted no part of it. Then about five years ago, we had this talk. I asked him why he waited so long for me. He'd been so patient. He'd never kissed me or anything and yet he had waited, why? He said he loved me. You could have knocked me over with a feather!"

Sueann said they would take long drives in his pickup or walks in the country. "Our meetings consisted of talking about being discovered by our families, the fear of becoming pregnant, how wrong it was to have an affair."

Sueann didn't say anything really about her husband. But she did say that when she's with her married man, "He makes me feel as though we're the only two people in the whole wide world. He whispers sweet nothings. I'm just overjoyed in every way."

Sueann said that she liked being a mistress. She liked "the newness of being with another man, the knowledge of a shared secret, and how good he makes me feel."

The brother-in-law match was common for the married mistress. In spite of the obvious complications—conducting a charade at family gatherings, the potential scandal and all—it was still prevalent. There were some days in my research when I had what I called a run on brother-in-laws. And while some married mistresses didn't say it was owing to a bad marriage, others did.

The Family Shoulder

It seems that in every family there are certain people who are the strong ones. Whenever there is a family crisis or hardship it is that tower of strength who rises to the occasion and smoothes things out. In addition to being a tower of strength, he or she is also a good person to talk to. The shoulder to lean on.

Chris rediscovered her brother-in-law as a good friend at a wake. She knew that he and his wife were having trouble in their marriage. It's not that Mike talked about it. His wife did—to anyone who would listen. God, everyone felt so awful for her! Everyone who didn't know the truth.

Chris knew Mike to be the victim, not the victimizer, in the bad marriage. After the wake they started meeting first in beer joints, then in motels.

"Our meetings consisted of talking to one another about our common problems—our marriages. I didn't feel that his marriage had anything to do with me, at first. I needed a friend. He was there, and so strong. I did not feel as guilty about his marriage as I did my own. In my house sex was just a word in a dictionary and for my husband and me communication was nonexistent. So why didn't I pack up and leave?

"Mike seemed to understand how scared I felt. How confusing life was for me. My husband says he loves me. I am not sure if I hate him or simply live with him because I have no alternative. I'm forty-six, you see, and facing Colorado alone is frightening."

Chris told me that she wanted more than a shoulder to lean on from Mike. But he seemed as immobilized in his bad marriage as she. Chris was looking for answers and depending on her tower of strength or me.

"Should I try to keep this farce together or simply forget it? And most important—what if I leave my husband, and Mike doesn't come with me? I love him but I need someone and if I can't have him then maybe I'd be better off staying where I am with my husband."

Even the family tower of strength can't provide the answers for Chris. Her story is not only common because of her filial choice, but because of her indecision. Getting involved with some member of the extended family is "natural" for some married mistresses. The capacity for friendship is there in the family organization. They know about each other through the family gossip grapevine. Friendships burst into affairs especially during periods of family crises. And then what?

The married mistress often finds that she has to decide whom to choose. How can she make that decision without losing the married man, the security her husband provides, or both? For Chris and other married mistresses who are riddled with indecision, I've designed a test at the end of this chapter: *To Divorce or Not to Divorce*.

One final pattern that I would like to dwell on involves the working wife who becomes a mistress. We've seen how work becomes a catalyst for affairs even to the most unsuspecting. Carol told me that working destroyed her marriage. In a way it did, but it can't be blamed on the job—not all of it.

Romantic Bondage

Carol said she had "the world on a string" back then. At twenty-eight in her little world in Wisconsin she had everything she had ever wanted.

"My husband had just turned twenty-nine. I had a daughter six and a son eight. We just moved into an old farmhouse that we always dreamed of buying. We had money in the bank and so on—nothing to worry about."

With both kids in school, Carol took a job selling land parcels part-time. She was a natural at selling. Things couldn't have been going better when...

"I started having these strange feelings come over me. I couldn't wait to see my boss every morning. It really bothered me. I got special treatment in the office, and loads of compliments. Little things like 'nice dress,' or a doughnut. Well, I guess I just couldn't stand these feelings I was getting anymore. They were different and so exciting, and were driving me crazy. I wanted to confess all this to him but I was scared."

One thing led to another as it often does and one afternoon over lunch the confessions were heard. Her married man felt all the same things. So began Carol's romantic bondage to Sam. Carol wanted Sam so badly that she couldn't think straight.

"It was May 7—isn't it funny how we remember dates so well? After a fantastic lunch we headed back and Sam said something about being left by me in pain and misery. I flipped. I brushed my fingers through his hair and told him everything that I was feeling. I'll never forget the magic of that moment when he said he knew exactly what I meant."

It wasn't all elation for Carol. Her husband was so proud of his working wife. She felt lousy because he shouldn't be so proud of her for what was going on at the office.

Carol tried living a lie, but after nine months she couldn't pull it off any longer. Those feelings were killing her.

"I told my husband I was in love with someone else. I didn't know what to do. He asked if I would give our marriage a chance. All I could think about was my romantic addiction to Sam. I said no and he moved out."

Carol felt some vague need to free herself. Romantic bondage has a way of creating those feelings. Only instead of freeing herself from her married man's passionate hold, she freed herself from her marriage. And although her married man felt the same romantic bondage, he couldn't free himself from his marriage. And so Carol is still enslaved by feelings. Different feelings now but with the same intensity.

"The tears won't quit and the nauseous feelings won't go away and the pain lingers. I feel lost and alone. This beautiful year wasn't supposed to end in tragedy for me. I was too willing to throw away my family for him. My husband still wants me back. He'd give me the moon, but I need time. I wish I could hate Sam for hurting me, but I don't. I still love him."

Carol is praying more now, she says, morning, noon, and night, hoping for some help to be freed from this romantic bondage.

Carol's tale is representative because many married women can't handle their own infidelity. An affair tends to make them question their entire lifestyle and marriage. Many, many wives separate from their husbands in the heat of passion and then find that their married man remains stationary. And it's not because the married man promises divorce either. You will see later that married men don't always promise divorce. No, the decision to leave for "love" is the married mistress' own judgment. The decision to end a good marriage in the wake of a great affair is risky. Romance sometimes makes us take risks without consulting reason.

All these married mistresses helped us see in what context the wife can become a mistress simultaneously. And yet none really clarifies just why this happens to some and not others. Of course bad marriages are easier to understand when the mistress issue comes up. But what about the wives who were "happy" and still got hooked up with a married man? Is there something about marriage itself that helps create the group of married mistresses?

Marriage is certainly not the simplistic answer to happiness that women were brought up to assume. Marriage is a beginning not an end. We all spend too much time longing for the event and organizing the rituals that celebrate the marriage. Not much thought is given to all the years that follow the honeymoon. To this add unrealistic expectations and women's new pressures and you have a very complicated institution. It is not uncommon for today's women to feel that fidelity is cheating them. Marriage's tedium, familiarity, neglect, and the little emotional struggles all add up to affairs with married men.

"I am a wife of twenty-six years, five children from fifteen to twenty-four. Evidently something was lacking in my marriage. For me the excitement seemed to have gone out of it. My marriage was really neither happy nor unhappy, just there. A man I work for asked me out for a drink. When I was alone with this man—and we talked and we touched—I fell head over heels, like a silly schoolgirl. This has been going on for two years now and I can't decide if the sheer pleasure of meeting once a month is worth it all. The worst is not being able to talk to anyone—even someone to tell me I need a kick in the ass." *(Kansas)*

"I'm writing these answers on a separate sheet of paper because my husband thinks I'm reading *The Mistress' Survival Manual* for kicks. I am thirty-five years old, a housewife, and married sixteen years to a wonderful man with two children of our own. Sounds fine, right? Wrong!

"I was bored with my everyday life—just paying bills, keeping my children clean and well and putting supper on the table every night. My husband and I decided to buy an old farm and remodel it for a summer hideaway. We hired a carpenter three years ago to do some advising. I worked closely with him on the plans, too closely. Before I knew it I was in love with a married man." *(small town, Missouri)*

Marriage offers security and a routine, an orderly organization that many of us need. Yet there is a price that is paid in terms of monotony and boredom. Some married women can't handle the passing of high-pitched romance and when it runs dry in their marriage, they find it with a married man.

"I met an old high-school sweetheart at our reunion. After twenty years that old flame was still bright. We picked up where we left off, in the back seat in our old parking spot. It's like those twenty years in between never happened. I love this guy and I feel that something so right can't be all wrong!" *(former prom queen from Illinois)*

I call this the Reunion Union. Some married mistresses give up on kindling romance in their marriage. They rekindle it with someone from their past. As if their lover being an old friend makes it less wrong somehow.

Being taken for granted is often a byproduct of any long-term relationship. A husband's neglect is often exaggerated in comparison to a new man's attention. Flattery gets some married men everywhere and some married mistresses right into an affair.

"In the beginning, my married man was so interested in everything that happened to me, everything that I would say. I felt great for some reason. I think it was because my husband never paid much attention to me. He never appreciated me no matter what I did or how hard I tried. He never had a compliment, only complaints. My lover was different. He complimented me on how I looked or whenever I did something right. I started noticing that I looked good for my age and that I wasn't useless. He would also enjoy talking to me for hours. I got so much attention from him I couldn't help but feel something." *(Bismarck, North Dakota)*

It's staggering to see how many triangles are set into motion, not by heinous husbands or insatiable wives, but by ordinary marital partners who have been sidetracked by emotional ruts. Nagging, belittling, lack of consideration, and petty power struggles. And add a new struggle, emerging female versus old-fashioned male domination. These marital liabilities spin out into triangles.

"I'm sitting by the phone waiting for my lover to call. He works with my husband. In fact he's my husband's boss. If my husband knew he'd be raging about how all this is my fault. In his eyes everything is always my fault. He always wanted me to change. Whenever I brought up something about him, it was always my fault that he was that way. My husband is always censuring everything I do or say. It's small wonder that I fell in love with someone else. I guess I feel my husband doesn't even like me." *(Cincinnati, Ohio)*

"I've done my domestic duty for twenty years. I've overmothered the kids, been the gracious corporate hostess, and the good wife. Now it's my time. My lover is younger than me and I love him, it, the romance. I have earned the right to have an affair." *(affluent Detroit suburb)*

That last case history resonated with the hair coloring slogan, "This I do for me!" Married women are sometimes reaching out for a piece of the sky and regard their liaison as a long-deserved vacation. Passion is the ultimate escape. I hope you are continuing to see it breathing life in and out of the married mistresses.

"He [my married man] wanted me so often, I was torn between wanting to see him and staying home and doing my housework. I was under a constant strain. I was being pressed by this affair. It was an obsession. I loved him better than

God. Being in each other's arms was heaven." *(Camden, New Jersey)*

The attraction to passion is of course the romance, the ecstasy of finding so perfect a love. Yet a part of the passionate attraction is the excitement, the danger, the intrigue. And still another aspect is the crisis state that so dramatizes the life of the married mistress. No choice dramatizes life for the married mistress more than choosing between romantic love and family love. That brings us to the children. Motherhood complicates the affair for the married mistress. It adds pathos, pain, and just the right amount of bittersweet despair.

"I love two men. I'm married and I have three children and I love my husband, but there is another man and I love him, too. I truly love them both. What love I don't get from one, I get from the other. I can't leave my husband. I'm afraid he would try to take my children away from me. I can't do without the love I get from the other man. I don't know what to do." *(Indiana)*

"My husband and I have little in common. I talk a lot, he's quiet. I drink more than he does. I'm impatient, he's calm. I'm quick tempered and easy to get over it, he's slow to anger but broods for ages after it's over. I like parties and people, he's a loner. I'm a strong person so I need someone stronger. My husband is not that. My husband loves me and has never had a mistress, and probably never will. I'm in love with another man and can't imagine life without my lover. Why do I stay married? I must because of the children. I need them as much as the air I breathe." *(Mississippi)*

"I don't like hiding the love that my married man and I have for each other. But with both of us being married, it's twice as complicated! I love him and life will never be the same since I met him even if he never marries me. Will I leave my husband? Only if I really got fed up with my husband, or if my married man got a divorce, or if my kids were older. I guess what I'm saying is I'm not sure." *(Pensacola, Florida)*

The maze of choices and possibilities that afflicts the married mistress is doubled. Often she feels pulled in a number of directions and is unable to strike a balance in her mind.

Triangles generate conflicts and lead to decision time. Triangles create ambivalance, dichotomies, and convincing illusions.

"My married man has really answered some questions for me about me. He has added a lot of confusion to my life. One thing that has been a plus is that he somehow made me see myself as more of a sexual woman. I feel more attractive and I believe it shows. But I feel like I am on a see saw or a merry-go-round and I don't know where or when I will get off. Or why I'm still on at all. But I definitely like myself more (in some ways anyway) than I did before."

Every statement has a contrasting clause in there. Loving a married man brings on massive contrasting feelings, especially for the married mistress. I continue to find interesting what women say they are getting from their affairs with married men. For so long one was led to think that only men benefited from affairs, in an explicitly sexual macho way. It's refreshing to see what women feel they are getting and to see the enthusiasm they have for their liaisons. All moral judgments aside, women are getting passion in a variety of ways: from attention to lust to drama, and to romance. For once they don't sound like unwilling victims.

Fidelity doesn't come naturally for women in today's world. They are approaching the concept with all the trepidation that was once characteristic of men. And they are succumbing to temptation in greater numbers as they find that marriage is cheating them. The married mistress in America reflects the change in American women in general.

One married mistress explained that "There is now a difference in the real me and the image of me. The image I, and everyone around me, had of me. My affair with Jack has given me lots of revelations, some good and some not so good. As you can guess I'm not the sweet little innocent girl down the block anymore, nor did I think I had it in me to be anything but that. But in a funny way, I'm glad I uncovered the other me. Just think she could have lain dead and the thought of that is very scary." *(Maine)*

The married mistress has to find her own compromise between marriage and passion. The marriage institution is perhaps more often the culprit than even the husband. But husbands have their role in the making of the married mistress. And the wives in their quest for identity and fulfillment have their role too. The married mistress is torn between two triangles, with children ricocheting everywhere. In between the ricocheting of those children, the passions are bouncing feverishly. Affairs with married men seldom remain static. So many wives who are mistresses separate and are immobilized by "Where do I go from here?"

How can the married mistress distinguish between love and passion? How can she negotiate her marriage license and her passionate license? Can she hope to align romance and reason with reality? I promised a test to help the married mistress assess her marriage and decide if divorce is perhaps the right direction. That test follows one on the Passion Factor. I have written about passion directly and indirectly and in the following test will probe your appetite for this spice of life. Hopefully, isolating passion and analyzing it will help you see it as a force rather than a destiny over which you have no control.

As for romance and reason, that in all likelihood is a lifetime struggle and temptation for some. Whether you choose the marriage license or the passionate license is your own choice. One out of four mistresses is trying to have it both ways, combining her husband and someone else's husband. Passionate license is changing the shape of many American marriages as triangles shape the making of the married mistress.

The Passion Factor

"What did you like about being a mistress?" *Romance, intrigue, lust, bliss.*

"What didn't you like about being a mistress?" *Yearning, fury, addiction, panic, suffering, despair, rage, pain.*

That is a slice of the questionnaire as answered by one married mistress. As I read her responses one thing struck me. Go back and reread her answers. There is one word that sums up each and every response. That word is PASSION. Passion is defined as any intense or overpowering emotion or feeling. That mistress was saying "passion" over and over again. She was the inspiration for this test.

You see, each of us has an appetite for passion. Whether

THE PROFILE OF THE AMERICAN MISTRESS

or not that appetite is starved or satiated, whether that appetite is large or small, has a real bearing on our actions. This test is designed to explore your appetite for passion. Then you can see if and how your life has been affected by the Passion Factor.

Directions: Read all the statements below and choose a multiple-choice answer. Fill in your choice in the space provided. Then proceed to the scoring and evaluation.

1. Passion is
   (a) a dangerous commodity (b) a precious commodity (c) an ephemeral or short-lived commodity
   1. _____
2. In a couple of words, my married man is (a) perfect (b) my escape (c) unappreciated at home
   2. _____
3. When I'm not with my lover, I'm inclined to (a) get sidetracked to other concerns (b) plot and panic (c) sing our song to myself and rekindle memories
   3. _____
4. Crimes of passion I feel are
   (a) no more excusable than other crimes
   (b) to be judged with the surrounding circumstances (c) to be treated separately because of the power of passion
   4. _____
5. How do you feel about marriage and passion?
   (a) In marriage, passion slowly gives way to other pleasures (b) Passion is impossible in marriage (c) Passion has to be cultivated in marriage
   5. _____
6. The times that my married man and I share are always
   (a) sublime (b) pleasant (c) romantic
   6. _____
7. The anxiety that I feel at times due to this affair can best be described as (a) frustrating disappointments (b) suffering in forms of despair and fury (c) a debate going on inside me
   7. _____
8. My private joys and sorrows are best appreciated by

(a) my husband (b) my lover (c) my girl
   friends   8. _____
9. A world where we eliminated passion
   would be
   (a) boring (b) stable (c) unbearable   9. _____
10. The most thrilling thing about being in
    love is that
    (a) romantic sharing (b) electrifying
    attraction (c) comfortable feeling   10. _____

Scoring:

In the column labeled Answers copy all your answers from 1 to 10. Then find the corresponding points and fill that in under the column labeled Points. At the end total up the number of points and proceed to the Evaluation.

Scoring Table

		Answers	Points
1.	(a) 1 (b) 10 (c) 5	1._____	_____
2.	(a) 10 (b) 1 (c) 5	2._____	_____
3.	(a) 1 (b) 10 (c) 5	3._____	_____
4.	(a) 1 (b) 5 (c) 10	4._____	_____
5.	(a) 1 (b) 10 (c) 5	5._____	_____
6.	(a) 10 (b) 1 (c) 5	6._____	_____
7.	(a) 5 (b) 10 (c) 1	7._____	_____
8.	(a) 1 (b) 10 (c) 5	8._____	_____
9.	(a) 5 (b) 1 (c) 10	9._____	_____
10.	(a) 5 (b) 10 (c) 1	10._____	_____

Total_____

Evaluation:

The Melodramatic Mistress. If your score fell into this highest range, from *70 to 100 points*, your appetite for passion is high. Your answers all reflect superlatives; your married man is seen as perfect, your time together sublime, a world without passion seems unbearable. Look at those words—even your vocabulary is melodramatic. Your hunger for passion is obvious in those answers about your life, such as love being electrifying attraction and suffering being fury and despair. In all probability you think that passion is precious, but for you it also is very, very dangerous. A high penchant for passion is often deceptive. You can be in love with love, as they say. Your affair may be satisfying your appetite for passion, but it may be bad for you in the long run. Watch out for the passion factor in your life. If you think that marriage and passion are impossible, that sets you up for a choice. If you feel that marriage kills passion, your extramarital passion is going to kill your marriage. Passion is often elusive as is love. If you don't learn to control your passion factor, your passion factor will surely control you. Life without reason and logic can be unbearable too!

The Romantic Mistress. If your score fell into this middle range, *from 35 to 65 points*, your appetite for passion can be summed up in the concept of romance. Your life hasn't reached the soap opera pitch of the melodramatic mistress. However, there is a rose-colored tint to your responses. Your time with your married man is romantic and he is unappreciated at home. Love is sharing, and life minus passion is boring. You have somewhat of a hold on reason, which is good. You realize that passion is ephemeral or short-lived. You do value passion as an important ingredient in life's mix and feel it can and should be cultivated. There's not too much danger here for you. You can find passion where you want to and create it when you need to. Passion can add the tingles and the breathlessness to living experiences. Aside from cultivating passion you should also cultivate a healthy respect for passion. Your passions can snowball, and when you score in middle ground you should give some thought to that possibility. The passion factor is part of your life, how big a part and how significant a part is up to you!

The Levelheaded Mistress. If your score fell in this lowest range, *from 10 to 30 points*, your appetite for passion is very low. The need for passion didn't get you into this affair and any explanations lie elsewhere. You see that life holds other pleasures just as enjoyable as passion. Passion is dangerously overrated. You weigh passion as you weigh most things in your life. Love is important because of that comfortable feeling it brings. Your married man may be an escape, and just what you're escaping from in your marriage is quite a source of debate at this point. Life may get the best of you at times, but not due to the passion factor. Your levelheadedness makes you and your world a little more stable than most. However, don't ignore your appetite for passion altogether. We all need a taste now and then. Absence can make the appetite greater and then the passion factor may surge and get the better of you for a while. Just because you haven't a problem with passion, don't ignore the other problems. But with your logical penchant you won't for too long.

In Conclusion... A Note for All:
The Passion Factor can be the single most influential factor in falling in love with a married man. Whether your appetite for passion is a craving or a romantic need, your affair may be the way you've been feeding it. Once you understand the Passion Factor perhaps you can see how it has led you into a triangle. Perhaps you can see how your husband has starved your need for passion and why your married man is a natural for it. If you have no trouble here, at least you've singled out passion and can go on to something else.

The married mistress cannot be understood without a thorough understanding of passion. Many of her motives, experiences, and desires can all be summed up in that one word... passion.

To Divorce or Not to Divorce

If your marriage has taken on another married man, in addition to your husband, chances are you are pondering the inevitable... the divorce or not to divorce question. It is common for a married woman who is caught in the grips of a triangle to do so. Perhaps, by candlelight with your lover, you are toying with the idea of divorce. Perhaps it is a long harbored desire you have been grappling with for some time. Whether it is a romantic fantasy or a serious frustration, you should take a moment now to delve into the question. Thoughts of divorce should not be taken lightly. Your whole life is at stake.

If your marriage has one too many married men in it, chances are you are all mixed up. Your lover and his impact on your life is probably your all-consuming preoccupation. It's probably hard to think about your marriage without thinking about your lover too. But just for a moment forget about your affair. Try to look solely at your marriage.

THE PROFILE OF THE AMERICAN MISTRESS

Directions: Answer the 10 questions below with a Yes or No response. Each Yes answer is worth 10 points. Each No answer is worth 0 points. Total up your Yes answers and multiply by 10. That will be your score. Then proceed to the evaluation.

1. Have you spent long hours planning life without your spouse; practically speaking with plans for lodging, income, and children? 1. _____
2. Have you considered going to some type of marriage counselor; a local minister/priest/rabbi, or a therapist? 2. _____
3. Do you feel trapped, rather than torn, by your present state of affairs (no pun intended)? 3. _____
4. Other than money and children, can you name three things that keep you in your present marriage? 4. _____
5. Have you approached your spouse about the troubled state of your marriage? 5. _____
6. Has physical abuse been a characteristic of your marriage? 6. _____
7. Has alcohol or drug abuse been a characteristic of your marriage; related to either your excesses or your spouse's? 7. _____
8. Have your close friends, or your parents, or any of your children suggested divorce to you repeatedly? 8. _____
9. Was your marriage sour long before the entrance of your lover? 9. _____
10. Have you logically and sincerely concluded that your husband, too, would be better off if the marriage ended? 10. _____

The total number of True answers is_____
X 10 = _____.

Evaluation:
No-Sense Divorce. If you scored between *0–30 points*, it seems that divorce would make no sense for you in the long run. This is not to say that your marriage doesn't have serious problems. A marriage that has turned into a spinning triangle

is a mess, but I'm sure I don't have to tell you that. However, divorce is more of a fantasy for you. You probably haven't calculated your financial losses or planned out where you would live and with whom the children would live. You have in all likelihood tried to approach the subject of the malaise with your husband. You may have even suggested counseling. There are reasons why you remain in that marriage, reasons that you should give a great deal of thought to. Your affair can bring all the problems brewing in your marriage to a head. If you so desire, your affair can be a learning experience and improve your marriage. Don't let the divorce fantasy deceive you; for you divorce makes no sense!

No-Fault Divorce. If you scored between *40–60 points*, the question of divorce for you only raises more questions. Whose fault is this mess? Who would be better off, if anyone, by the decision to divorce? Your marriage is really up in the air and where it lands only you and your husband can know. You are inclined to find all of these questions difficult to answer. Torn, trapped? Has the marriage deteriorated slowly or rapidly? Whether to begin honestly sorting things out or just end the marriage; you don't know which way to go. This is the worst possible range to fall in, because there is no clear-cut advice that I can provide. The best I can advise is that you spend some time thinking seriously about what keeps you in the marriage. How bad are its problems? How much do you want to mend the torn relationship that you have with your husband? You can either confront all your conflicts or go on in utter confusion. In the end your *no-fault divorce* dilemma will be your responsibility. Your fate, whatever it is, will be your fault!

No-Contest Divorce. If you scored between *70–100 points*, it seems that divorce is in your future. You could win a bad-marriage contest easily. The behaviors inside the marriage exhibit physical abuse, your throwing things at him or his throwing punches at you. None of this should be taken lightly. Possibly an addictive pattern of alcohol or drugs has crept into the lives of either you or your spouse, or both of you. You have probably wanted to get out of this marriage for a long time. You have probably plotted out the economics, the logistics, and the effects on the children. You think dispassionately that your husband would be better off too, and that's in all likelihood right. You may have tried counseling or decided that even counseling couldn't help. All signs lead to divorce. And yet you have hesitated in taking the final step. Why? Of course divorce will bring many problems for your family, emotional hardships and financial strains. However, you and your marriage have so many problems now that you had better start something. Listen to the good advice that you've probably heard more than once from those who love you. Divorce for you—there should be no contest!

In Conclusion:
This test was about you. It focused on your behavior in your marriage. We already know about your behavior outside your marriage. Sometimes it's very hard to distinguish between the two. You must learn to explore your marriage, your husband, and your future. Only then can you answer for yourself the question—to divorce or not to divorce—perhaps the most important one of your life.

CHAPTER 7

Jaded Lady—The Divorcée as Mistress

Divorcées account for one-third of the mistress population. Many divorcées suffer what I will call a nuptial hangover. "Something old, something new, something borrowed, something blue" seems to become a refrain which directs the pattern of many divorcées' lives, only with a slightly altered connotation. The divorcée who becomes a mistress finds new meaning in that old nuptial custom. Only now the something old is the way she feels about life: old and jaded. The something new is the renewed vigor she finds in loving a married man. The something borrowed is someone else's husband. And last of all, the something blue is a cascade of blue sensations that she now feels. These azure hues range from feelings of bright to feelings of brutal sadness.

The divorcée-mistress is a jaded lady indeed. She has often become dulled by her life experiences, meaning the failure of her marriage. Her values and expectations often shatter in the heat of marital discord. She feels hung over, disoriented by the new "single" life. She is often sated with marriage. Divorcées characteristically flounder for a while. And in that floundering many seize a married man.

In understanding why divorcées are especially vulnerable to affairs with married men, we'll explore the divorcée from a number of different angles. Yet at every turn you will see how the divorcée's present is shaped by her past. Her jaded perspective often shapes her life into a triangle. Many divorcées who opt for mistresshood are still locked away somewhere in their yesterdays. They seem incapable of seeing a bright future, instead just fixing themselves on surviving one day at a time. Even if they are not conscious of how much the past is ruling them, it is the driving force toward mistresshood for many.

As you read about divorcée-mistresses in particular you will see similarities in these jaded ladies. We'll look at some common paths that divorcées try to follow. And hear how they cope and choose; struggle and survive.

In my research an odd corollary has begun to surface, one I'm going to suggest and ask you to help me explore further. The corollary casts a jade shadow over a portion of the divorcée-mistresses. It seems that if there was a mistress in your marriage, your odds of becoming a mistress after the divorce are higher. In other words, if adultery existed in your ex-husband's behavior, its impact on you tends to linger and color your post-divorce behavior green. It tends to become the greening of your mistresshood. Very often the unmaking of an American wife results in the making of the American divorcée-mistress.

Divorcées initially feel married men are safe. Are they? They try to avoid repeating the same mistakes. Often that means making new ones. Romantic illusions have a way of persisting in new forms.

Imprisoned in a Prism

Clair lives in a city of 250,000, very New England. She feels older than her years at times. She has been divorced six years. She has no children. She teaches in the field called special education. It was her work that saved her after the divorce.

Clair met Bill at a singles bar that she had gone to for about a year. At thirty-five she had to end this life that she described as being "like the proverbial ostrich with its head in the sand."

After a year of meeting what seemed like worthless men to her, "Bill was different. He was gentle, tender, rich, interesting. And only as a last priority: married." Actually Bill was remarried, with a new son.

Clair sounded very much like the typical divorcée imprisoned in a collective experience. "The sexual aspect of my affair with my married man was important to me because not only did he turn out to be caring after our first sexual encounter, he was more gentle, more loving than the parade of men I had known of late, and he called the next day."

Clair put away the fact that he was married, and his wife

was no more "than a picture in his wallet." She told me that.

"We have laughter, friendship, sex, love, romance, and most of all the comfort of each other. He's kind to me and he cares for me. After my lousy marriage and my lonely divorce, even my mother is relieved there is someone in my life."

Clair's affair is in its third year. Bill lives in another state but travels a lot and therefore seeing Clair isn't really a problem. Secrecy isn't a problem either. They often socialize with Clair's friends. Everyone asks Clair why they don't get married. Clair sees Bill about two times a month. At first she was grateful for those times. Now, it's not enough.

"At first his being married was immaterial. Now it absolutely kills me. How can I ask him to leave *another* family? He has a new baby boy. Divorce is a fantasy. I wish and hope for it, but I know he dreads the idea of leaving children again, and all the rest of the divorce crap."

Clair knows that she is imprisoned in a triangle, but life seems to be a succession of prisons. First marriage, then divorce, now a triangle. Clair calls her affair a "prism."

"It's a prism. All of our experiences are refracted through the obstacle of our situation, and yet they remain worthwhile and they shall always be cherished in my mind. I wouldn't trade a minute of this affair. Even if we have to end, I can't foresee any bitterness. Nothing would diminish this relationship which will always be special and awesome to me."

This prism imagery is quite beautiful to me, but I don't like to see anyone describe their destiny in terms of prisons. Being imprisoned in anything is difficult, even a prism.

A Turnpike Romance

Vera didn't say how long she had been divorced. It wasn't too long ago, though, because the smoke was still rising from her burns. That smoky smell seemed to rise from her comments. Vera was twenty-six years old. She was an inhalation therapist and a CB radio enthusiast. Now you may think that one has nothing to do with the other, but that's not exactly true.

You see, driving home from the hospital one evening, she heard a call for a doctor to tend an accident victim immediately. The scene of the accident was a mile out of her way, so Vera reported ready to help if she could. A trucker was at the scene too, George. That trucker became Vera's married man.

After that chance meeting Vera would pick up George on the CB. They became instant friends and then much more.

"I chose to date George even though he was married because I had a fear of marriage. He was safe for me. I had felt broken up after the divorce. I felt unloved, unwanted, and unneeded. I was in a transition state of mind and very lonely. Yet I knew I was afraid of another attachment."

Not only were George and Vera both CB enthusiasts, they were sexually compatible, comfortable totally with each other, and both obsessed with the concept of divorce. Vera was reeling from it and trying to understand it. George was contemplating it.

Their schedules meshed well, too. Vera managed to coordinate her shifts so that she could get free blocks of time off. They were able to go on his road trips together. A few days here, sometimes a few weeks there. They had the open road, adventure, and romance. It was a turnpike romance of motels and diners and friendly voices over the CB radio.

"We often talked of divorce. He always brought the conversation there, not me. We talked about the difficulties, the strains, the fears and of course about how hard it was on children. At first divorce didn't matter to me one way or the other. In fact I felt secure in a way that he was still married. I just thought I could help him with his problems."

Vera moved out of state so that things might be easier. George had told his wife and she was interfering. That move made the distance between them greater. George did too much driving to be able to drive more miles to see Vera. But when he came he stayed a few days. Or he picked her up for an extended trip. After a while Vera moved back into the state. George needed all the help he could get.

"He just kept bouncing back and forth between his wife and me. I don't know why he doesn't divorce. I know he wants to; at least half of him does. Now each time the subject comes up, it's a different reason. One day I think he'll just keep driving and never come back."

Vera realizes she's still young and wants a future. Well, right now all that means is she wants to survive.

"I need help, that's why I bought your book. I am determined to survive with or without him. But I hope it will be with him."

I'm rooting for Vera. I like the sound of a turnpike romance. Only one without the painful detours. Breaker, breaker, I hope she doesn't get broken again.

While the last two profiles delineated more of the negatives for the divorcée-mistresses, this next story turns out to be thoroughly positive. Denise's becoming a mistress changed her entire life for the better.

New Growth

Denise's marriage was a case history in atrophy. Oh, she didn't say marriage was the culprit in making her atrophy, but that's what she meant.

"Marriage was totally frustrating for me. I was eighteen when I moved out of Daddy's house and into Don's. I don't think I ever thought about anything back then. After five years of marriage, I had no desire to get up in the morning. I was twenty-three and dying, kind of. I didn't understand it at the time. Don couldn't take it anymore so he left. I don't blame him."

Denise got a job working in a pharmacy as a cashier. She got a cute little apartment just outside her small Pennsylvania town. She pinched pennies and bought trinkets for her place and lo and behold began to think. Then she met her married man, the biggest influence ever on her life.

"My cousin introduced us. It was love. I was most certainly in love with him. I experienced the feelings that the songwriters and poets wrote about. It was a first for me."

Love was far from the only lesson, although it was the nicest.

"I trusted Ralph. He valued my intellect. I never even knew I had one. The mainstay in our relationship was friendship. I could tell him whatever I was thinking with no fear of being laughed at or judged."

Denise and Ralph lived rather far apart, so meetings weren't frequent. They met about once every other week. It was usually a rendezvous in her apartment. He would arrive in the early afternoon. They would make a fire in the tiny wood-burning stove, listen to some music, make love and have dinner. It all may sound mundane, but to Denise that would be a vast understatement.

"Ralph encouraged me to grow in so many ways. From little things to big things. I became a gourmet cook so our little dinners would be memorable. He made me aware of my own worth and that made me more outgoing. I even made new friends, and easily. The main change he made in my life was emotional. He made me realize that I really don't need a full-time man to be happy. In fact I am happier dating several men."

Actually divorce did for Denise what marriage does for so many. She blossomed. She found everything in life exciting, from balancing her checkbook to doing grocery shopping for one. She was thriving on her newfound self-sufficiency. The last thing I heard from her was that she had secured a loan from her ex-husband so that she could go to college. She was thinking about becoming a pharmacist. Her affair had ended.

"Ralph ended it. He said he couldn't handle the lows that came after we were together. But I think it was guilt that did us in. He ended it by phone on, as it turns out, an emotional critical day for him. (If you're into biorhythms.) But I'll never regret knowing him."

What are endings for most people are beginnings for Denise. Being a mistress started her on a growth pattern that is just beginning.

Most divorcée-mistresses like the ones here are looking for something different from what they found in marriage. They are running away from their pasts, or rebounding, or trying to erase them. They are feeling older and wiser.

"As a divorcée and former battered woman, I do not have a great desire to remarry. My married man has been good for me emotionally since my divorce. He has given me my self-confidence back. My husband had battered that as well as me physically. I know this man would be different." *(Charlottesville, Virginia)*

Certain divorcées are vulnerable to the Reunion Union—taking up with an old flame. We discussed that in the chapter of married mistresses. For the divorcée-mistress it is an attempt at wiping out the past by just erasing it. As if picking up with a former sweetheart can make the interim seem nonexistent.

"When we first fell in love he wasn't married. When we broke up he got involved with another girl, she got pregnant, and they got married. So did I. Now after six years he found out I'm divorced and he started calling. The old feelings are all there. It's like neither of our marriages mean anything, like they never even happened." *(upstate New York)*

It seems to be the consensus among divorcée-mistresses, at least at the outset, that married men are safe.

"Marriage is not for me. I've learned that. I wanted a married man because he couldn't do to me what my husband did again." *(Cambridge, Massachusetts)*

"It seemed simple enough. I never wanted to be anybody's wife again. I could never be his wife because he had one. So we could have love and romance without the ultimate bummer-divorce." *(Buda, Texas)*

"I was scared of making another mistake. Divorce taught me I was a lousy judge of character. A married man relationship had limits, so how much damage could I do to myself?" *(Tuskeegee, Alabama)*

Divorce is so steeped in trauma that the divorcée-mistresses often feel that affairs are better, safer. They have lost already and are afraid of losing in the same way again. Afraid of losing anything more. Sometimes it is those very fears that set them up for more losing almost like a self-fulfilling prophecy.

"I wanted the divorce, but afterwards I was so lonely. I was totally vulnerable. After I met my married man I got lost in him. I lost myself and all my fears in his problems. It all backfired. Most of the time I'm depressed and still lonely. All the wasted time I spend waiting for a call from him. I'm no longer important to myself. I'm no fun to be with. Right now I'm very afraid. The thought of not having him terrifies me. If I lose him, I have nothing, not even myself." *(rural town, Vermont)*

It seems that the one thing the divorcée-mistress holds on to is romantic illusions. When marriage betrays those wonderful illusions, instead of giving up on them, divorcées project them onto their new lovers. Just as husbands rarely can live up to these fantasies, married men suggest the romance but often fail to deliver too.

"I just knew almost immediately that this was it. Ken was married but so what. Even if he divorced I'd just want to live together. Our meetings were exciting, naughty, and yet relaxed. The communication on every level was unparalleled. I liked the arrangement." *(Miami, Florida)*

"This man is the answer to all my needs. I love him as I never thought I could love any man. Because he's married, at times I feel like everyone sees the large red "A" that is plastered to my forehead. But overall, I'm delirious. The problem is now I am thinking about marriage again to him. He's not thinking about divorce, though." *(Columbia, Maryland)*

Before we leave the subject of illusions, and get to the outlook projected for the divorcée-mistress, let's get to that corollary I mentioned. Part of being that jaded lady is developing a jade cast. This does not apply to every divorcée-mistress, but to enough to make it significant.

The Greening of Mrs. Williams

Mrs. Williams told me that she had been married for eighteen years when she found out that her husband had had a mistress for six years. Mrs. Williams was forty-four years old at the time. Her husband was forty-six; his mistress thirty-nine.

"After the shock I had to admit to myself that my marriage was far from any idyll. I had been living for a long time for my children and for the day when the marriage would either start working or end. It ended when my husband asked for the divorce and told me about the other woman."

Mrs. Williams said she had an insatiable curiosity about the mistress.

"I didn't want my husband back, but still I wanted to know everything about this other woman. What restaurants they went to, where she shopped, where she lived, what kinds of gifts he'd given her."

In time, with the "help" of consoling friends, she knew lots. Two years after the divorce, Mrs. Williams began seeing a married man. She had known him for years. He had delivered her children. He was her gynecologist.

"My married man was different from my husband, up front and his own person. I was everything to him and he needed me. He appreciated me. When his secretary quit, it seemed perfect for me to quit my job and go to work for him. Then we were together every day. I lived to be with him."

In the first four years of all this, Mrs. Williams floated on a cloud.

"I have emotional security. I have freedom, too. Who needs marriage!"

Recently things have changed.

"About a year ago, my married man told me that he could never leave his family. I have a home where he never comes. I have spent virtually every weekend and holiday alone for the last five years. I am not the pleasant gay divorcée I once was. I am now nearly fifty years old. I feel my time is being wasted. I want to date and live the life of a single woman, but I don't know how. I thought an affair was better than marriage, but it didn't turn out that way for me. I was sure mistresses were treated better than wives, but that hasn't happened to me. I am bitter and it hurts that what was once a perfect romance is now over. My ex-husband has been happily married for years now. I feel betrayed by him and my own stupidity about being a mistress."

Mrs. Williams was characteristic in thinking that the mistress' life was more romantic than the wife's. After finding only disaster in the wife role, she figured the mistress role had all the good stuff—freedom, romance, and endless attention. What was the greening of Mrs. Williams turned out to be an empty harvest.

This pattern as it repeated itself among divorcée-mistresses started me thinking. It is a corollary that I would like to research further. Your odds of becoming a mistress are higher if your husband had a mistress while you and he were married. In my search to see if this hypothesis is supported by further investigation, please answer the following questions. If you are a divorcée-mistress with this relevant history, it will further help you understand the making of your mistresshood.

Please either tear out the questionnaire or photocopy it and send it to me: C/O Berkley Publishing Corp.
200 Madison Ave.
New York, N.Y. 10016
I welcome any of your thoughts or observations here.

Was There a Mistress in Your Marriage?

1. In your marriage experience, are you certain that your husband

was involved with other women?
2. Was your husband's adultery at the time limited to one particular woman?
3. Were you curious about the other woman?
4. Did you attempt to satisfy your curiosity, and if so, how?
5. Did you and your husband discuss his affair openly?
6. Was it the reason for the divorce? Or part of the reason? Please explain.
7. As a wife at the time, did you feel that the other woman had distinct advantages? (for instance, age, glamour)
8. Did you feel that your husband treated her better than he treated you as his wife? If so, how?
9. Do you think any hint of revenge played a part in your becoming a mistress?
10. Has your image of the mistress changed since you have taken off the wife's shoes and donned the mistress' shoes? How?

In reading over the questions, you will probably see that the divorcée-mistress' experiences are important, as well as her illusions. A question of some vague notion of vengeance comes into play, too.

"I felt a sort of 'right' to love a married man since I lost my previous man to another woman and I felt that since she wasn't keeping him home in bed, it was my turn to have fun. It was a sort of revenge." *(Ozark, Alabama)*

"When I first learned my husband was sleeping around with that woman I hated her. Now it's odd because I am a mistress myself. Looking back now I feel sorry for her. As for my married man's wife, I don't feel guilty at all. I survived, so can she." *(West Allis, Wisconsin)*

"I chose a married man on purpose. I wanted an affair, no commitments, no strings, just affection and a good time. His wife? Who cares about her. The woman who stole my husband didn't give me a thought, so why should I be any different? All's fair in love and war, right?" *(the Bronx, New York)*

The concept of revenge has surfaced sometimes in the vocabulary of the divorcée-mistress. Other times the concept is suggested in a rather unconscious way. Singled out, it sounds cruel. But with divorcées you should remember that it is all mixed up with disappointments, expectations, and the confusion that divorce leaves in its wake. Divorce leaves behind bad experiences and some illusions. Illusions, however, are like the phoenix. Out of their ashes new illusions or more illusions rise up again strong and eternally elusive. The divorcée-mistress has excess baggage as far as illusions go. She has lost illusions from her marriage failure. Yet, although she may have lost illusions about marriage, she has new illusions about affairs, married men, and mistresshood. The future for the divorcée-mistress is very much related to how those illusions last or disintegrate over time.

Experience and illusion are the makings of the divorcée-mistress. Unfortunately, a great many divorcée-mistresses can't lose their illusions without losing other things as well.

"I thought that any woman who got involved with a married man was a real dope. She would get what was coming to her. After my divorce, I fell in love and lost my fiancé. He died of cancer suddenly. I felt lost and I needed comfort, understanding, and physical contact. I got involved with this married guy at work. He offered no attachments and I was satisfied because I was still in mourning most of the time. Then I started feeling miserable with him and miserable without him. I wish I could crawl into a hole and never have to face another day. I have been a little dopey maybe, but I didn't deserve this on top of everything that's happened to me." *(Mansfield, Illinois)*

"I did my homework. I read all the magazines about how delicious loving a married man was. After the blahs I felt after the divorce I was ready for something delicious. Becoming a mistress has made me the happiest I have ever been in my life and the most miserable I have ever been too." *(Parma, Ohio)*

"I saw my ex-husband's mistress once. She looked stunning. I decided that that was for me. I envied her and I wanted to be just like that. Beautiful and distant. She seemed mysterious. Now it's a mystery to me how that woman ever survived a nine-year affair and our dirty divorce. I am now a mistress and it is too many sacrifices. It's lonely and depressing most of the time. Some days I think I'm going to crack." *(Costa Mesa, California)*

"I had the new job and my children. I needed a lover, but nothing full time. A married man fit the bill. Now, he's ruining everything; my job, I have no patience with my kids. All I do is scream." *(Deer Park, Long Island, New York)*

"I'm not a college graduate. I don't have a real important job. I got divorced five years ago. I guess I thought being a mistress would be fun. My mom always taught me that no matter what, I should keep my dignity. I've got no money, and no future with Chuck. And now along with losing my mind, I'm gonna lose my dignity 'cause I can't give him up no matter what." *(small town, Alabama)*

These divorcée-mistresses are all talking about losing something. Whether it be dignity or peace of mind; the quality of their parenthood or the image of what a mistress is; it is a list of losses. Divorcées have lost enough after their disappointing experience with marriage. Oftentimes, mistresshood adds to their losses when the pros and cons are weighed. And yet, the failures and bad experiences in their past have colored them jaded or jade enough to make them mistresses before they have a clear picture of the role.

Marriage frequently doesn't live up to our romantic fantasies of it. Affairs are the same. They can't match over time our expectations of freedom and endless romance. Husbands often don't live up to their "forever and always" promises at the altar. Married men don't always verbalize promises but their kisses make promises and their passions make promises that they rarely can ever keep. The jaded divorcée-mistresses live in a transitional state just trying to survive. They don't have much faith left in traditions. They don't have naive high expectations about men and marriage. They have a void in their emotions to fill and affairs seem like the best elixir. They have a past to escape and a future to fear. The present becomes the best gameboard. All these variables make the divorcée prime material for becoming a mistress.

There are no statistics about how many divorcées become mistresses, but one-third of the mistresses are divorcées. In becoming a mistress they find love, growth, comfort; disappointment, betrayal, and passion. One thing is certain. No matter how jaded a woman feels after a brush with divorce, the divorcée-mistress is rarely too jaded to be blasé about her affair with her married man.

Are You Mistress Material?

You are divorced. Are you mistress material? If you are already a mistress, why did you become mistress material?

The divorcée in America has a unique blend of variables that make her especially vulnerable to becoming a mistress. In my travels and correspondence I've encountered thousands and thousands of divorcées who are head over heels in love with married men. I have also been asked countless times by divorced women if they should begin seeing a married man. Therefore this test is twofold.

If you are a divorcée who finds that all her prospects are married men, is there some logic to this? If you are a divorcée who is already in love with someone else's husband, how did this happen to you? How did your life experience lead you right up to the threshold of a married man? It is hoped that this test will help you understand that you definitely are mistress material and why.

Directions: Read each statement *carefully*. Some will apply to you. Some won't. After each statement write True or False. Then proceed to the scoring and evaluation.

1. A satisfying affair with a married man is better than an unsatisfying marriage.   1. _____

2. Freedom is harder to find within a
   marriage than within an affair with a
   married man.   2. _____
3. Married men are safe.   3. _____
4. Married men treat their mistresses better
   than they treat their wives.   4. _____
5. I survived my ex-husband's affair; his
   wife will survive his.   5. _____
6. A man should be judged for himself, not
   for his marital status.   6. _____
7. Affairs are easier to get out of than
   marriages.   7. _____
8. I learned my lesson: marriage is not for
   me.   8. _____
9. Independence is easier to retain in an
   affair with a married man, easier to
   retain than in a marriage.   9. _____
10. Being a mistress is more romantic than
    being a wife.   10. _____

Scoring:
True answers are worth 10 points. Count them up and multiply by 10 to get your total score. False answers are worth no points. Every False answer takes you further and further from being mistress material. Let's look to the evaluation of your score to see the significance of those True statements.

Evaluation:
 The Immune Divorcée. If your score fell in the range of *0–30* points, you have a trace of mistress potential. However, in all likelihood you will never become a mistress. Divorce is at best a difficult process. A few True answers just display the scars that you bear from one unsuccessful experience with marriage. Perhaps you feel marriage is not for you. Beware if you feel that affairs are easy to get out of because they are not legalized—look at the Lee Marvin case. Luckily, your low score shows that you don't buy the classic myths that make you mistress material. Are married men safe? You probably don't think married men *or* unmarried men are safe! Keep up those defenses for a while anyway, until you let time heal your wounds. Right now you seem immune to the attraction of a married man. However, no test is foolproof so I suggest you

read the other scores so you will be well informed about the divorcée's special vulnerabilities.

The Vulnerable Divorcée. If your score fell in the range of *40–60* points, you are somewhat vulnerable. Your mistress potential seems ambivalent. The best thing for you to do is to go back and check your True answers. That's exactly where your vulnerability lies. Do you think that affairs naturally encourage the growth of independence and freedom? Do you think that married men treat mistresses better than wives? Do you think that married men are safe and that mistresses are glamorous? Do you think that marital status is less important than friendship? If you are saying yes, your inclinations are taking you into the arms of a married man and the complexities of a triangle.

For the divorcées who are mistresses now, see how these beliefs led you into your affair. You can tell the prospective mistresses, I'm sure, that affairs have their own set of problems. Affairs are not all freedom; married men have none. There is another side to the romance and glamour; a side of loneliness and disappointment. For the divorcée who is contemplating mistresshood and scored here, I suggest you do a bit more research into the affair with a married man. You are vulnerable to myths that are the essence of this test. You are vulnerable, also, to the drawbacks of mistresshood for which you are a likely candidate.

The Ripe Divorcée. If your score fell in the range of *70–100* points, you are ripe for mistresshood. In fact you probably are already deep into a love affair with a married man. Why did it happen or why is it going to happen to *you*? Just look at the beliefs that you hold. They all point up a preference for being a mistress rather than a wife. They describe married men as safe, and marital status as incidental. Affairs are defined as free, with room for independence and growth. Romance and satisfaction are your goals and marriage just didn't deliver these. You definitely have a disenchantment with the institution of marriage and a curiosity about affairs. Perhaps there's even a tinge of vengeance, especially if your marriage had a triangle in it. It's no wonder you are a mistress. Your life experiences and how you reacted to them made you ripe. Unfortunately, becoming a mistress isn't the answer for most people. It doesn't always bring happiness all of the time. Like marriages, affairs have problems, pains, and passions. They are just as emotionally binding as marriages and can be just as difficult to break out of.

In Conclusion:
The American divorcée makes a good candidate for mistresshood. You, in particular, can understand why by reading and rereading those True answers of yours. You can digest this chapter on the divorcée and learn to step outside yourself and grow. Self-understanding is very important for the divorcée. All learning doesn't have to come the hard way, even if it seems that way now. Learning the whats and whys of being a mistress are very crucial to you. After a bad marriage, I want to help you get more out of life, not less. If you are mistress material, look before you leap!

CHAPTER 8

The Young, the Old, and the Tradition

In the course of my commitment to mistresses, I have been cross-examined by literally thousands of wives. One question that is fired at me incessantly with cold condescension is, "Why should mistresses be helped?" I have explained that many women are seduced unexpectedly into mistressing. That stirred little sympathy. I have delineated the suffering that many women find in the triangle. Still not much sympathy. I was often told that mistresses deserve that suffering. They should have known better. However, in time my research provided an answer to that question that ended all argument. And even where it did not ensure sympathy outright, it did put a question mark in the mind that previously was all vengeance.

If you have had no sympathy for mistresses, beware. If you think they shouldn't be helped, watch out. Because the mistress you are condemning and denying help to may be your daughter or your grandmother.

Teenagers make up approximately 16% of the mistress population. Yes, that figure describes young women between the ages of seventeen and twenty-one. Another 1% are even younger, under seventeen.

Senior citizens of sixty years and older account for 2% of all mistresses. Many of these older women are widows. Widows of all ages comprise 3% of the mistress population. I shall talk of the two, older women and widows, synonymously because the two often go together.

I decided to include the old and the young in one section because they often seem like flip sides of some coin—a mistress coin. They provide interesting similarities, ironies, and contrasts.

Age is such a relative commodity. There were times when

I read such wisdom in the writing of a teenager on Mickey Mouse stationery. At other times such schoolgirl passion and folly came from the pen of a septuagenarian. You will see what I mean in a minute.

What's it like being a teenager in love with a married man? Not only do you have to keep your secret from his wife, but from your parents, too. And how do such young women get mixed up with married men in the first place? How does the triangle affect the shaping of those formative years?

How do grandmothers wind up wearing a scarlet letter? They wind up hiding their affair from their children! How do our prejudices affect senior citizens? Why do situational factors make married men so appealing?

After we look at the making of the younger generation of mistresses, and the making of the older generation of mistresses, we'll look at a new tradition. It is a mistress legacy that is being handed down from one generation to the next. It is a phenomenon that merits our attention.

Without another word let's look at a teenager who is a mistress. In Donna's case she was a teen-mistress for nearly three years. Now it's over, but I'll let her tell you all about it.

Back to Basics

"I am twenty-one years old now. I'll be graduating soon. The affair began in the latter part of my eighteenth year."

Donna's married man was one of her college professors. Even though she didn't say what he taught, even though it wasn't the Humanities or Fine Arts to be sure, there was still a trace of Pygmalion somewhere. Because to him, Donna wasn't just another student. She was a woman with something he needed, and it was all as magical as if it were the handiwork of Aphrodite. Or the machination, depending on your perspective.

"I was in a work-study program and I worked for him for a while. We started spending more and more time together on campus. I was afraid of seeing him more and also afraid that he was going to say that we couldn't let anything more happen.

Sounds pretty confusing, eh? I was confused. I was falling in love with him but hated to admit it to myself because it was against my upbringing and my morals. I was scared to death and I kept telling myself that I wouldn't make love with him. But we ended up making love one day. I remember it perfectly."

Donna's professor was thirty-one. He was highly regarded on the faculty. His bedpost was not noted for the number of notches he accumulated from the student body. He was industrious and serious about his work. He was an authority in his field. While he taught Donna in some ways, she taught him in others.

"What he gave me, no other man had. Here was a man who wasn't only attracted to me physically. He needed me for comfort and understanding. He made me feel like I was somebody. He was a man of power, of knowledge, of confidence, good looks, even money. I had him on a pedestal. The perfect man. Although he seemed to have everything, he was lacking and he turned to me. An absolute child. He was my strong oak tree protecting and guiding me."

Donna has mixed feelings now that it is over. She's trying to make sense about how she felt and how he felt.

"I must admit there were moments when I enjoyed the sound of the word 'mistress,' but mostly I dreaded hearing it. At times I wanted to think that I was having a nightmare and I would soon awaken. I wanted to be a little girl again and have my daddy take care of me. Yet I loved him so much and he showed me so much love.

"I think the main reason for our relationship was simple. I brought him back to the basics of life. Kindness, caring, concern, sincerity, simpleness, understanding, and companionship. It all had nothing to do with money or materialism. All he had was me. Someone who would listen to him and be there when he needed to have someone hold him. I was there for him all the time. I don't know where his wife was, but she couldn't have been where he needed her to be."

The affair between Donna and the professor was profound and natural and yet it was scandalous and improper. His wife found out and they all separated; Donna and the professor, the professor and his wife.

Donna says she'll survive and they (the professor and his wife) will probably get back together. He will always be to her "the man who tried to explain things in life that were confusing to me. The man who held me when I hurt. The man who taught me I was someone and pushed for my independence. I hurt now. In good time I'll get it all together. I'll start slowly and get back to basics."

Falling in love with a teacher, a mentor, isn't anything new. There have always been crushes in the classroom. Even the Pygmalion experience is rather traditional. There have always been teacher's pets. But now we live in an age of greater sexual freedom, especially for young women. As they discover their sexuality in high school or in college, sometimes it happens in an educational context with their teacher. Some teacher's pets become teacher's lovers. And it's not all lechery and lasciviousness. It's also loving and learning. It makes teenagers teen-mistresses. Of course there are risks and drawbacks that we'll look at a bit later. In the meantime, let's look at another teen-mistress. This story had nothing to do with the educational experience, but it was an experience.

Ships in the Night

Susie lives in a very small town. She is seventeen and works as a receiving clerk at a department store. Her married man is twenty-four. He is receiving and shipping manager at the same department store. There was nothing too unusual about how they were attracted to each other or how they got started.

Susie knew him before they started working together. She recalled that his wife had chaperoned the Senior Prom. Her father was on the school board or something.

"When we started out I was still an innocent little Donny Osmond fan who didn't even know how to French kiss. I've come a long way. We met on dark avenues usually. He's really hilarious. Every time a car passed he would duck. He always looks over his shoulder before we do anything. It's like dating I-spy. He says some afternoon we're going to get a motel and spend the whole day together. But if I held my breath I would have been dead months ago."

Susie and her married man don't do much or have much. Mostly it's just shipping and receiving. Only I would have to say that he's on the receiving end in this one.

"The only way I can see him whenever I want is to sit on the no-through road above his house and look through a pair of binoculars. Some nights he said his wife was going to work so I'd sit up there and wait. Once I sat there till two in the morning waiting. Then all the lights went out. They're in bed and I'm in the dark making up some story to tell my folks."

Susie's affair has been going on only for six months. But to listen to her talk it sounds like a lifetime. She certainly doesn't sound like a carefree teenager to me.

"These days futures are very hard to see. Right now I don't want to love anyone but him. For every ten-minute coffee break we spend together in the morning, there's a week of loneliness. I've tried to date a couple of guys, but I can't stand them even touching me. All I want is him."

Susie knows that there is no future for them, only a continuation of this secret voyage.

"He'll never divorce. He's afraid of losing his wife and his kid. So don't ask me why he does it. He's mysterious about himself; and me, I'm too in love to ask any questions. I'm in so deep I'm drowning. I cry continually when he's not with me. I never want to let him go when I'm with him. It's hard to get time with him, but when he snaps his fingers I run. I can't be mad at him for more than two seconds. Then he's perfect again."

It was odd how Susie knew nothing really about her married man. He didn't have a story—a bad marriage or a nagging wife. In all probability there was nothing to tell. This was just one of those things for him. One of those things that he perhaps shouldn't have done, but the temptation was too much at the moment. It's obvious that he wasn't making promises to Susie or even leading her on too much.

Susie's married man hadn't much to say because most of his life was irrelevant to her. It was only her life that was wrapped up all around him.

"The problem is loving him is killing me and giving him up will kill me. I can't take just waiting and waiting. I just go crazy. If I live to see eighteen I'll be lucky."

Susie and her married man are just ships passing in the night. Only Susie sounds as if she is ready to retire to a sanatorium for a rest. And while he sails into port every night, Susie is drowning. So young for such a bad experience!

The teen-mistress is so young that her story seems inexcusable and incomprehensible. The married men in these cases seem even more heinous. But you must be careful in judging the young. Their emotions and needs are just as real as anyone's. It's only naiveté or innocence that misleads them. Vulnerability to an affair occurs without regard for age. Of course the teenager shouldn't get involved; of course the married man shouldn't compromise such youth; but the world is not made up of shoulds and should nots. It is made up of things that are. I point this out because young women are falling for married men in large numbers. 16% is nearly one out of five. If we are to halt this trend, it has to be done with compassion, understanding, and logic.

There are drastic drawbacks for the teenager who is desperately in love with a married man. Her formative years are too often affected adversely when her life takes on the form of a triangle. But preaching isn't going to prove that. I wanted to design a test, but I found it impossible. Why? Because testing has to involve a reality for comparison. Teen-mistresses are too young yet to have much in the way of a mode of comparison. Often this married man is their first "love" experience, or their first sexual experience, or an experience like no other prior. The intensity is so awesome; it's difficult to get them to see any drawbacks through the impetuosity and the tears.

Adolescents place a high value on the opinions of their peers. Therefore to illuminate the drawbacks of teen-mistressing, I bow to their peers. No one says it better than the teens themselves. They are honest, highly perceptive, and right on target.

"It's not fair. I have never been so unhappy in my whole life. All I want is the man I love, but then again that is all his wife wants, and she has him and I don't. I am only halfway through your book but everything is there. I have close friends but they don't understand and they are tired of listening to me. I see my friends with their boyfriends being happy, planning their weddings. My older sister is planning hers. It hurts. If my boyfriend wasn't a married man I would be planning mine too. It's not fair!" *(Rhode Island, eighteen)*

"Did I ask him to divorce? I'm only nineteen, and divorce is a little out of my territory. I know for a fact he'd never marry me because he'd feel he was tying me down, and I'm too young for that yet. Isn't he sweet!" *(Wisconsin, nineteen)*

"I am white. My parents are very much against my ever dating a Black person. They are very strict. I fell in love with a Black married man—I was reaching out to be needed, I guess. It just about ruined my life. Taking on race, a married man and my parents was too much for me." *(Mississippi, sixteen)*

"I had dreams about my geography teacher in 11th grade, but I never thought about them coming true. We became friends and then one day we got to talking about our fantasies and dreams and finally we decided to meet out of school. I saw him for the next two years and then I went away to college. That freshman year was miserable for me. On vacations I'd come home and he'd pick me up because I couldn't get the car. I missed him too much so I dropped out of college and moved back home. I don't get to see him much even now. None of my friends are around, they are all away at college. I'd end the relationship but not only would I be losing a lover, I'd be losing my friend and even my family at this point too."
(Tennessee, nineteen)

How does a mother or father cope with that type of adolescent dilemma? Teens are old enough to make their own decisions, but not always objective enough to see the consequences. The things that teen-mistresses do for love are often not in their best interests. They are old enough to feel love, but is it love that they are feeling? Who is to say it's love or it's not?

"Am I in love with my married man? A tough question. I guess it's a matter of faith, not knowledge. I believe I love him because no other explanation (crush, infatuation, affection, respect, admiration, pity, regard, sympathy, etc.) seems to fit. Also because I recognize the feelings as the same sort I have toward people I know I love, such as my parents, family, and close friends. Also my feelings seem to be the same as those described and illustrated in biographies, autobiographies, histories and in some cases, fiction. Finally my feelings seem to be the same ones that my friends and family tell me they have experienced with members of the opposite sex." *(New York, twenty-one)*

That case for "love" is one of the most thorough and thoughtful I've ever read. And while it's not a point of contention that there is love in the teen-mistress's affair, it is a point of contention whether the love should be pursued. Love has to be give and take for it to be beneficial. For the teen mistress, she has a whole life to give, and for what? Poems and promises aren't enough.

Getting through to teenagers isn't easy. It was not so long ago that I was a teenager and I still remember the self-righteousness of it all. At the risk of sounding preachy, there is one point I am compelled to make for the teen-mistress and her parents. Teens are young women, old enough to love, and to express that love in all ways emotionally as well as physically. Morality doesn't stop them from falling for married men or making love. It can stop them from using contraceptives, though. Teen-mistresses labor under the double fear of being discovered for their sexual activeness and being discovered loving a married man. That can make them less inclined to seek birth control. Teenage pregnancies are an acknowledged epidemic. One million teenage girls become pregnant yearly. One out of five new mothers each year is a teenager, and 370,000 teenagers undergo abortion. Until we learn to see teenagers as women, and teen-mistresses as women, too, our morality will only further complicate their dilemmas.

Loving a married man can happen at any age. And at each age there are unique sets of problems and passions. Loving a married man can lead to learning and acquiring lessons from that old school of hard knocks. The highs of it all are equaled only by the complications.

"I don't care if the whole world says we were wrong. It was right. It also ruined everything. I wrote him love letters. He took pictures of us at a party. His wife found them and she had a little talk with my parents, my boyfriend, and the principal. He substitute taught on rare occasions. Now my parents will never trust me or forgive me, my boyfriend broke up with me, and my friends ignore me. I just can not understand how something so damn beautiful caused so much hell. It's not right." *(Canada, seventeen)*

Sometimes the only thing that teenage mistresses don't grasp is that triangles aren't fair, life isn't fair, and love isn't fair.

Widows, on the other hand, know that lesson all too well. Losing a husband taught them about life's injustice quite well. Unlike the teen-mistress, the grandma-mistress has life, most of it, behind her, rather than ahead of her. And ironically hindsight doesn't discourage her from falling into a triangle. Often it encourages her.

A Sigh Is Still a Sigh

When I was reading Hedda's letter, an invisible orchestra started playing the theme from that movie classic *Casablanca*, "As Time Goes By." Long afterward the memory of her story and the music lingered.

"One day I walked to the shopping mall near our apartment complex and I heard a loud sigh from a man walking alongside me. I turned to see if the person was ill. He was a nice-looking elderly gentleman. I ventured, 'Are you alright?' He said, 'Yes, I'll have to get over that habit of sighing.' I've teased him many times since that he sighed on purpose to get my attention." In Hedda's case a sigh wasn't just a sigh.

"He asked me if I would sit on a bench with him. I was in a hurry to get my errands done, but I said yes. I thought the man was upset. We sat quietly for a while. Then he told me that his wife didn't give him love and affection. I thought, now that is a peculiar thing for someone to say to a person he just met, but I'm soft-hearted. So he continued to tell me his first wife died thirteen years ago and now his second wife of eight years makes him miserable. I could empathize because I lost my dear husband just six years ago. After an hour or so, we shook hands, he held mine for a long time, and, looking right into my eyes he said, 'I'll be here next Monday.' I didn't answer, just smiled and left. The next Monday I was there, so was he and that's how it began."

Hedda said she has a rather large extended family, but she doesn't see too much of them. She's in Miami and they're up North. She says none of her friends would believe this of her. Yet she needs to talk about it.

"I see very little of him, only on Mondays. Sometimes his wife decides to go along, then I sit waiting like a fool. We can't do much. He has very little money, which his wife manages. So we sit in my apartment, have lunch and eventually have sex, such that it is. I stopped the sex part because I thought that's all he wanted, but he still kept calling and begging to see me. He says that he loves me. He says that I have brought something into his life he hasn't had since his first wife of thirty-two years died. I know exactly what he means."

Hedda is entitled to love and so is the married man in a way. Yet it's not as simple as that.

"There are many activities where I live. We have Senior Citizen dances. I love to dance. There are very few men so I have to settle for women partners. Married men don't ask other women to dance. I would love my married man to accompany me, but he can't go.

"Lately, he's been talking about divorce, which I refuse to discuss. I will never marry again. I certainly won't live with him. What am I really getting out of this? I'll tell you—more guilt than anything. I want more than anything to get back to the decent normal life I had before I heard that sigh. But I can't hurt him, he needs me."

What Hedda needs too is that feeling of being needed. She knows that her loneliness was really responsible for this. She closed by saying that "Everyone would be shocked." Again that worry over popular opinion. Well everyone shouldn't be shocked, because moonlight and love songs are never out of date. Violins up. The fundamental things apply to senior citizens, to the grandma-mistress and her married man as time goes by.

A Timepiece

Edith was obsessed with time, with clocks, with watches. It could have had something to do with her Swiss ancestry, but it definitely had something to do with her age and her affair with her married man.

"Perhaps I should tell you that I have been widowed since 1955 and am just sixty years old. After the death of my husband, I buried myself in a job where I would not meet any men and stayed with it for fourteen years. Then I moved to Washington to take care of my sister. I have worked at my present job for six years, but in the last three years I have had close contact with the supervisors. There are no single men in my age group although there are 350 people at our plant. My sister died in 1977 and we had been very close. Guess I have been more lonely than I realized since her death. In all my wildest, I never thought I would get involved with a married man."

Edith said that Sky is "kind, sixty-two years old, affectionate, a fantastic lover, and is very good at his job. I never dreamed that there would be another man in my life ever. Sex was long buried, I must confess with some difficulty, as I am passionate by nature and always enjoyed that part of life. We like the same things—reading, music, plays; he likes camping. In short, he is everything I want in a man."

The fact that Sky is married is even more complicated by the time factor. Their affair is contingent upon their working at the plant. Retirement is the impending heartbreak.

"The plant has a mandatory retirement policy at age sixty-five. Sky always had a dream of building a house to retire to on a lot out in the country of our beautiful state. He owns the property. His wife will not do this because she tells him if anything happened to him she'd be stuck out in the middle of nowhere. In my opinion no wife should say such a thing to a husband. She should go along with the dream for as many years as they would have together. I would love to live that dream with him. I live near woods and feed the birds, squirrels, and anything else that comes along—red fox, raccoon, chipmunks, etc. His dream of retirement has become my nightmare, because I would never see him again.

"I can't imagine life without this man now, never to have him hold me again, kiss me again. These things are just too painful to think about—as a matter of fact I'm crying as I write them down. At most we have three years left till he retires. It's been over two since we've been lovers. I might as well get used to the idea that I'll be alone for the rest of my life and get it over with now. Why after all these years surviving without a man, not living maybe, but surviving, why did I have to see how life should be with two people sharing love? Why did I have to fall in love with a married man? Oh, maybe this affair will die a natural death in the next few years, I doubt it but I hope so. Why did I have to find a man now with no hope of a future together? I just don't understand."

Divorce isn't in the picture. Sky's been married thirty-eight years. There is a lifetime of inertia behind him. For Edith that means a lifetime of aloneness ahead of her. For a sixty-year-old that may not seem like a long time, but it is the only time left. Lifetimes are relative. One day soon her affair will be nothing more than an antiquated timepiece stored away somewhere.

The grandma-mistress, even the label, suggests such dichotomy. Our images of black negligees and orgies are so far removed from the shawls and knitting needles that we see woven around senior citizens. We forget that age does not harden emotions and passions like it hardens arteries. Things like love and loneliness don't wear out.

The grandma-mistresses have futures, too. A part of that future is the concept of death. That is difficult to face without the man you love. Health considerations are always a reality for the senior citizens in the triangle.

"My married man wants very much to divorce. But because of a heart ailment we wouldn't risk a court fight. We will wait until he can convince her that a no-fault divorce would be best for all concerned. I'm in no hurry to get married as I'm not in good health so for the present we just cherish what we have found so late in life. Also because of financial considerations we would probably just live together. Marriage would decimate our incomes. She may have his name, but I am more his wife. When he's hospitalized, I'm the one they call." *(small town, Ohio, sixty-eight)*

"It's interesting to imagine that after seeing you on television this morning, literally thousands of women are sitting down just like me and writing to you. I just wanted to reinforce what you said about women from sixteen to sixty-five. I'm in my seventies and just a couple of years older than my married man. Our friendship began twelve years ago and intensified every year. Sex didn't enter into it until five years ago. Waiting that long wasn't my idea, but as everything else in this kind of relationship is waiting for the man, so was that. Everything you mentioned is true. I am his best friend. I'm the only person he can be honest with, I know more about his life than anyone in the world. I relax him so much that even his ulcer doesn't act up when he's with me. He loves me, etc., etc., etc., but all of it is meaningless when I have to face my 'twilight' years as some mistress said alone." *(Michigan, seventy-one)*

"In reality I do not think he will ever divorce. If his wife passes away, then I would indeed marry him. That could be forever, and with the strain I'm under, I could die before she does. Or he could, and take the easy way out of all this." *(Arizona, sixty-two)*

"I'm seventy years young. I've been married three times. Now I'm in love again with a married man and it's the best yet. He is my fountain of youth. If you ask me love is better every time around, not just the second." *(Iowa, seventy)*

Grandma-mistresses may be old in years, but still they are fighting for love, a future, and their married men. They have lived long enough to see that life involves compromise. Compromise and mistresshood go together. They realize that death is near enough to make them savor the present and prize the love they feel. That present-fixation adds to the making of their mistresshood. When it comes to triangular passions we seem to go through life young at heart. In the twilight years, many feel it's not wise to pass up a married man. It's foolish to miss out on a romance with someone because he's married. In that age bracket, with comparatively so few men around, sometimes wisdom points to mistresshood.

While we are fixing our attention on generations, I'd like to spend some time talking about a new tradition that is emerging. I call it the Mistress Tradition. I am finding that there are daughters who are following in their mothers' footsteps as far as mistressing goes. If your mother was or is a mistress, your odds for becoming a mistress are increased. Now at first this seems illogical. If a daughter watched her mother go through all those lonely Saturday nights, and all those torturous frustrations that go along with loving someone else's husband, you would think she would be smarter. You would think that a marital-status examination would be first and foremost even before a hello. Yet, the opposite is true.

This is not the first instance of self-debilitating behavior being passed down from one generation to the next. The same is true for alcoholics and child abusers. Alcoholic parents tend to raise children who manifest a weakness for and often the same addiction to alcohol. Child-abusing parents breed children that grow up to become abusing parents themselves. It seems so contrary. You would think that a child who saw the destruction that alcoholism can cause would never even sip wine. As for the child who experienced bruises and scars of parental beatings, you would think that as a parent that cruel memory would never turn into a repetition. The reverse is the documented sociological reality. It is logical when we realize that children learn what they see. No matter how perverse the lessons, if it's the only curriculum, that's all there is to learn. Learning occurs in the environment, which is made up of parents, and sometimes that means learning is limited.

Matched-Set Mistresses

Unlike the dishwashing-liquid commercial, there was no contest about age. The mother was clearly older, but the daughter looked old, too. The mother was forty-two; the daughter twenty-three. They both worked. They both looked worn. They both loved married men.

I met Sheila, the mother, and Sharon, the daughter, at a regional television program in the Midwest. Sheila had been through sixteen years of the agony and the ecstasy of the triangle with her married man and it wasn't what she wanted for her daughter. But at the start of our meeting, she wasn't looking to talk about her affair, she was concerned with her daughter, who was now locked in the agony stage.

Sharon had taken off from work for the day, not only to see me but because she was too upset to function at the office. She had been involved with a co-worker for two years. Of late he had separated, moved in with her for a few months, and then did an about-face and returned to his wife, bed, and board. Sharon had commented during the show about her dilemma and was now obsessed with "Should I call him and tell him to watch?" "Should I set up another meeting so he can explain why he's decided to stay married?" "Will he change his mind again?"

I must say that at least Sharon was able to talk to her mother about her problem. Sheila knew exactly what her poor daughter was going through. She'd been there. She'd seen the patterns. She'd felt the anxiety and the obsessive panic. But she was no help. She was well educated in mistresshood and had kept her married man through a marriage, a divorce, and still had him at the center of her life. She was less miserable about it all because she had adjusted. She knew the rules and the sacrifices that being a mistress entailed. But she wanted more for her daughter, not this. What Sheila had done was to pass her education on down to her daughter.

It was not an easy twosome for me. It triggered off an alarm that my sociological backlog had installed. I took them aside and said what I could.

I told Sharon to forget about him for a minute. I told her point-blank to go home and watch *herself* on television. Look long and hard at her face, whose expression was so full of pain. All this about setting up meetings and investigating his capacity for mind-changing was nonsensical. It would only bring on more of this same scene over and over. She felt her mother was a comrade in arms. I told her, "Look at your mom. Do you want to wind up like her? A lifetime of fantasies, waiting, hoping, compromises?" Poor Mom stood there shaking her head.

I could not wave a wand and make Sharon see that her value was lost in her plots and plans about him, his feelings, his fate. I asked her when she had laughed last. She couldn't see the significance of so trivial a question. That is a very significant meter to evaluate your mistresshood. I could only give her a copy of *The Mistress' Survival Manual*, a hug, and a plea to read the whole book before doing anything.

As for Mom, she was old enough to know what she was doing as far as *her* life went. In the end, remaining a mistress for a lifetime is a possibility if that is what a woman wants. What Mom *didn't* know was that her experience as a mistress set Sharon up for following the lifestyle.

All the while Sharon grew up, she saw that the main relationship her mother valued was the affair. The affair canceled out the marriage. The affair kept her mother preoccupied, happy, miserable, etc. She had learned along the way to equate love with affairs with married men. The agonies as well as the ecstasies were all part of that definition of love. Love to her therefore came to mean, naturally, loving a married man. An affair was even more natural than anything. That is what she saw, she learned, and she understood as normal.

Mistresshood, just like alcoholism and child abuse, seems to be following a proven sociological pattern. It is a tradition that is passed down from one generation to the next. It is a legacy that well-meaning parents don't mean to transmit, but it is transmitted anyway in the environment.

I haven't run across the mother-daughter mistress phenomenon in any great numerical way. But seeing it several times was sufficient. Mistresses who are raising daughters should be aware of the impact that their affair can have on the future of their daughters. Fathers who see mistressing in the mother should do their best to see that daughters learn other things about love. Otherwise as the mistress population increases, the Mistress Tradition will be passed down more and more. Mistresses will breed more mistresses. People will say that it's some Dante-like justice. However, it's not justice, but injustice and compromise inherited.

Some women choose mistresshood aware of the alternatives. Daughters who have mistress-mothers are not capable of making an objective choice. For some of them mistressing is the only way. It's a tough choice for those who choose. For those who don't choose, it can be a tragedy. The Mistress Tradition is not the heirloom that mothers treasure and save for their daughters to inherit one day.

Among women, the young and the old and those in between are often looking for the same things. The young have life ahead of them and naiveté guiding them. The old have life behind them and a limited male pool and loneliness guiding them. Naiveté, experience, and environment can all add up to the same thing—a triangle. The young are often perceptive about their married men but not old enough yet to be perceptive about themselves. The old know themselves and life too well to give up a man they love. All mistresses want love.

"I guess we all have a need to be loved and to be the most important person in one person's life. That's how we get into it. While I don't necessarily want marriage, I do want some Saturday nights." *(Oxford, Ohio, fifty-nine)*

Everybody's looking for the heart of Saturday night, young and not so young. The difficulty is that married men have no Saturday nights to give. Some have too much heart, some not enough, and some none at all. The young mistress is oftentimes aged by the mistress experience. She's too young for a past, and mistresses are seen as women with a past. The older mistresses are frequently revitalized by the mistress experience. But the grandma-mistress usually can't count on a future, and she's never too old to have a future.

Be careful in what you say about mistresses. Your daughter or the grandmother in your family could be one. If not today, then tomorrow or in the next few years. It may be in your family's best interests to educate yourself on the making of the American mistress, to cultivate sympathy, and to watch for the Mistress Tradition. Your family coat of arms could someday soon be decorated with a triangle!

CHAPTER 9

Title, Position and Fringe Benefits: Career and the Mistress

Is mistressing a career? Are all mistresses "kept"? Is mistressing a position that involves service and years like other career climbs? Are there fringe benefits? Does the title of mistress describe the lifestyle? The word "career" encompasses several different concepts. We are going to look at them and how they apply to mistresses in particular and the mistress phenomenon in general. In doing so we are going to update the myths regarding the mistress. We are going to personalize any occupational tendencies. And we are going to clarify differences between career mistresses and the mainstream.

First and foremost I would like to address myself to the entire concept of "kept." To most people the definition of mistress is "a kept woman." That definition assumes monetary compensation for some sexual service. It is assumed that mistresses work at pleasing their married man and are paid in money, trips, luxury gifts, and a diet of caviar. Thus, the mistress, it is assumed, always exists in an upper-echelon world, a world of glamour. This concept of the kept woman is subscribed to by professional psychologists, by women contemplating mistressing, in fact by most people. However, it is only women who become mistresses who know the real story. Where did this mythical image of the mistress originate?

Mistresses are like blue jeans. That may initially sound like an inane comparison, but recounting to you the history of blue jeans is the best way I know of explaining the historical development of mistressing and the making of the myth.

In 1495 King Henry VIII went to Janua, Italy. He bought 262 bolts of a heavy cotton material which was new at the time. The material was named after the city of Janua, and called jean. His royal tailors made trousers out of the jean.

They dyed the material blue and the blue jeans were the most popular idea yet. Henry VIII was a sensation in his novel blue jeans. Soon all the gentlemen in court wore them. Then the material and the popular blue jean trousers were made available to the lower classes. The look and the durability fitted their lifestyle too. So finally, in sixteenth-century England, everyone followed the trend initiated by the king who wore blue jeans.

Mistresses have followed the same distribution trend. Once the mistress was found only among royalty. She lived in royal style. In America she lived in upper-class style, since executive suites are the closest we have to royal chambers. So "mistress" came to represent a title signifying wealth and luxury. She was a sort of appendage of wealthy men, a status symbol, an expected part of some men's lives.

Traditionally royal marriages were pragmatic. Mistresses were romantic. In America's upper echelons and right on down to the plebeians, the appeal of romance was ever popular. Marriages that didn't measure up to the right romance quota started to add the mistress. Poor men found that they needed a mistress and that having a mistress fitted into their lives. Money wasn't plentiful, therefore it was not an issue. In our times of moral relativity, feminism, and opportunity, more and more married men find more and more willing mistresses. Triangles are even more prevalent among the less privileged. Having a mistress doesn't take money. It takes appeal, romance, and passion. And while the title of mistress has retained that historical image of wealth and privilege, the real mistress is far from that myth. The phenomenon of mistresses has become widely disseminated, popularized, and a uniform experience very much like the phenomenon of blue jeans. That is why we have this myth of the kept mistress and why it is so outdated.

Statistically speaking, about 2% of mistresses are financed according to the kept concept. That percentage came out of my questioning the mistress about her financial relationship with her married man. I asked on the questionnaire, "Did your married man give you any money? For what? (rent, expenses, etc.)"; "Did you want him to give you money or gifts?"; "Did you refuse to take money or gifts?" The answers that came across the board can be summed up in the following excerpts. They were the majority feeling and express the reality about being kept.

"Richard has never given me any money. As a matter of fact, he owes me $410 and has owed it to me for some time. I would have liked for him to give me a gift, money no. He has never offered me any gift or money so I cannot say I have refused." *(Austin, Texas)*

"Mike gave me gas money twice because he used my car to go to Detroit. I don't expect or need any tangible things from him. I mean gifts would be nice, I wouldn't refuse anything, but I do fine without them." *(small town, Michigan)*

"I wanted gifts, sure—everybody likes little presents. Yes, he has offered me money for groceries, because he knows I have a tight budget, but I always say no. When you are a dinner guest you don't pay for the meal in my house. It is a big sacrifice for him because he is deeply in debt." *(Pueblo, Colorado)*

"Did he give me money, no, but I gave him twenty bucks once to hold him over till payday. He gave it back. Did I want gifts? No, all I wanted was his love. He didn't offer me gifts. He didn't exactly have a pile of money to squander on me." *(Columbia, Nebraska)*

"I don't expect money. He loves me. That's all I expect from him. I gave him gifts, though... & I still do. I love him. He doesn't owe me anything but his mutual love. And I have that." *(Sunnyvale, California)*

"No, he never gave me money really. He would lend it to me if I needed help though, but I always paid him back whether he knew it or not. Sometimes I would slip it into the money bin if he said that I could keep it. Once, my dress got ruined at work and he handed me money to buy a new one. I didn't want to feel like he was paying me for my love. I didn't want to feel any cheaper than I did. Instead he'd buy me flowers or plants even though I have a black thumb. He used to draw me pictures and write humorous captions underneath the drawing. He'd write suggestive notes and drop them on my desk at work. Those are the things I cherish because only he and I shared them. I miss that. I still have every one of those silly pieces of paper. I didn't want or need materialistic things. I just wanted to share with him and to hold him." *(Pennsylvania)*

"As I had a house provided by the military, and a job, he never had a reason to give me any money. I never wanted his money. The gift I got was more beautiful than anything he could ever have bought me. I had a piece of his soul." *(Riverview, Michigan)*

"He gave me money from time to time. Things were rough for me after the divorce. He paid for motels, for dinners. He was a generous man. He would have done more if he could but he didn't have much money himself." *(Houston, Texas)*

"Money wasn't ever mentioned. I would have been real insulted. I couldn't be paid for the love I gave him. I've never been for sale. His wife's the one who cares about money, not me." *(Oregon)*

Do you get the financial picture? Most mistresses are not looking for financial compensation. The reality is that they don't get any. You'll see why when we discuss in depth what married men have to give. Mistresses value their love to a superlative degree that is beyond any mundane realm of accounting. They expect reciprocity in emotion and passion, not in tangibles. Most answered my monetary questions in terms of grocery bills, gas bills, dinners, etc. The 'kept" vocabulary of luxury items, penthouse rents, was virtually nonexistent. It was the farthest thing from the minds of most of the mistresses.

For 98% of the mistresses who entangle themselves with married men, there are no fringe benefits in a financial sense. What about that 2%? What is it like being kept? Is it as luxurious as the imagery? Is it a desirable position? I can't answer, because although I was once a mistress, I was not of the kept variety. So to explain the experience I've chosen someone who has been there.

A Real-Life Mannequin

Models flock to Manhattan. Karen was just twenty-six when she flew in with all the predictability of a Capistrano swallow. Like millions before her, she found that being beautiful wasn't insurance that she would succeed. Everyone was a beauty contest winner somewhere along the way. Everyone had a portfolio which included at least one exquisite photograph. Everyone seemed to be out of work. All except the mannequins in the store windows. They seemed to be the only well-dressed, poised models around.

Now and then Karen got a modeling assignment in the garment district. During one of those assignments she met her married man. He was the president of his own company. In the course of the fashion business they met several times. Finally Karen started the ball rolling.

"He suggested that we go out, but then he never followed through. One day I said it's now or never so to speak. I thought I could handle seeing a married man. I said I didn't want to be married yet. We'd see each other nearly every day. He kept an apartment in town that his wife never used. So we'd meet there or at my place. It was really lovely for me. I'd been so depressed about my modeling. There were restaurants, nites on the town. He was fun and he had an incredible mind. Not at all like the boys I'd known back home."

Her married man was forty-one. He was apparently generous. He paid Karen's rent. He was always bringing her beautiful clothes, but after all that was their business and he got them at cost or for nothing. They made a beautiful couple, dressed to kill and dancing around Manhattan. A still of one of Karen's nights on the town could have been a magazine ad. She was a real life mannequin, displaying high fashion and romance and love.

According to Karen, though, it wasn't all fairy tale material.

"I am definitely the 'golden' girl-mistress, kept mistress, but the pain has been no less. I want to commend you on a long overdue book. I'm sure you've heard it before, but I could have written it too. It is indeed a subject of taboo, but just the same is a fact of everyday life. There is so much I could say on and on but I won't bore you. I am choosing to continue with my relationship. It has its ups and downs, but for me it has many pluses in between. If it weren't for my married man's help, I'd have to go to work and forget about modeling. And besides I love him. If it weren't for him I'd be crazy by now. Thanks for helping me make sense and logical order from all those thoughts, hurts, and fears. I stare in the mirror and have those talks to myself. But for me it's good for now."

Karen's monologues with the mirror are characteristic of many mistresses. But mirrors are mere shadows for a model. And if her life resembled a mannequin in that she displayed a part of his love, or an illusion of a whole life together, for Karen it was natural. Mistressing, modeling, mirrors, and mannequins all added up to a position that Karen could pose for perfectly.

"I still haven't found out how to enjoy Saturday nights or weekends, which are actually the only times we are not together." But for Karen Saturday nights aren't so important and besides she needs her beauty sleep.

It seems to me that Karen had a calling to come to Manhattan and a calling to modeling, but a calling for married men, not necessarily. That was her first mistress experience. As for another married man in the future, Karen said maybe. Does being a mistress even once prove that a pattern will follow?

Mistressing is conventionally defined as a pattern. It is assumed that mistresses have other married men in their pasts. And it is assumed that their futures will be populated by more married men. It's like bouncing from one job to another. People assume mistresses bounce from one married man to the next. Does loving a married man lead to a career in married men? I spent a great deal of time researching whether or not a pattern existed in the world of mistresses. Are American mistresses making a new career, all of them, part of them, and why?

I asked, "Was he the first married man you dated?" And again, further along I asked, "Is he or was he the first married man with whom you became involved?" And, "Would you ever date a married man again?" My data was split on the pattern theory.

Approximately 65% of the mistresses said this was the first encounter they had ever had with a married man. Approximately 35% said this was not the first married man in the past. Of the mistresses with a married man in the past, most tended to be divorcées: 44%. The next largest grouping were singles, 33%, and then married mistresses, 19%. Widows accounted for 3%. So as for a married pattern, a little over one-third of the mistresses do suggest some pattern of becoming involved repeatedly with married men. Two-thirds don't suggest any pattern at all. The vast majority of mistresses don't plan on having an affair with a married man again. Again there are the exceptions, the women who do plan on remaining mistresses.

Let's take a closer look at some of the rationales for those mistresses who seem to suggest a pattern with their past and their present.

The Beat Goes On

"I will give my name because I am proud of being what I am, a mistress. I don't feel as though I should be ashamed, have guilt feelings, nor try to run around as an anonymous person. I've had many relationships with married and single men. I've been married and divorced. The best love's always been with the married ones."

Even though this mistress wanted to use her name, I won't. I'll call her Jennifer. She is twenty-eight, a registered medical assistant. She comes from Coram, New York. Her current married man is a musician and a CPA. He's twenty-eight.

"I haven't been this happy in years. I go to work every morning a happy person. My social life feels full. I'm happy and contented with my married man and therefore need no others. I have no complaints—sure, disappointments happen, but be glad you have your man now, my motto is 'Live for today—not the future.'"

I'll let Jennifer backtrack a bit about her former married man. It sheds light on her philosophy and her career goals.

"When I was eighteen years old I fell in love (sort of love at first sight) with a married man. I had a beautiful eight-year affair. I was brought up by very strict parents as the only daughter. We never planned or 'chose' to meet, we just saw each other and bam! He got married because his wife was pregnant, so when his daughter was born, I kind of resented her because she was the reason he never left. But throughout the eight years, his wife, not me, hated me, called me, threatened me but I knew I was the loved one so therefore considered her 'the other woman.' When my parents found out, I was treated like an infant. I was constantly watched, punished, etc., until finally I got married to get away from them. Since it was not a marriage based on love, I ended it soon enough. My parents are still angry at me and say I disgraced the family name. The only reason that beautiful love affair ended was because my married man was killed, an automobile accident. I cannot cry as I think about it simply because there was so much love and joy. I remember the good times.

"Maybe that's why I am so fulfilled being a mistress again. I know that I live for today. I meet my married man at clubs. We love dancing, just sitting and talking. What is the sense of issuing ultimatums which only lead to fights? Why plan for next year? You should be happy for the time you have now. There may never be a tomorrow."

Jennifer liked, and continues to like, being a mistress. She feels that married men make you feel "like someone special." In comparison, the things that life has taught her are worse lessons than the drawbacks of mistresshood. Life does go on. For Jennifer the beat of a married man goes on. She doesn't much care if it is the beat of a different drum.

The point in Jennifer's story is that a pattern of married men often has logic to it. Some women find that mistressing is fulfilling to them. It measures up to their expectations. For these mistresses the pros outweigh the cons. A pattern of married men is not always documentation of some classic psychosis.

What other kinds of expectations are fulfilled by affairs with married men?

"This particular time as in others, the man was appealing, attractive. Back to that old issue of intimacy. He was very open and trusting, very human. Definitely unlike single men who're so caught up in games and defensive maneuvers; he wasn't afraid to show tenderness or his human frailties and vulnerability." *(single, thirty-two, Flint, Michigan)*

"Your book started out to be a joke gift from my married man. I'm glad to know I'm not alone. It's helped me understand him and vice versa. Still I've learned a lot of new things and been places I never would have had he and I not met. I get a chance to be sophisticated and have him pay attention to me. Most guys are more interested in getting attention and looking at other girls. Conversations are limited and shallow. With my married man I'm it. We can talk about anything and know there's no hidden meanings. I feel married men treat you like a person and I'm not being taken advantage of. We can be honest about what we want." *(single, twenty-five, Washington, D.C.)*

Among some mistresses who make a career out of one married man or out of several in succession there is indeed a preference for married status. Many women are telling me that married men are better—better lovers, better friends, and better companions. Married men do have special things to offer, as we'll see in their section.

Some mistresses see a pattern of married men as a vulnerability, not a choice. Nevertheless they see logic.

"It has been my rose-tinted ill-fortune to have been involved with various married men since the age of nineteen. It took over a decade to kick the habit, and that is exactly what it becomes. Once hooked and hurt, though becoming a little wiser in the process, many women like myself are even more vulnerable and tend to fall into the trap again and again. It is my observation that a sizable group who are particularly susceptible to illicit liaisons are so-called career women. It seems the more independent the lady is between nine and five, the more emotionally vulnerable she becomes from five to nine. She is attracted to equals. More often than not they are married. My experiences have given me the dubious reputation of being a sage in these matters. I have spent many hours and drunk innumerable cups of coffee with acquaintances and friends who need someone to listen." *(single, thirty, Sacramento, California)*

Mistressing as a career in terms of time and commitment can bring ill fortune and it can bring good fortune. It seems to depend upon the mistress. The pattern is more complex than a Freudian catch phrase. It is subjective. It has to do with training, experience, and objectives.

One last concern is the future for those 65% of mistresses

who are in the grips of their first triangle. Do they see a pattern for themselves? Do they plan on spending a lifetime with this one married man? Would they fall for another married man, even consider dating one?

"Are you kidding? I would never again date a married man. That is if I survive this time." *(Des Moines, Iowa)*

"No, I would never let this happen to me again. Loving a married man is all the hell you write about and more. I would try to discourage any friend of mine from dating a married man. They just don't realize where it leads." *(Harvard, Illinois)*

"I probably would go out with another married man. It's not a matter of choice. It just happens sometimes. I can't say what will happen in the future for me." *(Vacaville, California)*

"No, no, a thousand times no." *(rural Georgia)*

"Yes, definitely. I like the feelings that my married man has given me." *(Milford, Connecticut)*

"I wouldn't date a married man again, knowing now what I know. But this man is worth it all. I will wait a lifetime for him if that's what it takes. I can't live without him." *(Round Lake Park, Illinois)*

"I won't go out looking for one again, but if I fall, well then I guess yes." *(Michigan, upper peninsula)*

Although more women said that they wouldn't date a married man again, there was still the "maybes," and the "yeses." And since mistressing seems to happen, you can count on some changing their minds if the "right" married man comes along.

The 35% who do have a pattern seem to be aware of that pattern and in control of where the future will lead them. Of course there are a number of career mistresses who feel out of control, unhappy, and desperate. A triangle can be a unique torture chamber. Yet that one type, habitual and unhappy all of the time, is the only type that is ever presented classically. Most career mistresses are thoughtful, unconventional, and leading lives that satisfy their needs. Mistressing, like any career, can be a wrong or a right choice. It is up to the individual to know his/her vocation and change careers in midstream if necessary.

Mistressing is not always a career, as people assume. There is not a clear-cut pattern for all mistresses limiting their diet to a straight menu of married men. Yet it can be a career for a lifetime. Mistressing is not a profitable venture as the kept image suggests, except for a mere 2%. Mistresses are kept in their role for other reasons. Mistresses are kept in cocoons, in nightmares, in illusions, in stalemates, in real-life *Dr. Zhivago* romances, in scripts that seem to be written by Dante's ghost. Mistresses are kept in heaven and in hell, simultaneously or periodically.

Mistressing is a position of honor and dishonor. It is a position of convenience and preference. It is a position of surprise. Or it is a position of transition. It is not a titled position resembling Madame de Pompadour's.

Mistressing has fringe benefits, though rarely the monetary kind. There is the intimacy, the honesty, and the love of someone special. There is being needed and feeling like you have a man's soul with you even when his body is elsewhere. There are similarly negative fringes: loneliness, jealousy, anxiety, and Saturday night.

The concept of career and the mistress is a diversified subject. It is often as diversified as the mistress. And the fact that career goals change as love affairs change makes discussing it all the more difficult. Every mistress should explore her relationship with her married man from a career standpoint. Affairs sometimes turn into decades. If loving that married man is becoming your career, make sure you realize it is your life. Trying to adjust to a career that is not suited to you can kill you.

Accurate career research is hard to come by as far as mistressing is concerned. The general information is mythical, misleading, and lacking reality. In the final analysis, only you as a mistress can decide if mistressing is for you, if it can make you more happy than unhappy, and if it is worth your time and possibly your life.

Are You Cut Out to Be a Career Mistress?

How about a career in the army of mistresses? Is it for you? There is a portion of mistresses who find that their affair leads to a career in a kind of triangular service. They pledge allegiance to the married man for a lifetime. "Career" has a number of different meanings. What does it mean to you as a mistress, or as a woman contemplating joining up? Are you cut out to be a career mistress? Take the following test and see if you qualify.

Directions: Read each statement. They are in paragraph form, with the salient statement at the end. Then choose your reaction from "always," "sometimes," "never." Proceed to the scoring and evaluation.

1. The way in which women view becoming a mistress varies. Some feel they were involuntarily drafted into the role. Love caught them off guard. Others feel it was a preference. How would you rate the decision to become a mistress? *Mistressing is a conscious choice.*

                always
                sometimes
                never   1. _____

2. Historically speaking, mistresses have been analyzed from a Freudian perspective. Unresolved Oedipal conflicts and rivalries are seen as the driving force. Mistresses are fulfilling some childhood destiny. How do you rate that explanation? *Mistresses are victims of Freudian destiny.*

                always
                sometimes
                never   2. _____

3. The term "mistress" usually conjures up money. In your view or your experience does mistressing bring an income? Are mistresses kept in high living, vacations, gifts, etc.? Can the role supplement the income of a working girl or divorcée?

How do you assess this?
Mistresses are kept.

         always
         sometimes
         never   3. _____

4. "Sleeping their way to the top." You've surely heard that about some women. For some women in today's moral climate that statement is unfair and unnecessarily harsh. Why not mix business and sex? The two can complement each other. So what if advancement is a byproduct! Others feel mixing the two is a definite timebomb, morality excluded. How do you feel about the mix?
A mistress benefits with career pluses: advancement, raises, privileges.

         always
         sometimes
         never   4. _____

5. Married men are different from single men. Some women think married men are better; more honest, forthright, romantic, and intimate. Single men pale in comparison. They seem shallow, egotistical, and guarded. Do you feel married men have greater appeal for you?
Married men are better than single men.

         always
         sometimes
         never   5. _____

6. There is a tendency to cast mistresses as habitual users. One married man means there will be others and there have been others. A mistress' past is seen to determine her future. Does one married man mean a lifetime of affairs with married men? What do you think?
One married man predicts a future of married men.

         always
         sometimes
         never   6. _____

7. The realm of parenthood is changing. Today single parenthood is on the rise. Some feel it is no longer necessary to have a husband before having a child. If you subscribe to that,

mistressing doesn't have to stop you from mothering.
A mistress can opt for single parenthood any time.
> always
> sometimes
> never   7. _____

8. An affair with a married man is set up to offer no commitments, other than an emotional bond. Some women feel this ensures assets like freedom and independence, others feel it only means boundaries and limits to the growth of the relationship. How do you see commitments, as an asset or a liability?
As a mistress I do not want commitment, other than emotional.
> always
> sometimes
> never   8. _____

9. Mistressing is rated by some as opportunity. By others it is defined as servitude akin to indentured servitude. Where does your rating system fit in?
The life of a mistress is a life of opportunity.
> always
> sometimes
> never   9. _____

10. A good man is hard to find. Many, many women still hold to that old adage. Finding a good man regardless of his marital status is a quest for many. They become mistresses because that good man is married and they can't be any more than that, owing to circumstances. Widows, career women, married women find a limited supply of men. The man is more important than his marital status. Supply and demand—do you think it applies to mistresses?
When men are in short supply, their marital status becomes irrelevant.
> always
> sometimes
> never   10. _____

Scoring:
For each "always" answer give yourself 10 points.

For each "sometimes" answer give yourself 5 points.
For each "never" answer give yourself 0 points.
Total your score. Total _____

Evaluation:

Tour of Duty: 0–30 Points. If you scored in this range, most likely your mistressing days will be a brief stint. You don't express a particular preference for mistressing as opposed to other forms of relationships. You don't feel that the mistress role has unique assets. Rather you see liabilities. You don't agree with the professional assessment that mistresses are destined into their plight and locked into a pattern. For you a tour of duty with one married man is enough for a lifetime. The real benefits are few in comparison to the myths and the limits. You are definitely not cut out for a career in mistressing.

Training Ground and Re-enlistment: 35–65 Points. If you scored in this range, most likely you do see possibilities in mistressing. Your career plans are still too nebulous to be certain of, though. However, mistressing does offer potential advantages. It may augment your life with gifts, promotions, and companionship as far as you can see. You tend to be ruled by impulses and situations. If men are in short supply, a married one is better than none. If your business includes an attractive man, why not expand the working relationship. Morally, you are flexible. You view mistressing as more than a tour of duty, it's become re-enlistment for you. There may be only one married man in your life or several in the past. The future, however, is still uncommitted. A career in mistressing for you? Maybe.

Career Soldier: 70–100 Points. If you scored in this range, most likely your mistressing days will turn into years. In your judgment mistressing has much to offer. You may or may not ascribe to the Freudian theories. It doesn't matter, because there are conscious reasons for your mistressing preferences. You value emotional commitment and need no more. You see mistressing as opportunity, as a choice. It can supply freedom, independence, glamour, and add to your job as well as your lifestyle. Your mistress experience may have proven this. If that is so, you are the exception. Or your attitudes may be based on commonly held beliefs regarding the mistress life. If it's the latter watch out. A career in mistressing demands a certain type. You are definitely headed for a career in mistressing. I hope your expectations fit your qualifications. Career soldiers have a tendency toward casualties.

In Conclusion:
If there isn't a married man looming over your mind already, in the future there may be some married man who wants you! Should you answer the call and join up? Some women are well suited and make well-adjusted mistresses for years or a lifetime. Others are mismatched to the "career" of mistressing. Mistressing has something to offer for some; nothing for others. Do career research and find out if you fit the mistress bill. Don't wind up AWOL—away without leave of your senses!

PART THREE

The Married Man/The Man in the Middle

CHAPTER 10

The Triangle Papers

The married man is somewhat like a spy who came in from the cold, looking for a receptive ear and a warm shoulder. In his mistress he often found these things. The married man responded with a coded communication that was secret and highly classified. The mistress may not have started out like a Mata Hari, but she found herself privy to intimate confidences by default. What kinds of confidences? What kinds of secrets? In this chapter you will see because I will declassify some of the Triangle Papers.

The Traingle Papers will show you an inside view of the married man. Mistresses have reported to me for quite some time now on the confidences of their married men. What do married men tell their mistresses during those clandestine rendezvous? Why don't they talk to their wives the way they talk to their mistresses? What do these coded communiqués say about the nature of the triangle? What do they say about the married man?

Some of the material I have included here is directly from the pen of the married man. Some is written and some is implicit. Most of the material comes from the pen of the mistress. Perhaps it might therefore have a certain bias or perspective, you might say. Well, even so, the Triangle Papers will give you a new insight into the married man. The Triangle Papers deserve to be revealed so as to dispel certain myths and misconceptions about the affair and the married man. The Papers are quite informative, especially for wives.

I'd like to make a rather personal entry. It's sort of an unwritten entry but pregnant with a message nevertheless. Permit me to reminisce for a moment, back to the days when I was a mistress. Often I have been asked what do mistresses and married men do in their hours together. What did we do, my married man and I? What did we whisper during our rendezvous? Well, on those few hours my married man and I shared on infrequent afternoons, one of his most ardent desires was to nap. Yes, nap. He would come over to my tiny apartment, stretch out, and sleep. I would cover him with my ragged fluffy quilt and silently stand romantic guard over his much needed rest and peace. This story is perhaps disappointing to those who expected a furious, frenzied scenario, but it is the truth. During one of those naps I wrote this:

Rest Easy in My Arms

Rest easy in my arms
Tune into this lullaby,
Take shelter in my arms
To all your cares just wave good-bye
    To tomorrow with its troubles
    And the struggles you encounter on the way
    Surrender to the pleasures
    That we treasure discovering today;
    I'll surround you with a calm
    Rest easy in my arms.
Rest easy in my arms
Unspin your head for just an hour
I'll chase away all qualms
And dull that hassling thinking power
    Take a breather from your escapades
    The cavalcade of where your life proceeds
    I'm designed for you
    My thoughts resigned to all your needs
    I'll surround you with a calm
    Rest easy in my arms.

Those naps meant a great deal to him. They were communicating a message to me. A message that was steeped in total ease and total trust. I have included my romantic interlude here to make the point that affairs are not what you might think. They aren't all passion and frenzy. Affairs between the married man and the mistress are an exchange of trust and confidences. *It is a confidential relationship*. My married man flattered me with many spoken confidences as well. Spoken or unspoken they were revelations, secrets, and emotions that were bonding us in a classified relationship.

Before I go any further, I am going to "declassify" a letter written by a married man which really illuminates what I mean when I say a confidential relationship.

"My Sweetheart,

It's taken me such a long time to be able to sit down and try to write a letter like this to you my love. I had to because I read and reread your ultimatum letter a hundred times this past week. I hope and pray I can say what I mean, express my love and understanding so that we can continue and have an even better relationship. These last twelve years have been wonderful and I hope we can go on.

First of all my love, no one knows better than I all the heartaches that you have endured for me as my mistress. I hate when you use that word. You know you have been so much more, you are not my mistress but my love. The strength you have shown over the last twelve years far exceeds anything I could have expected. It proves to me what a wonderful, loyal, and sensitive person you are. You have supported me in so many instances that it is without question that no one else could have done it.

As for my feelings, need you even ask? I have never had to hold back or hide any of my feelings with you. They have never changed, not from the beginning. I have always viewed you as a beautiful human being. You have always been my own personal Rock of Gibraltar during the trying times I've had in my life. You are the only one I have ever completely trusted with all my confidences. You have that quality that assures me you would never do anything to hurt me or betray a confidence regardless of how small. Your tenderness and your sharing were always there when I needed them both.

Again darling I love you and I want you. I can't imagine living without you. I would have to bottle up my very soul if not for you. I do sympathize with your feelings but please reconsider. You more than any other person know how unhappy my life is. You surely know that I do not love my wife the way that I love you. You also know why I cannot abandon my responsibilities no matter how little joy they bring. It is you to whom I go for the joy.

See me when we can and talk to me when we can so that we don't destroy the bond that has glued us together all these years. I believe deep in my heart that it was our destiny to be like this. We were assigned to this task of communicating which in my eyes is wonderful. I have wanted to call you. The only reason I haven't given in is my desire to honor your wishes to stay out of your life if that is what you truly want, but I can't.

This letter may not make sense to you my darling. I hope it says what I should be saying in person right now—I love you.

YOU KNOW WHO"

Leave your judgments aside for a moment. That letter epitomizes the definition of the confidential relationship. I have labeled the affair between the mistress and the married man a confidential relationship for several reasons. Most affairs are clandestine by necessity. Secrets are a matter of course. They are implicit in the very nature of the affair, in every rendezvous. They are the meat of many conversations. Confidentiality is the code name. It augments a very basic, deep pattern of verbal communication and deep intimacy. Married men remind me of some modern version of the Lone Ranger or Zorro. These triangle protagonists, too, have a faithful partner, but that partner never sees beneath the mask, never learns the true identity. The masked men of the Triangle Papers have marital partners who may not see the identity that the mistress sees. Some married men only unveil for their mistresses.

"My married man said it once—'I can take off my mask when I'm with you.' I feel that he finds me the one person he can be himself with. The main reason for our relationship is friendship. I like and respect him deeply. I, too, have a background in the social sciences. You seem to zero in on traits of importance for mistresses and for married men. The thing my married man said fits right in. It seems men do value friendship and the need to take off their masks." *(Brooklyn, New York)*

At times the confidences are light. Conversation is often an art to a mistress and a married man. It is a tool to explore each other's depths and heights.

"We saw each other several times a month at restaurants or motels. Sometimes we would travel into town and go to a museum or a concert. Many a long evening was spent sitting and disucssing ancient history, the Renaissance Period, Egypt and the Pyramids, the Inquisition and the Dark Ages. And we also talked of us as individuals, our home life, work, children, his relationship with his wife and why he chose to have an affair after twenty-six years of marriage, never having had an affair before." *(East Haven, Connecticut)*

Confidences go from light intellectual explorations to thorough life examinations and philosophy. The married man eventually uses the mistress as a sounding board for decisions, conclusions, and advice. There is no subject, except divorce for some, that is out of bounds.

"Our meetings consisted of mostly talking, talking about our lives in general, business and personal. He would come to my home to relax, to get away from the pressures and demands of his wife. We would talk about our hopes, our dreams, our frustrations—just everything. There were our love sessions, which he told me were better than those with his wife. And I believed everything he said at first. Now I believe less except that I'm sure our conversation was better than any he ever had with anyone; man, woman or child." *(Tulsa, Oklahoma)*

"My married man and I have so much in common. We each have three children. Our children are exactly the same ages, isn't that amazing? We talked at length many times about them, giving each other advice about the various problems and consoling each other about the difficult stages and laughing with each other about the antics. We have the same ideas when it comes to raising children. Sometimes we even have the same disagreements with our spouses about certain tactics used to raise the kids." *(Hillsborough, North Carolina)*

"One of our lengthiest topics of discussion was his son's bottle. He was very upset because his wife continued to give the child a bottle at bedtime even though he was nearly four years old. Apparently he and his wife argued about this frequently, to no avail. This was a stepping stone to talks about motherhood, fatherhood, psychology, and child-rearing. As I'm writing I'm chuckling because it's hard to imagine two breathless lovers talking baby bottles, isn't it? And I don't even have a baby." *(Norfolk, Virginia)*

Affair participants seem to focus on any crisis they are having in their life. If the affair goes on for years, so do the discussions. Mistresses are often invisible partners in the passages of the married man and helpful with his adjustments.

"Through the years we have seen each other from time to time. Our affair has been one of those on and off kinds for seventeen years now. Yet each time we feel that certain something that we knew we had always felt for each other. It is friendship, caring about how the other person is doing in life. I am a confidante he can trust, someone to be completely open with in any area of his life. I feel the same way with him. We have talked of this often. We communicate to the fullest and are, because of it, extremely close. I guess we'll be like this always." *(Green Bay, Wisconsin)*

How does the mistress exact such confidences from a gender that doesn't open up easily? Does she have some magical truth serum underneath her fingernails or a special flavored lip gloss spiked by Ian Fleming? Actually the mistress does facilitate intimacy in a way, which we'll come to in a few pages. However, her tactics aren't mystical or mysterious. And the married man isn't as stonewalled as he is reputed to be. We'll get to that too. First, though, the affair itself plays a significant role in the language of confidentiality and total communication.

Affairs are clandestine. They must be conducted in places where the married man won't be recognized. Usually that means rendezvous must be scheduled in seclusion, in isolation, and in private. Likely places are off the beaten path or in invisible motels. What this means is that the married man and the mistress have no distractions. They have no social life except each other. They have no conversation except a dialogue. They have to communicate verbally. Married men are taking risks in launching an affair. Oftentimes they take these risks because they have needs. Needs is actually a whole other chapter. However, the need to communicate is salient. Married men are immediately intimate. They need to communicate desperately in verbal as well as tactile ways.

"It was really weird for me. I was beginning to think that something was wrong with me or with him because all he ever wanted to do was talk. I knew his whole life story before he even attempted to hold my hand." *(Iron Mountain, Michigan)*

Taking a risk with a mistress demands trust. The longer the affair goes on, the more and more trust builds. After all, the mistress holds her married man's secret, his infidelity, in her palm. She protects that secret as she protects all the others. So as the trust grows, the list of confidences lengthens. Soon she knows every Achilles' heel, every dream, every mistake, every regret her married man has. Over and over I hear the same vocabulary.

"We are best friends. He tells me everything." *(Caroline, Wisconsin)*

"I call us soulmates because we have shared our very souls with each other as well as our bodies." *(Jacksonville, Florida)*

The very social organization of the affair as it is conducted in America breeds intimacy and profound communication. Not all the credit can go to an intangible structure, though. The married man and the mistress do respond to the intimate atmosphere.

It says something very interesting about the nature of men. I've heard that men have no feelings and that men can't talk. I've heard it a hundred times from women who are in the process of raising their consciousnesses. A new wave of rage has been articulated throughout the women's world at men for not being communicative or sensitive. Novels such as *The Women's Room* have captured that rage. The sales figures for that book alone attests to its author's touching a feeling and a judgment of men that literally millions of women relate to. It's a classic cameo to picture the husband deliberately ignoring the wife while he hides behind the newspaper or in front of the television set. Women by the millions have concluded that this is the way men are. They don't have feelings. They don't talk about their feeling or much of anything except sports.

Well, I've never heard mistresses characterize men that way. Never. In fact it has always been the opposite, as you've seen in these excerpts. Married men do talk, and talk and talk. They have feelings about everything—their jobs, their children, their wives, their goals. Verbal communication is the basis of many affairs. Married men do most of the talking. Their confidences are the glue that bonds them to their mistresses. Mistresses have seen their married man laugh, cry, connive, manipulate, console, and express all the emotions that human beings express. If you doubt me go back and read that letter. That married man articulated a gamut of all these and more. Married men do talk, and if your husband isn't talking to you that doesn't necessarily mean he is incapable of verbal intimacy. One of the biggest myths to come out of the feminist outpourings is that men as a gender are deficient emotionally and verbally. It's a fallacy. Don't take my word for it. Ask any mistress. Any mistress who has been involved with a married man will tell you. Each and every mistress has her own document to add to the Triangle Papers. Each and every mistress has heard privileged information, sensitive secrets, and seen the sensitive vulnerability of the married man. In fact it was those very confidences that hooked the mistress.

"My married man really threw me. I was used to dating single men, hearing the same questions and having the same meaningless conversations. Then when I met this married guy, it was like meeting a new species of animal. He wanted to talk about important things like feelings and art and happiness. I'd rather have my married man less than put up with the singles world any day." *(East Peoria, Illinois)*

"I'm no brain and I know that. But I like to talk about how I feel and things, you know? Sal is married but he talks to me like I'm smart. He asks me questions and wants to know what I think about things. I like that. I'm afraid if I walk out on him, I'll never find a guy who'll talk to me again like that." *(Mt. Upton, New York)*

Needless to say, hearing secrets can be spellbinding. Being treated like a confidante is a flattering role. Being trusted and being needed can be addictive. Married men need to talk and mistresses find that they need to listen. Intimacy breeds intimacy, until both are talking, listening, and are bonded together by their communication.

The quality of his conversation often sets the married man apart from his single competition. It even makes up for the lack in quantity of time that he can offer her. Since he is giving his mistress his soul, his essence, how can that be measured in terms of Saturday nights?

The making of many a mistress is directly related to hearing the confidences of her married man. It's hard to turn your back on someone who is unveiling himself so intimately. And so mistresses dedicate their lives, in months and in years, to compiling and making entries in the Triangle Papers. The married man is like a sacred trust. To mistresses their work is as important as the medieval monks who hand-copied manuscripts to preserve history throughout the Dark Ages.

The married man and the confidential relationship he offers the mistress are spellbinding and captivating. His truths and confessions ensure her loyalty. That is why mistresses view their affairs as a friendship or as a communion of souls. The married man's ability to communicate verbally so intimately is at the very heart of his potent appeal. He means it when he tells her she is his best friend and number one confidante. However, the confidential relationship is often a one-way street.

Mistresses do tell some secrets, but rarely all. For instance, many mistresses can't let on how badly they want their man to divorce. This is their ultimate secret. Or how much pain jealousy brings them. Mistresses more often put on a happy face and choose conversational topics that are going to please, free, or interest *him*. His problems take precedence. Therefore the married man is not the mistress' best friend or prime confidant. She may think he is, and often does. But his loyalty, his friendship, is too often more illusion than truth. How can he be a best friend when he is rarely there in an emergency or when you need him most? A confidante is useless when you have to hold back for fear he'll judge you too pushy. A mistress often has her confidential relationship with the mirror, another mistress, or me. Yet she holds on to this illusion that her married man is her best friend. And that illusion and his appeal make her a mistress for as long as she decides.

If you don't clearly see the logic in this go back and read that love letter once again, the one from You Know Who. He extolled his mistress for her loyalty, for always being there, for her friendship, etc. He obviously could tell her everything and did. Yet when she finally revealed her deepest anxieties, he dismissed them in a manipulative attempt to continue for another twelve years. He was indeed intimate, vulnerable, and also self-centered, selfish, and conniving. Without villainizing the married man, one must realize that he is looking out for himself first. That letter illuminates his need for the confidential relationship and his lack of regard for his mistress' welfare.

The married man often stops talking when the mistress starts asking the wrong questions. Hence, too many mistresses know this instinctively and don't ask. The friendships in affairs are therefore imbalanced. Realizing this is the first step for the mistress in exploding the triangle; demanding equal friendship and equal communication.

When it comes to the Triangle Papers and their married man, mistresses tend to be a selfless breed. All their loyalty goes to their man until none is left for themselves. They listen, they give, they attune themselves to the vibrations of their married man. Wives behave differently.

One mistress had some valuable observations on the married men she came into contact with, and how their vulnerability to a mistress developed.

"What a coincidence I caught you on television while I was a patient in the hospital last summer. I watched every second of it with delight and fascination—all the time never knowing that it would soon all apply to me—as I was soon to become a MISTRESS.

"There are a few things I want to say. I work as a secretary in the headquarters of a large corporation. Over the four-year period that I have worked there, I have worked with approximately 270 people. I have seen many affairs and even more attempts at affairs. I, myself, have been approached by at least eight men in the office and I'm certain there are other women here who could claim a larger number of interested men. The number of unhappily married men that I know personally is quite alarming. I have developed sound friendships with most of these same married men who have approached me through the years we have worked together. Their stories are fascinating, their excuses lame, and their lives mostly sad. Their desperation to communicate is amazing. I cannot help but wonder what keeps them at their wives' sides as I watch them reach out to other women so hungrily to fill a void. I think another interesting book would be one written about the married man and his motivations, as I know I can only shake my head in disbelief as I listen to some of their realizations and witness their sadness." *(Quincy, Massachusetts)*

Many married men are walking around with a void to fill. Why don't wives fill that void? Why don't wives draw out the realizations that splatter all over strangers at the office? Are wives at fault? Or is it a deficiency in marriage? Or is it a husband's doing? Why can't wives hear the confidences at first hand instead of from these Triangle Papers? There are quite a few relevant entries in the Triangle Papers on possible answers to these questions. It's difficult to avoid sweeping generalities here. So let me caution you. Wives must make their own personal judgments. The judgments of the mistress and the married man are here already. Many are hypothetical and many are hearsay. However, they will give you a better understanding of why some married men seek confidential relationships outside of marriage and inside a triangle.

Sweet Nothings and Sweet Everythings

Jackie was bursting with her story.

"Where do I start? I have another story for you because I am involved with a married man. Two days ago, I picked up your *Survival Manual*, and I haven't been able to put it down. I have so many emotions pent up inside that I've got to share them. I can write more fluently and more expressively than I can talk, and I can type almost faster than I think."

You guessed it, Jackie is a secretary. And as you will see, she isn't the only one pent up with feelings that are bursting forth. She works for a university complex in Boston. She fell in love on the job, not with her boss but with another married man in the administration department. Jackie is twenty-eight; Eli, her married man, is forty-two. They have a confidential relationship, or at least he does with her. Let Jackie backtrack.

"Eli always used to ask if I could fix him a cup of hot chocolate. One day he couldn't find me at my desk, and I saw him going through all my drawers looking for the hot chocolate mix. I thought that was the cutest thing. He looked like an addict having a chocolate fit. Christmas was coming so I wrapped up a package of hot chocolate, saying it was from Santa's elf. It all started out harmlessly enough."

Apparently underneath his chocolate drive, Eli sensed something else about Jackie.

"Well, Eli stopped to talk. We flirted a bit, I guess. He was really interested in how I liked my job, how I got along with the people in the office, my boss and all that. He began telling me things about himself. He was going through a real crisis in his job. We recently acquired a new director who was going to make some changes. He started to fire and hire. Eli felt for a while that he was going to be phased out of his responsibilities or even his job. He told me he didn't know if he could stand to be cut out of the picture. He considered several job offers from other companies. He talked to me of his thoughts, anxieties, and worries. I couldn't do much more than listen, because I wasn't qualified to make suggestions or recommendations about his life. Our friendship became closer.

"On Valentine's Day Eli started bringing me those little hearts with the messages on them—'Be mine,' 'Say yes,' 'Only you.' I had some of those little hearts too, but I was careful which ones to give because he was married. I saved all my chocolate kisses for him and would leave them on his desk when he was out of the office."

Well, as you can probably guess, one day they ran out of chocolate kisses and improvised with the real thing. Jackie said the first kiss was "electric." They met on campus where and when discretion allowed.

"We used to meet at the Mausoleum. The Mausoleum was isolated enough and we could be alone. It's a beautiful setting—green lawns, hedges, thickly grown trees. We spent a lot of time there, lunch hours, just after work before he would have to go home. We talked a lot. Eli was still undecided about the fate of his future and his job. He told me his feelings, the doubts he had about this choice or that. I tried to hint at why he wanted my advice, what about his wife? He said he couldn't talk to her and always dismissed it."

Then came National Secretary Day, which was an eye-opener for Jackie in more ways than one.

"Eli handed me a box obviously from a jeweler. I remember thinking it was just like in the movies, where the boss gives the secretary a diamond bracelet. It wasn't diamonds, just a simple gold bracelet. I wouldn't have traded it for the biggest diamond in Liz Taylor's vault. I was overwhelmed. I didn't feel right taking it. Eli insisted. He said I deserved it for listening and if it wasn't for me he'd have no one to talk to. I found it hard to believe but I didn't argue. Then I noticed some fresh pink scars on his arm. It looked like a cat had scratched him very deeply. When I asked him about the scratches he laughed in an odd way, shook his head, and wouldn't say anything. I started guessing—the cat, a dog, he fell? Finally he told me his wife had done it. He had gone home and found her drinking. They got into a big argument about where his job was going. My eyes almost popped out of my head."

Jackie said that National Secretary Day marked when she stopped feeling guilty about loving someone else's husband. Here was a wonderful man who deserved better. Yet Eli had no intentions of divorcing. They both intended to continue the affair. So far as I know Eli is still talking. This crisis has passed but he still has confidences to reveal at the Mausoleum. Jackie is still listening. They're still drinking hot chocolate and exchanging sweet nothings and sweet everythings.

It seems from this profile that Jackie became a confidante by default. Eli didn't have a sympathetic ear at home so he found one at the office. Yet, he didn't characterize his marriage as horrible. What makes a good wife a bad listener? What makes a faithful partner a bad confidante?

In the case of Eli's wife it probably had something to do with her security. In all likelihood she viewed his tenuous position as a threat to her financial and emotional security and that of their children. Therefore she had little patience and lots of fear, which ruptured into anger. She couldn't afford the same objective sympathy that Jackie had because she wasn't in an objective position. Jackie had no stake in the crisis. Eli's wife did, and her stake was unnerving and not conducive to passive listening.

Mistresses, unlike wives, have no vested interests in a married man's problems. Therefore they are open to his wide range of fears, desires for change, or upsets. Nothing he does will threaten the mistress' lifestyle or standard of living for the family. A mistress' position on the outside gives her the distance needed for compassion, patience, and good listening. A wife's position on the inside often makes her react selfishly, or emotionally, because she is personally at stake somehow.

"My married man confessed that he hated being a lawyer. Secretly he wanted to change his career in midstream. He had wanted to buy a grocery store upstate and go back to simpler living. His wife knew none of this, he said. They had separated once because of his negative cash flow. He didn't want to risk even suggesting it." *(Atlanta, Georgia)*

Husbands and wives know each other well and can sense the limits of their confidences. This is partly owing to the nature of marriage. Familiarity teaches spouses exactly what the other will think long before the thought is even expressed. This familiarity also breeds boredom, which can hamper self-expression.

Wives have heard all these daydreams, likes and dislikes, philosophies, and opinions a thousand times. Some wives lose interest in what their husband is going to say because it's all repetitious, in theme anyway. Sensing this disinterest, many husbands stop trying to have conversations. They find a new listener who won't be bored.

"My married man is kind and sweet. He's one of those men who loves to talk. He talks a great deal although he's not particularly interesting. He says he loves to talk to me because I'm a good listener. I guess I'm good at listening because I love him and I know how much my just listening means to him. And at our age, late sixties, talking is one of the few pleasures left." *(Iron Mountain, Michigan)*

Husbands aren't always right in their judgments of a wife's capacity for confidences. In all fairness to some wives, some husbands don't give their wives a shot at their most intimate thoughts. This can be all tied up in some macho self-image that the husband feels he must maintain. His silence is all mixed up in that view of himself and his responsibilities. He may not view his wife as a person, but more as another responsibility. Weakness can't be spoken about within the marriage.

"I don't think he [my married man] could just turn around and become the center of my life, because I am too independent and I am not dependent on him. This makes me his oasis when things become too much for him. He uses me as a shoulder to cry on. That is my function and according to him not a wife's. Maybe if he looked at a wife as a partner, not just a responsibility who produces more responsibilities, I could stand a chance of becoming Mrs. So-and-So." *(Portsmouth, Ohio)*

"My married man will never divorce. He may need me as a friend to turn to but that's all it will ever be. He also needs to be the center of someone's life who needs and depends on him for everything. He's old-fashioned. He likes that superior role. Without it he'd be lost. His wife must like it too. That's not my idea of communication, but that's his. I'm sure I'm not the first or last friend he'll find to talk to." *(San Mateo, California)*

It is still true that men hold a double standard with regard to women. You may be familiar with the double-standard terminology with regard to sex. You may not be familiar with it with regard to confidences. But there are some men who feel that verbal intimacy is not for wives; it is for mistresses. This breed is the masked man who divulges his secrets only to the stranger. You will never know what goes on inside him unless you read his excerpt from the Triangle Papers. This type of man does not see marriage as a confidential relationship. He's colonial, territorial, protective, and uncommunicative with his wife. The wife is not to blame for his verbal reluctance.

Then there are the wives whose husbands' judgments of them are accurate. Some married men know exactly what they are doing when they go outside their marriage for a friend. They know what their marriage is and what it is not. Many marriages out there are family arrangements, with financial clauses and sexual clauses but not confidential agreements. If you listen to the mistresses, that description is quite common.

"My married man says his wife is the enemy. He told me there are things he'd never tell her. Can you imagine? To me that says he has a horrid relationship. How can you go through life guarding against the enemy, or worse, conspiring with the enemy?" *(Aurora, Colorado)*

That example may be extreme, but many men feel a barrier in their marriage. Their suspicions may be of their own making or real. Either way that barrier will lead them into a triangle and a confidential relationship with an extramarital friend.

"My wife doesn't understand me." That statement is in the

Triangle Papers a thousand times. It is a cliché. Of course many married men throw it up for sympathy. But how many really mean it? How did it get to be a cliché? The point is that married men are not stereotypical bums fast-talking their way into the bedroom. Thousands of them believe that statement. They have a long list of confidences, rationales, and judgments that come after it. How you react to that statement, "My wife doesn't understand me," can tell you if you are confidante material or not. Mistresses rarely dismiss it immediately, even if it is a cliché. Clichés attain that status for a reason—that is something we tend to forget.

The married man is really a controversial subject. Nothing is as controversial as his confidences and these Triangle Papers. Men need to communicate and they do. They are spies looking for a warm retreat. They are double agents whose loyalties are an impenetrable maze. Married men often live by odd codes which mistresses and wives both try to decipher. Affairs tend to bring out the depths in most married men. Mistresses seemingly have an added talent for truth-getting although it is a talent that is not in their own best interests.

Declassifying the Triangle Papers is instructive. I would like to declassify more, but married men are careful and selective about their confidences. They carry their secrets and their mysteries, looking over their shoulders furtively seeking the right shoulder to lean on. The insides of the married man can't always be seen from the outside. Sometimes it takes an outsider like the mistress to get an inside view. Men are a mystery; married men aren't as simple as you might think. That is if you understand the Triangle Papers.

CHAPTER 11

The Moment of Truth: Marriage and the Bedroom

There is one bedtime story that has been handed down for years. It is a bedtime story told whenever the subject of triangles comes up. Perhaps you've heard it; perhaps you haven't. Either way this bedtime story has permeated our culture. It is written into the family fabric of Americana even though it is obsolete.

This bedtime story is about marriage and the bedroom. It has Victorian roots. It's the story of how wives don't like sex. According to the plot, frigidity grows soon after the first few marital years. Wives' sexual desires atrophy or are channeled into the sensual aspects of having and nurturing children. As the metamorphosis transforms lovers into mothers, husbands are left out in the cold starving sexually. Husbands have no choice but to stray. It's the natural order for men to want sex and for good women not to like sex. Married men have to resort to extramarital territory to fulfill their sexual drives.

This bedtime story is clearly a lesson in causation. Husbands stray because wives leave them no alternatives. The culprit in this tale is the frigid, neglectful wife. This version of the classic bedtime story may be too allegorical for you, but its theme is prevalent nevertheless. How many times have you heard a husband's affair chalked up to a wife's sexual inadequacy?

That bedtime story may have been true generations ago, but women today have outgrown Victorian strictures. The outdated story does a disservice to all types of women—the "good" ones who hate sex and the "bad" ones who hate marriage, men, or both.

One can't begin to discuss married men who take mistresses without paying homage to the classic bedtime myth. Is the sex life between the husband and wife the sole determinant in his taking a mistress? Just how responsible is the conjugal record for the affair with a mistress? Is sex the key to understanding the married man who gets in the middle? Is there a correlation between the married man's age and his sexual prowess or his insecurity? Is age therefore a significant influence for the married man who strays?

I asked mistresses some questions about their married man's conjugal life. One question in particular zeros in on a wife's possible culpability: "Did he complain that his sex life with his wife was unsatisfactory for him?" That gave rise to mistresses commenting on marriage and the bedroom. Do any conventional studies agree with what the mistress' consensus decided? What do these conclusions say about the impact of marital sex on the triangle, on wives' inadequacies, and on husbands' drives?

Again I want to make the point that we are not talking here about a married man's one-night stands. We are talking about a relationship with another woman, his mistress. Just how many men is that? How many married men live inside a triangle?

In triangular questions statistics are always a problem. It's not exactly a status married men readily admit. Fifty percent of all married men have an affair at some point in their marriage. Actually, that now goes for married women too. However, the 50% applies to short-term affairs. The only statistic I've seen about "the middle man"—or the married man in between a wife and a mistress—is found in Lewis Yablonsky's book *The Extra-Sex Factor*. According to his study of 800 men, 16% of married men carried on their relationship with another woman for more than a year.

All I know is that I've received thousands and thousands of responses from mistresses over the last three years. For each of those mistresses there was a middle man. How many does that suggest, or how many more are loving in silence? I wouldn't even venture a statistical guess.

What is the sexual context of the marriages in which these triangles exist? What are the married men saying about the sex lives they have with their wives at home? Married men have complaints, to be sure. However, my research didn't find that sexual complaints were the prime cause for the affair with the mistress. Let's see why.

First let's air some of those complaints, as reported by the mistresses based on attitudes from their married men.

"She [his wife] would hardly ever engage in sex and when she did, according to him, it was only because she felt it was her duty and, he said, she would just lie there and when he was 'done' she would leave their bed and finish the night alone on the couch." *(Tucson, Arizona)*

"His wife is a Mormon and sleeps with him only to reproduce, not for pleasure. I fill that aspect of his needs." *(Burlington, Illinois)*

"Sex, with his wife, is as quick as sex with my husband. He says that she [his wife] never moves or makes a sound. It's like making love to a pile of old clothes." *(North Andover, Maine)*

"He said their sex life was indeed unsatisfactory. His wife felt it was duty and their method of birth control was withdrawal. Need I add anything else?" *(Midwest)*

"For many years he said his sex life with his wife was scarce at best and I know that is true from her as well as from him. A few years back he had a prostate operation much to her joy and encouragement, for she thought that would end the whole sexual hassle. Between her and the doctor he was also convinced. After the operation he tried with her several times and they were failures. When we first got back together he told me he couldn't perform. That wasn't true, to our mutual delight. He blames her for the whole problem because she refused him for so many years and so often." *(Concord, New Hampshire)*

"His wife had broken her pelvis so she was unable to have sex for a while after their baby. Several months later he told me that he tried having sex with her, but it had been very mechanical. He was very sad. He said he thought it should have been a beautiful experience (the first time they'd had sex since before the baby and all) but it hadn't been. After that, or so he tells me, he went to her less and less. He told me they had relations every few months and then only out of a sense of duty. Yesterday he said that now he has not one iota of desire for her anymore sexually. Zero. He said it's never been zero before. The latest is that his wife made a doctor's appointment for him to discuss his sexual problem." *(Mt. Berry, Georgia)*

"For several months he was unable to perform sexually. It was almost like he'd forgotton how and he told me his wife made him lose all interest in sex. I was very patient with him and finally he came around. What a glorious triumph for both of us. He hasn't forgotten how or lost interest since then!" *(South Orange, New Jersey)*

"He says that he has not had sex with his wife since long before he met me. Not long ago he told me that his wife said she might turn into a virgin because they never have sex." *(Millville, New Jersey)*

"From the very few things he's said on the subject, his sex life with his wife was limited. He said he never had a chance to have sex too often. It ended some years ago, after the birth of their last child." *(Sioux City, Iowa)*

As you can see, there is a definite trend of complaints. Sexual dissatisfaction at home is prevalent among middle men, as I coin the married man who takes a mistress. However, there is another trend that is just the opposite. If complaints were solely the majority experience, we could suggest that conjugal behavior was the significant reason for the mistress. But what about all these noncomplaints!

"He didn't complain that his wife didn't satisfy him sexually. Maybe that he didn't get enough, but is that a complaint or an advertisement for her ability?" *(Wyoming)*

"He would never discuss his wife and sex with me, felt it was none of my business. After reading your book I know what that means and I wish I didn't." *(Marshall, Michigan)*

"He didn't complain, just said that one woman wasn't enough." *(Salt Lake City, Utah)* No surprise there!

"He's basically happy with his marriage/family/life the way things are. I haven't heard complaints about his sex life at home or about anything at home for that matter. As I've said before, he is uncertain about just exactly what he does/doesn't want in life." *(Sacramento, California)*

"No, he didn't complain that his sex life with his wife was unsatisfying. He never mentioned their sex life." *(Newcastle, New Brunswick, Canada)*

"He said that his sex life with his wife was the same from the beginning, and that he had really married her because she would make a good wife and mother, which actually isn't an uncommon phrase. Is that a complaint or not? I don't really know." *(Scottsdale, Arizona)*

Then, in all fairness to my research method, I must mention that the complaints and the noncomplaints are at times questionable. Some married men complain for sympathy while others are scrupulously honest. Some mistresses want to hear complaints or read things into remarks because it makes them feel more secure.

"He never complained; however the surprise and wonder he felt during our lovemaking showed that he *must* have felt unsatisfied at home." *(Reading, Pennsylvania)*

"He's been having affairs for years. I'm the first one he has fallen in love with and has lasted so long at. He's never complained about his sex life with his wife. But the fact that I'm not the first one indicates, to me anyway, that he's not terribly satisfied at home. He's told me that I'm the only woman that's stopped him cold in his tracks. As far as I'm concerned he's been faithful to me, that is if you don't count his wife." *(Sweet Springs, Missouri)*

It is interesting to note that women, too, in this case mistresses, believe the old bedtime story about a wife's inadequacy. Surely that must be the key to understanding a man's extramarital love affair. Mistresses have to continue to believe this so as to reduce their jealousies and ease their pains as they crawl into bed each and every night alone while they know whom their married man is crawling into bed with every one of those nights.

From my inferences about the married men and their sex lives at home, I conclude that sex is sometimes a source of dissatisfaction, but not the sole determinant in taking a mistress.

If a married man is looking for a sexual outlet, surely there is an easier way than conducting such a risky, complicated liaison. The sexual aspect of the affair is only a part of it. The mistress' appeal and the married man's attraction isn't as one-dimensional as sex. A less risky pattern of short-term affairs could end sexual deprivation. A lengthy relationship with another woman suggests more than sexual need. That explains why some married men have complaints and others don't. Men have a sexual drive but they have other needs as well. The following chapter will look at those other needs of the married man. I think it's difficult to isolate the sexual factor completely where men are concerned, especially married men and their mistresses.

It is overly simplistic to place the burden of guilt on the wife for the development of a triangle. What about the married men who want variety? It is overly simplistic to analyze the mistress phenomenon solely in terms of sex. What about the married men who hate their spouses but nonetheless adjust to their marriage? Human behavior is complicated. We forget this when it comes to the mistress and the married man. We still classify them in the same old caricatures: sex-deprived husband, nymphomaniac temptress, and in the background somewhere a frigid wife. These limited sketches don't adequately explain the diversity in human motivations.

Are my conclusions unique? I'd like to include a bit of research here from Lewis Yablonsky again. It covers 367 men and addresses why they chose extramarital sex. 48% of the men said they enjoyed relationships with other women and that sex was only a part of it. 23% said they wanted some romance in their lives. 31% said their sex lives at home were satisfactory but they need more. 23% said their sex lives at home were inadequate.

To underline the findings, approximately half of the men in the study sought companionship, with sex as a part of it. While those percentages refer to extramarital sex and not specifically to the affair with a mistress, I feel their conclusions do apply. Before we leave Mr. Yablonsky's work, there is one more interesting fact.

Some 80% of the married men who strayed either in long-term or short-term affairs said that their sex lives at home were satisfactory. So if you doubt my claims that the conjugal scene doesn't determine a husband's outside sexual behavior, here is more proof from a conventional source. That should get wives off the hook, sexually speaking anyway, once and for all. A wife's sexual performance is not the sole criterion for a husband's affair. However, a wife's behavior in its totality, with sexual response included, is another matter. You will see the ramifications of that in the other sections on the married man. A married man's reasons for taking a mistress are far broader than merely a bedroom scenario.

Before we leave the married man as seen in the context of his marriage and his bedroom, there is one more related topic. Part of the bedtime stories about big bad wolf hungry husbands who go out looking for little red-lettered riding mistresses is the age hangup. This fairy tale says that some husbands may not even have frigid wives. Instead they have nagging fears of aging that drive them out into the forest to recapture their youth or prove their potency to younger girls. When the fear of aging hits a married man, his wife can't appease his ego, only a new young conquest can. People often assume that married men take mistresses as part of an aging crisis. Turning forty and middle-aged is the most common passage that comes to the majority of minds. If a married man is forty, it figures that he has a mistress. That is basically the logic.

I spent a good deal of time focusing on the age statistics for mistresses and married men as well. What I came up with, based on questionnaires and case histories, didn't support any of the theories that married men stray from their wives to feel young again. Why? Because the vast majority of men who have mistresses are not forty and just hitting "middle age." Nor are they taking up with ingenues.

The age breakdown looks like a bell-shaped curve. Approximately 12% of married men described to me by their mistresses were between twenty and twenty-nine. 40% and the largest grouping were between thirty and thirty-nine years old. Approximately 30% were between forty and forty-nine. Approximately 13% again were between fifty and fifty-nine. Married men sixty years and older accounted for 5%. Under twenty years old the number of married men was statistically insignificant.

Peak vulnerabilities were in the thirties and forties. Then again mistresses tended to be in the same age bracket. The older man rekindling his youth in the youthful sighs of a mistress didn't surface. Married men out on a quest to prove themselves sexually may well be, but it is not a quest that hits the male gender like menopause, at forty or middle age. Personally I don't agree with the conquest theories, regardless of how chic the social biologists are becoming. Human beings are animals, but emotionalism is part of our instinctual nature. Married men have needs, but I don't think sexual prowess and conquest urges are a function of chronological passages. I don't think that the mistress phenomenon is fixed by age or the pursuit of youth.

One last reason is that in my research I didn't hear many quotes about how a married man feels young again in the arms of his mistress. I've no bias on the age issue. I would gladly report it if it had been suggested by mistresses. Married men were looking for many things. Youth didn't seem to be a pervasive goal for the middle men. Romance, love, companionship, friendship were mentioned over and over. Fountains of youth, rejuvenation, images of aging and feeling young again just weren't part of my research experiences.

At any age romance can be an amphetamine. It can give every age-bracket of married man a new spring in his step. Affairs often have a euphoric effect on their participants. I'm certain that has quite a bit to do with married men and mistresses continuing their affairs. As far as an inducement to begin an affair, a married man can feel old and bored at thirty-one as well as at fifty. Feeling old and feeling alive, with regard to triangle players, has little to do with chronology.

The purpose of this chapter is to clarify the myths with regard to husbands and wives and sex. The object of reporting my research is to dispel the ice-cold reputation of the wife. It is also to dispel the sexually starved image of the husband as well as the type-casting of men who have mistresses as all "freaking out at forty." This in no way means that I feel there are no marriages with mechanical sex or no married men who are sexually insecure about aging. These types and motivations do exist and do lead to affairs. However, the converse is not necessarily true. Not all wives or husbands fit the mythical bedtime fictional legacy.

Every married man and every wife and every marriage has its moment of truth. But the moment is not the instant some sexual peak is reached or not reached. The moment of truth doesn't always occur in the bedroom. Affairs have something to do with sex. Married men certainly tell mistresses that the sex with them is great and it probably is. But the sex at home may be great too. Affairs have something to do with wives and urges, needs and marriages. Affairs are influenced by what goes on before and after the sexual act. That holds true whether we are talking about the husband and wife or the married man and the mistress. Allegorical prototypes are useless. Triangles are complicated treatises, not fables or fairy tales. Once upon a time husbands may have had to go elsewhere for their sensual fulfillment, but wives can't get all the blame for triangles now once and for all. Especially since night tables all over America contain copies of *The Joy of Sex*, *The Hite Report*, and, I hope, *The Making of the American Mistress*.

CHAPTER 12

Of Triangles and Trapezoids

The married man in the middle is imprisoned in a triangle like the other two players—the wife and the mistress. And yet his angle is quite different from theirs. His dilemma has some of the triangular complexities, the boundaries, the jealousies, and the anxieties. In addition his position as "middle man" takes on a new geometric dimension. The man in the middle is trapped in a trapezoid, too.

A trapezoid is a four-sided geometric figure with two sets of parallel sides. Many middle men live in a trapezoid with two parallel sets of needs pulling them in opposite directions.

A trapezoid isn't the most commonly known geometric figure. And that is exactly why I have chosen it to demonstrate the married man's dilemma. Most people think that the middle man has it made. He's got the best of both worlds. Although that may be true for moments at a time, his position is far from enviable. He also has the worst of both worlds. Middledom is not like some royal kingdom all the time; it is like serfdom too.

In this chapter we are going to dissect the trapezoid and look at the middle man from both parallels. What keeps him in his affair with the mistress? What keeps him in his marriage? What is he getting from each of the women in his two worlds? The married man's barter with his mistress is not what most people think. And he definitely pays a price for playing both ends against the middle. He winds up in a Gemini Bind. Then comes a bargain with the devil. Some needs have to be compromised or cultivated elsewhere. The middle man's needs are his joy and his pain. Trying to meet them is how most married men get into triangles and then into trapezoids.

The making of the American mistress is intrinsically related to the needs of the married man. How? Everyone likes to be needed. More than anything else, the married man makes his mistress feel needed. Most married men are articulate about their needs, as you have seen. They have a vast array of needs that mistresses are expert at filling. For being needed, mistresses labor within triangles. Actually they get little else than being needed and being able to ameliorate the neediness of the married man.

The barter between the married man and the mistress mythically was one of sex and money. However, hopefully you have outgrown those myths. Mistresses don't have to outgrow any myths on that score because they have lived the true barters. What in reality is the married man giving and getting in his affair? He's not giving money or time. Married men don't as a rule have much of either. It has long been assumed that married men were giving promises. My research shows that most middle men don't promise divorce. Yet I must add that unspoken promises or planting seeds of hope can't be documented in my research or anyone's.

The married man is giving intimacy, honesty within limits, and affection with clear-cut strings. He is opening up and laying his vulnerability out for the mistress to see. In return he is getting those needs he so clearly revealed met. He is getting a special type of love that only a mistress can give by virtue of her triangular position. Rather than list those needs, I shall call upon the mistresses to report different categories of needs. Then we'll define that special brand of mistress love.

"I watched you on the Phil Donahue Show. I found myself so frustrated by the narrow scope of understanding by many of the women in the audience. As you know, human relations are so complex—there are few people who know what love is. When I was in my early thirties (I'm married then and now) I fell in love with a psychologist. He had always been a stoic, aloof, hungry man, never allowing closeness with anyone or maybe just never getting it. I'm not sure exactly which it was. I'm sure only of his desperate need for closeness. To see this forty-year-old man discover the gift of intimacy (as you said, it has very little to do with just sex), come down out of his lonely tower and experience tenderness and closeness, was a marvel to watch.

"He actually said to me once, 'You gave me a gift that

changed my outlook and all my relationships, my work, and my friends. I'm an entirely different man, I see things in a different light. Thank you for making me human. How did you know and how did you ever get to me? I was buried in cast iron.' I knew cause I could hear screams of loneliness." *(Leavenworth, Kansas)*

"He [my married man] is basically a lonely man and I am a lonely woman. He doesn't get much love or acceptance at home. I give him what he needs." *(Pueblo, Colorado)*

"The sexual aspect of our relationship was important to him I'm sure because he found it difficult to warm up to his wife. His wife is a gorgeous woman and I used to find his remarks hard to believe. I've grown up a lot and I now realize beauty is nothing compared to feelings of comfort and understanding. Closeness and warmth were missing in his life. I was there with them." *(Villanova, Pennsylvania)*

"Our secret life together brings out his great need to be wanted and loved. There is a great desire on his part to be accepted for what he is and approved of. He says his wife hasn't been too thrilled with him lately in most respects, sex being one of them, and he feels whole when we are together." *(Pompano, Florida)*

Married men need love and affection. That seems rather odd, given their marital status. However, taking a more realistic look at marriage, it becomes clearer. One can be lonely in a crowd and one can be lonely in a marriage. Marriages aren't all love affairs and best friendships. Some marriages are allegiances between strangers. And marriages, too, have their cycles. There are some marital stages when needs just aren't fulfilled within the union. Wherever there is a marriage of strangers and incomplete needs and poor communication, there is likely to be a middle man and a mistress.

Some marriages have love but they don't have enough romance for the husband. Affairs never have a shortage of romance. It is an easy need for a mistress to fulfill. Wives have to work at romance. Romance often comes along automatically with the triangle territory. Therefore mistresses tend to be good at recognizing that need.

"He always told me I was his own Lara. My mirror told me I didn't look like Julie Christie, but maybe I was like Lara—snowblind and blindly in love. I guess he needed that romantic role of Dr. Zhivago. His life was a mess." *(Peekskill, New York)*

"The only thing I'd like to say about our sex life is that he described it as an oasis from the real world. I think this is why he fools around—to escape the weight of his responsibilities. I'm his fantasy." *(Linden, New Jersey)*

"My married man often told me that he had not felt a passion like this for a long time. He sounds like an old man but he's only thirty-four. It's just his marriage that is old." *(Kansas City, Kansas)*

"His wife and I are the same age, but we are generations apart sexually, emotionally, in every way. Loving a new person is like having a new life. I am a different world of freshness and romance. We have a new kind of love." *(Galesburg, Illinois)*

Some married men are looking for something out of the ordinary, while others are looking for the basics. Some married men have marriages that are good, if not continually exciting. Others have marriages and mates that have stripped them of their ordinary feelings of self-worth. Ego-building is one of the most common functions of the mistress.

"I was a good ego-builder for him. I loved him more than life itself. I put him on a pedestal and he needed that for a while. I knew that in reality he was only a mere man who made as many mistakes as anyone. I don't think he realized that because I was always telling him how perfect he was. It was hard in the end for him to live up to the ideas that I had of him. But I wanted him to see that he was important because he is a person, even though she [his wife] never treats him as such." *(Cinti, Ohio)*

"When I met him he wanted to kill himself. He used to be a fireperson. Now he lives on a disability pension and works part time. I was in love I guess with the idea of loving an ex-fireman. In two years I brought him up from the pits of life and made him spiritually a King. Yes, he wanted to kill himself when I met him; now I do. No, but I am disappointed so awful much." *(Saylorsburg, Pennsylvania)*

"I make him feel admired and respected. I don't know of anything I would change about him except his marital status. I accept his faults, hangups, good habits, as being a part of him along with all the wonderful things about him. I make him feel good about being himself." *(Topeka, Kansas)*

Married men don't always need a complete overhaul of their self-image. Some men want to be able to pursue an interest or express some creativity and be understood and appreciated.

"Gifts, more than anything I cherish his doodlings. He could have been a really talented artist. He never had the money to go to art school or anything. He drives a bus, that's how we met. I love the artist in him. Those silly drawings or cartoons he brings me are more valuable to me than anything. I'm trying to get him to draw me a real picture for my apartment." *(Bellrose, New York)*

"My married man and I are both musical. We've had a group for eight years; I play piano and he sings and plays guitar. I do all the arrangements for the group. We perform at granges, churches, and home weeks. We just get along great. We never compete or conflict, like him and his wife. He has written 50–60 gospel songs. Some of them are very good. His wife thinks it's foolish. I'm very proud of him and he is very proud of me." *(small town, Tennessee)*

The salient point about the married man's needs and his mistress is that he states those needs and she caters to them. That is the barter in the affair.

Each affair may have a unique barter of needs, tailored to the special needs of each married man. Each married man is looking for a particular something; each one has a particular point of view that is driving him outside his marriage and into the arms of a virtual stranger. That virtual stranger becomes his mistress. Suddenly and unexpectedly she begins hearing the confessions of her married man. Those confessions reveal how he struggles through his own jungle of demands to see his mistress. They reveal exactly what he needs, be it understanding, affection, or adulation. The mistress fulfills a set of needs that her married man does not disguise or hide.

For a mistress, knowing exactly what his special needs are can be very enlightening. So if you want to know just what you are giving that is keeping him in your affair, turn to the end of this chapter and take the test, *The Confessions of Your Married Man*. It will zero in on his needs and your handling of them.

Then there is the mistress' love. That keeps many a married man in the middle. A mistress' love, you see, is different from a wife's love because of the mistress' angle in the triangle. A mistress has absolutely nothing to gain by loving a married man except his love and a few hours. A wife, on the other hand, does have things to gain—a home, a family, an income, respectability, a future, and the list goes on. This is not to say that a wife's love is all selfish and mercenary. However, when a married man looks at his loving devoted mistress he can't help but see a woman who wants nothing more than him; his love, his personality, his conversation. He is the total love object, the center of attention and the prize. Mistresses tend to live on standby, waiting for their married man. The very structure of the triangle makes this setup standard. She patiently and faithfully waits for the opportunity to express her love and shower the married man with his needs. The mistress' love responds to her married man's needs. She is dedicated to these. It is ego-swelling for any married man to be wanted solely for himself. That is the mistress' special brand of love. In return she merely asks to be needed and that the married man does. Actually that feeling of being needed is all some married men can offer.

When the mistress begins to confront her own needs, she gets to thinking she may want more than an affair with such restrictions. That is when many mistresses look at why their married man stays married. If he loves her, and most married men do love their mistresses, then why doesn't he rearrange his life to accommodate that love? That leads us back to the trapezoid.

Although the mistress is naturally equipped with powerful magnets of affection and image and romance, the wife too has magnets of her own.

Many wives hold in their persona a sense of security and continuity intertwined with their family role. The married man is usually a family man, and his sense of belonging lies with his wife and family. Regardless of the quality of the marital relationship, his sense of where he fits revolves around his membership in a family. Therein lies his respectability, his citizenship, and his lifestyle. His wife and family represent a large part of his social identity. And the more important the extended family and his in-laws are in all this, the stronger the magnet is.

Human beings are naturally driven to reproduce and protect their offspring. Those drives are part of emotional identity. The married man has created his family and devoted himself to protecting it and rearing the children. The package includes his wife. It's almost unnatural in a sense to "abandon" the family as divorce demands to various degrees. The decision to divorce may have a severe impact on a married man's image as a protector, provider, and father. To divorce may mean lowering of his self-esteem. Some married men cannot face forfeiting their lifestyle. Some cannot handle disrupting their sense of continuity and the past. Then of course there is finances, a problem for nearly everyone.

For many married men divorce means shattering the very foundation of life. The wife personifies a structure, both fiscal and filial, that is the substance of that foundation. Choosing the mistress means beginning all over again, and what's worse destroying all that was built during the marriage. Property, business, investments, complicate divorcing. Yet so do human commodities and emotional investments.

A married man's emotional makeup is central. His psychological disposition may keep him married or make it easier to divorce and break away from his wife's magnetic field. Some personality characteristics that are crucial are his inertia threshold, loyalty, guilt quota, and his interest in what others think. A wife's magnetic field becomes more powerful when he values her opinion of him and her family's, or if he's loyal and guilt-inclined. If his professional standing requires a family label, his wife's get more points in her favor. The magnets possessed by the wife often have little to do with her as a person, but more to do with her as a central part of the married man's life philosophy, his progeny, and his projections.

Some married men wear wedding bands for all to see. Others don't wear wedding bands on their fingers. However, an invisible wedding band is there around their mind, their heart, and their whole being. Even if a married man is not committed to fidelity, his commitment is to his wife and family and all that goes along with it. It is these magnetic pulls by the wife, by virtue of her role, that keep many married men in the middle.

If you are a mistress and want to know exactly what is keeping your married man in his marriage, turn to the test at the end of this chapter: *What Keeps Your Man Married?* The test analyzes all the wifely magnets based on your man. If you are a wife trapped in a triangle and wondering why your husband is vacillating, you should take the test too.

Many mistresses, I found in my research, have pretty good ideas about why their man is staying married. From the questionnaire, here are some of their hunches.

I asked, "Why do you think your married man hasn't divorced?"

"Obligation. He has a German background and is rigid. He believes in the family institution. I really believe he is the kind that gets set in his ways and is afraid of change. Also financially he would be hurting, but aren't we all?" (*Cheviot, Ohio*)

"Religion, family criticism, objections. Strict Catholic upbringing—his and his wife's. No divorce on either side of the family. He is very attuned to 'what people think'; business and political friends. In fact now that I answered the question I'm surprised he has a mistress in the first place! Obviously he's not the type, at least from the outside." (*Roslyn, Pennsylvania*)

"I never thought my married man would get a divorce, because he is too hung up on duty." (*Baltimore, Maryland*)

"My answer to this is rather long. He and his wife were married when she was only nineteen. He was her college teacher then as he is mine now. The reason he divorced his first wife was because the wife didn't want children. He still pays that one alimony. After his divorce he eloped with this young girl and they had three beautiful children. But now she has a career and neglects the family and him. He is the full-time babysitter, housekeeper, etc. He needs a mistress but would never leave his children. They were the reason for the first divorce and they are the reason that divorce is out of the question ever." (*Wendover, Utah*)

"He says it's because of their baby. It's his second marriage and his second shot at fatherhood. You should hear him talk about the little darling. How could I blame him for this feeling? How could I ask him to divorce knowing what it would mean for him and his baby?" *(Corpus Christi, Texas)*

"My married man is basically a passive person. He used to fantasize that his wife would throw him out or that he could somehow have a separate half of the house, but he would never act. He was that way in everything. He wanted for life to act upon him. Is that clear? He feared change; he feared financial loss. Perhaps if in the beginning I'd made it a condition, he would have divorced, but it's not in his character really." *(Thomson, Georgia)*

"He [my married man] says that his wife is a habit, but she takes good care of him, otherwise, and makes good money. That is making his dream for the future come true. In six years he will take early retirement and they will live on the ocean-going fishing boat that they are building, which takes all his spare time. I tell him he can get all except her financial contribution from an aunt or a sister, or hired help for that matter. He feels he and she have too much stake in their years together. Besides, he says, what would she do alone as he is her whole life which I know is true. Even though I love him deeply, I wouldn't hurt my husband or family so 'we' will never really be unless we both outlive both of them, which is unlikely." *(Cape Cod, Massachusetts)*

"Fear of change; weakness; guilt; not wanting to hurt his wife and children; not wanting to hurt his parents; not wanting publicly to shatter his self-image of a paragon of moral virtue and respectability; religious scruples from a Jesuit upbringing; mistrust of his own emotions—fear that it may be a midlife crisis or lust; indolence; inertia; financial worry; fear of community and colleague reactions; fear that it would break his mind to take such a drastic step and a morally questionable one; also he's so busy he doesn't have sufficient time." *(Ithaca, New York)*

"After my married man left home and moved in with me I thought things would be okay. When his wife found out it was me and that we were serious about all this she turned the children against him. I saw him turn away from me. He said the problem has always been he loved those children so much and that I had to give him time . . . Well I sent him home after I could not stand to see him so sad all the time and nervous." *(Tampa, Florida)*

"I think he's very secure in his marriage. He loves his daughter very much. His wife also received a $61,000 trust fund after they were married a year—that helps." *(Oklahoma City, Oklahoma)*

"My married man seemed to complain endlessly about his wife those first few years. After a while I realized something. His wife had her faults, sure. But the marriage didn't make him miserable. He wasn't deliriously happy, but he wasn't uncomfortable either." *(Baldwin, New York)*

I'm sure that mistresses did quite a bit of soul-searching before coming up with the answers to what keeps a man married. They searched their souls and married men's too. Mistresses too often look to the middle man for the answers. They look to him to decide when the "right time" to divorce is. They look to him for Someday. They wait and hope he will come up with some answers soon. That is one of the mistress' biggest mistakes. The married man, you see, doesn't have the answers. If he did he wouldn't be imprisoned not only in a triangle but a trapezoid, too. Trying to find the answers for himself and his own life is difficult given the two sets of parallel needs that are pulling him in opposite directions.

Middledom is not really some grand kingdom where a man is lavished with attention by the wife and the mistress at his beck and call. In time he is graced only with scenes, demands, arguments, and hysterics from two unhappy women. Affairs don't go on for years in isolated bliss. Mistresses tend to want more. Wives tend to get suspicious. Mistresses exert pressure. As one mistress put it, "It's like calling up for information from a company and being put on hold indefinitely." *(Phoenix, Arizona)* Mistresses can't stay on hold forever. Wives can't either, knowing that their husband is in the arms of another woman.

Most middle men wind up unhappy in their bondage to two women. They wind up in what I call the Gemini Bind. This is fairly simple. Married men in the middle will recognize the position. The Gemini Bind means when the middle man is with his mistress all he does is think about his children, his wife, their life together. Then when he is with his family all he can think about is his mistress. What is she doing? Is she out with another man? The middle man can not be two places at once. Whichever place he is in is the wrong one. He would like to be two separate people. Then and only then could he live both lives, satisfy both women, and meet both sets of needs. Married man can't become separate entities. They, therefore become victims of the Gemini Bind. They want two lives, two women, simultaneously.

"I couldn't bear seeing him like this anymore. He was so torn up I could almost see the seams bursting. I know the end is near for us or for them. If he leaves, I wish him love. I wish him God. I wish him health. He's so complicated at this point I don't know where he's at. I don't think he knows either. He's tame and wild. He's a walking contradiction." *(a mistress from San Jose, New Mexico)*

The Gemini Bind is indeed a turning point, but it is far from an instant phase. It marks the point when the married man knows that he can't have it both ways. He knows if he chooses his mistress, he'll lose. If he chooses his family, he'll lose. He's lost much already. The romance is gone from the affair and the serenity is gone from his marriage. Amid all the demands upon him to make a decision, he's immobilized in indecision. Some middle men live within the Gemini Bind for years. I called it the Eternal Crisis for mistresses. It's a period during which he bounces back and forth from the wife's home to the mistress' haven. He can't make a decision that he can live with. The bouncing phase of the Gemini Bind will go on sometimes for years, for as long as the wife and mistress will take it.

"I'm the married man who supposedly has the best of both worlds. I saw you on TV today and possibly you could give me some pointers on what to do. Your morning show seemed to deal with people in their twenties and thirties. I am sixty-five, my girl is fifty-nine, and my wife is sixty. We are all in the same boat as you described. It seems that there may be some hesitancy to act here because of our advanced ages. Anyway people in any age bracket need help too.

"I'm not happy with having both worlds. I have been coasting along as it is, but it is killing my girl and it's not good for my wife either. As for me, I don't know what's good for me. I've no time to think lately about me. The obvious answer may be divorce or termination but are they the only solutions? I am wondering about the effect of a compromise. Instead of a divorce with its hassles, how about a separation? I realize that many women and wives would not be happy with this arrangement, but in reality aren't you really doing better in this case? You are not sacrificing all your possessions and giving up your wife due to divorce, but you are still giving your girl (assuming you move in) your undivided time and concern. I'll try that I guess. It sounds like I'm seeking help and I guess I am. I guess, though, there is no answer that you can give me that is going to be easy. I can't do the right thing for them both. No fool like an old fool." *(suburb, Minnesota)*

The Gemini Bind is indiscriminate. Sooner or later it gets most married men if they feel love and have a conscience. Living the Gemini Bind can't last forever and sooner or later some path is chosen. The odds are usually stacked in favor of marriage. It is a cold fact that mistresses are more easily expendable. Many marriages get a shot in the arm by the triangle experience. Many mistresses go on a casualty list of forgotten wounded that no one cares about. The married man has to choose one set of needs over the other. He has to destroy his trapezoid before he can ever effectively break out of his triangle. It is really rarely easy; it is always inevitable. One married man provided a poignant afterthought.

"I was deeply in love with my mistress. I even separated for a few months. Then my wife inherited two million dollars. Within my grasp was a home on the shore on the island, complete financial security. I sold out. I promised to give up my mistress and make a go at the marriage again. I have always been a safety-first person. I fasten my seat belt to put my car in the garage. I have always done predictably socially acceptable things. With an alcoholic wife, even my affair fits that. I discovered there was such a thing as love. I tried to take a risk for it, but a leopard doesn't change its spots. Have mercy on the lover that doesn't get his divorce. He knows he is a coward. He knows he has compromised his soul and sold out his heart." *(Maine)*

Most married men pay a high price to get out of the triangle, whichever way they go. It is the needs of the middle man that get him into the grips of the triangle and needs that eventually get him to break out. Double living has a personal cost. Ask any married man. Double dealing in the end compromises the middle man more than anyone else. The Gemini Bind has a distinct flavor of Dante.

"No matter what I do I'll be unhappy. If I stay married I will forfeit my love of a lifetime, my mistress. If I get divorced, I will lose the closeness of my children, my family's approval, and heaven knows what financially. Anyway I go I'll never be truly happy again." *(Pueblo, Colorado)*

That line of reasoning keeps many married men in the middle for an eternity. It embodies fallacy as well as truth. That is why no matter how much suffering I have seen mistresses go through, I have some compassion left for the married man. Being a mistress as well as loving a married man has taught me about trapezoids as well as triangles. But, married men, take heart because in the long run nothing is worse than the Gemini Bind, the inherent torture of the trapezoid.

As a footnote to this section, I've included one test to help the married man who is in the middle this instant. They are usually seen as the culprits, and so little help is offered to them. Certainly they have their share of responsibility and blame to shoulder, but they have their crosses to bear too. They could use a book on how to get out of the triangle and the Gemini Bind. Their angle in the triangle is complex. It is triangles and trapezoids. The test, "The Right to Spite," is a beginning effort to help the married man. It is coming up in a few pages.

The Confessions of Your Married Man

What's keeping your married man in your affair? You are nourishing him with something he needs, but what? This test is designed so you can make sense out of his confessions and understand the needs those confessions convey.

Directions: This is a multiple-choice test. After each of the following statements or questions you must choose one answer.

THE MARRIED MAN/THE MAN IN THE MIDDLE

List your answer in the space provided. Then proceed to the scoring and evaluation. Remember—only one answer. Some may be hard

1. What is the most common, repeated experience in your sexual encounters? (a) in your relationship you discover each other's special preferences (b) your lovemaking is a spontaneous outburst that erupts anywhere the opportunity arises, be it an automobile, an office, wherever (c) you marvel at his performance and express that no one has ever made you feel as he does   1. _____
2. Do the majority of your dates tend to be (a) in ordinary places—the important thing is your communication (b) in surroundings where he can show you off (c) romantic escapades in clandestine and exotic places—isolated beaches, hidden-away hotels   2. _____
3. Since you began seeing your married man, has his appearance (a) changed drastically—weight loss, new clothes, new interest in his physique, etc. (b) not changed at all (c) changed a little   3. _____
4. Does your married man complain that his wife (a) has let herself go as a mate, putting all her energy into the kids (b) has no interest in his dreams and conflicts (c) downgrades him and is never satisfied   4. _____
5. What does your married man seem to enjoy most? (a) your listening to his theories, his feelings (b) your pampering him by cooking favorite meals and giving little gifts (c) your flattering him sincerely   5. _____
6. The time that you and your married man spend talking is (a) not much, minimal (b) devoted to his problems and desires (c) designed to

make him feel better about things   6. ____
7. His attitude toward your problems can best be described in which of the following statements?
(a) he says he can solve all your problems in time (b) he advocates kissing all the problems away (c) he probes your problems with you in search of solution   7. ____
8. What quality would you say your married man admires most in you?
(a) glamour, your special something (b) warmth (c) sympathetic nature   8. ____
9. When he alludes to his sex life at home or complains outright about it, are his allusions or complaints that
(a) he never mentions their sex life to you (b) his wife has her likes and dislikes and that's it (c) sex has become routine, quick, and almost mechanical   9. ____
10. Would you say that your married man's lifestyle
(a) doesn't express his real character (b) bores him (c) degrades him ever so subtly   10. ____
11. If your married man lost you, what do you think he would miss the most?
(a) your counsel (b) your approval (c) your excitement   11. ____
12. A woman should
(a) be the spice in a man's life (b) stand by her man (c) know her man   12. ____
13. The dream vacation that you and he would most like is best described how?
(a) anyplace so long as you and he could be alone and intimate (b) an isle of sunsets, moonlight, and lagoons or a lodge of firelight, furs, and frozen daiquiris (c) a week to paint the town, hit the night spots, dress up, and dine in style   13. ____
14. You and your married man are first and foremost

(a) lovers (b) confidantes (c) mutual
admirers   14. _____
15. Does your married man have a starved
(a) body (b) soul (c) ego   15. _____

Scoring:
Each answer that you have chosen is equal to a certain number of points. The following table lists the point value for each answer. Fill in all answers from 1 to 15 in the space provided under the column labeled Answers. Then look up the point value and list it in the space provided under the column labeled Points. At the end total up the points column and then read on for the evaluation.

								Answer	Points
1.	(a)	1	(b)	5	(c)	10		1. ___	___
2.	(a)	1	(b)	10	(c)	5		2. ___	___
3.	(a)	10	(b)	1	(c)	5		3. ___	___
4.	(a)	5	(b)	1	(c)	10		4. ___	___
5.	(a)	1	(b)	5	(c)	10		5. ___	___
6.	(a)	5	(b)	1	(c)	10		6. ___	___
7.	(a)	10	(b)	5	(c)	1		7. ___	___
8.	(a)	5	(b)	10	(c)	1		8. ___	___
9.	(a)	10	(b)	1	(c)	5		9. ___	___
10.	(a)	1	(b)	5	(c)	10		10. ___	___
11.	(a)	1	(b)	10	(c)	5		11. ___	___
12.	(a)	5	(b)	10	(c)	1		12. ___	___
13.	(a)	1	(b)	5	(c)	10		13. ___	___
14.	(a)	5	(b)	1	(c)	10		14. ___	___
15.	(a)	5	(b)	1	(c)	10		15. ___	___

Total_____

Evaluation:
15–60 Points. The confessions of your married man are painting an emotional need for understanding. If he's always saying "My wife doesn't understand me," you can believe him. He has chosen you because you are fulfilling his deep need to be known and understood. He loves your ability to empathize with him, your willingness to explore his dreams and problems, your listening, your counseling, etc. His marital relationship is probably set and shallow where this man needs to be deep. He is longing to be discovered sexually as well as intellectually.

His soul is starved. He is looking neither for glamour nor for inspiration, just sincere affection and understanding. He doesn't need weekends in Las Vegas or rendezvous in the Caribbean; all he needs is you, your ear, your shoulder, and your heart.

65–105 Points. The confessions of your married man are saying that he has a need for fun, excitement, and passion. His lifestyle has frankly become boring for him. Perhaps his wife has directed all her energies to the children. Certainly he is not the recipient of much attention at home, not the kind of attention you are providing anyway. He likes being pampered with favorite meals, little gifts. You have an aura of glamour for him. He loves spontaneous passionate sex more than long, hand-holding talks. Problems have no appeal for him; he wants to kiss them all away. (Probably he's good at it when he's around.) He'd be lost without your spice, your excitement, your passion. He wants you and moonlights and music and lagoons and all that romantic stuff. He's a man who really needs a woman in an earthy, physical way.

110–150 Points. The confessions of your married man are saying that he has a need for ego-boosting. Psychologically his self-image is in need of adulation and adoration to get it up to where it should be. His marriage is not a happy one most likely. He is subject to degrading remarks and downgrading behavior. He may not have a sexual problem at home and then again he may be even too embarassed to mention it, thinking that, like everything else, is his fault. Since you came into his life he probably looks like a new man because he feels like one. He thrives on your flattery and your knack for making him feel better about things, especially himself. He would like to show off both you and his newfound self. Your warmth has been an inspiration for him. He probably hasn't been this happy in years. His ego has been starving till you. You make him feel like he can handle all the problems in the world. Maybe he can!

In Conclusion:
Confessing seems to come naturally to the married man. Chances are you've felt like some Roman Catholic priestess locked in a dark curtained confessional. Married men are open about expressing their needs. They come to a mistress immediately intimate so to speak. This test narrowed down exactly what his confessions mean. It showed you how you are

fulfilling those needs of his. The confessions of the married man are sincere, vulnerable, real, and captivating. So captivating sometimes a mistress can forget she has needs too!

What Keeps Your Man Married?

What keeps your man married? If you are hooked on your married man, you have probably spent an eternity pondering that question. Now that you've read what some mistresses say about their married men's future, what is your married man saying about his future and yours?

This test is designed to structure your probings and supply you with concrete answers. Knowledge of what makes your married man tick is the key to your understanding what keeps him married. At the end you will know what magnet his wife has that keeps your man immobile.

Directions:
Following each of the statements below, answer either True or False. Answer to the best of your knowledge.

1. I have heard my man speak often of the scars of the "broken home." 1. _____
2. My man is obsessed with his wife—love or hate are all part of the same coin. 2. _____
3. My man has strong feelings on what a father should be and intends to fulfill that image no matter what. 3. _____
4. What other people think of him is of prime importance to my man. 4. _____
5. His life is really a network of his family: cousins, in-laws, siblings, etc. 5. _____
6. Coming up with the money for a divorce is a real problem. 6. _____
7. His income could hardly handle child support much less finance a new life for us. 7. _____
8. My man has told me he's spent a lifetime building his present lifestyle, step by step. 8. _____

9. For him marriage and his business are intertwined. 9. ____
10. His profession demands the identity of an intact family. 10. ____
11. My man is an extremely loyal individual. 11. ____
12. His personality is basically one that is resistant to change of any kind. 12. ____
13. My man has guilt running through every vein in his body; he's fatally infected with it. 13. ____
14. Romance seems to be a concept that is separate from marriage entirely, in his view of it. 14. ____
15. His ethnic legacy is ill-disposed toward the concept of divorce and destroying the family. 15. ____

Evaluation:

There will be no points assigned to any of your answers. True answers provide the clues you are looking for as to what keeps your man married. False answers indicate that these issues are not particularly relevant to your man's future where divorce is concerned. The more True answers you have chosen, the sturdier that invisible wedding band is. Your man may be locked in his marriage by either his family bonds, his pragmatic realities, or his emotional makeup. Go back and concentrate on where those True answers are.

Family Ties. Questions 1–5 probed what your man thinks about family life and exactly how family life influences his schedule. Does he harbor the "broken home" syndrome? By that I mean does he still think divorce scars children permanently and that bad marriages don't? That can be crucial, especially if in addition he has a strong image of fatherhood. For some men being a good father is very important to a healthy self-image. If your man lives in a world populated by relatives, watch out. This means not only must he divorce himself from his wife and proximity to the children but he has to divorce himself from all his relative/friends too. Family-network living makes divorce even more difficult. Their opinions of his actions may be meshed with his opinions of himself. Their codes regarding divorce may govern his behavior. Some men are family members first and individuals second. A man whose filial

THE MARRIED MAN/THE MAN IN THE MIDDLE 217

identity, ties and dependencies are primary isn't a man who can easily adjust to divorce. Family ties with his children, his wife, and his extended family are definitely keeping him married.

Business and Finance. Questions 6–10 focused on your man's pragmatic realities. Finance can be an obstacle in any income bracket. Poor men can't afford a divorce. Middle-class men may be reluctant to risk everything that they have spent a lifetime acquiring. Wealthy men may find that their lifestyle is impossible to leave. Finance is relative. Your man may stay married because he has no other option financially or sees no other options for himself that are satisfactory. If you can contribute financially you may be able to release him from this angle that keeps him married, and in a triangle.

Business, on the other hand, is more complex. Some occupations—politicians, for example—need a family identity as part of their professional itinerary. Of course divorce has lost most of its stigma nowadays, but for some professions it is still a handicap. A handicap that may be keeping your man married. Another complicating factor may be that your man's business is all wrapped up with his wife. He might be employed in her family's enterprise or they may co-own a business. Or his wife may be the invisible partner, brains, or tradition that is a requisite for his continued success. If that is the case, his career may demand marriage to his wife for survival.

Emotional Makeup. Questions 11–15 explored some of the personality traits of your man. There are certain characteristics that keep a man married while others make it easy for him to change his life. Loyalty, inertia, ethnic legacies, and guilt can keep a man married no matter how bad the wife or the marriage. His personal emotions make him more inclined to stay than to desert a sinking ship even if he's drowning in the process. Some of us are overly endowed with loyalty, guilts, and fear of change. Unless you can change your man's emotional makeup, he will be destined to be victimized by his own characteristics.

Romance deserves a separate paragraph. Some men don't expect romance within the structure of marriage. They don't expect mistresses to become wives, or wives to cater the way mistresses do. And they don't expect to leave a marriage for romance because the romance will die as soon as the wedding vows are spoken. If your man doesn't see the possibilities of a marriage with romance in it, he will not divorce. Emotional dispositions and emotional definitions can be salient in destining some married men to stay married.

In Conclusion:
Your man may be in the middle, but he may be wearing one of those invisible, invincible wedding bands. Its layers may be from family ties, his financial portfolio, or his emotions—or all three.

Some of the forces that keep a man married you will never be able to change. Others you can work through if he is willing. How loud he sings the wedding-bell blues is meaningless. It's why he sings those blues and does nothing that counts. Knowing what keeps your man married is important to both of you. It may keep you from finding happiness as individuals or together. Learn to see more than the wedding band on his finger, or worse, that illusion of no wedding band at all.

The Right to Spite

I have been suggesting to my husband, Michael, that he write a book called *The Married Man's Survival Manual.* Why? Because he suggested this test, which is an excellent idea. As I have been the confidante of mistresses, he has become that of married men and fathers. He was formerly my married man. Therefore he has had to grapple with all the conflicts and vulnerabilities of the triangle from the male perspective. His advice, as demonstrated by this test, could be extremely valuable to any man caught in the middle.

The right to spite was claimed by the Almighty in a biblical directive, "Vengeance is mine for I am the Lord." However, many creatures down here on earth cannot wait for the Almighty to exercise his/her right to revenge. While spite is not a feminine monopoly, ex-wives can excel in it if they have an innate capacity and can get astute legal advice. Therefore, for a married man's future it is important that he assess his wife's capacity for spite. Much must be weighed before a married man can resolve his triangle.

Directions: Read each of the following statements carefully. Choose one answer and circle it. The answers measure degree:

THE MARRIED MAN/THE MAN IN THE MIDDLE   219

"absolutely," "somewhat," and "not at all." Then proceed to the scoring and the evaluation.

1. My wife is a possessive mother; at times I feel excluded as a parent.

1. absolutely_____
   somewhat_____
   not at all_____

2. Our home and property is in her name.

2. absolutely_____
   somewhat_____
   not at all_____

3. Spite is a behavior I have already seen in my wife, directed at me or at others.

3. absolutely_____
   somewhat_____
   not at all_____

4. My wife has a poor relationship with her own father.

4. absolutely_____
   somewhat_____
   not at all_____

5. My wife has family or relatives that live in a distant state or country that would take her in if she opted for a "new life."

5. absolutely_____
   somewhat_____
   not at all_____

6. Our assets are owned jointly.

6. absolutely_____
   somewhat_____
   not at all_____

7. I don't think my wife values fatherhood as much as she values motherhood. She feels children are her domain as a woman.

7. absolutely_____
   somewhat_____
   not at all_____

8. My wife hasn't cultivated any marketable skills that could translate

8. absolutely_____

into a job for her if we were to end our marriage.

somewhat_____
not at all_____

9. My wife has a great deal of pride.

9. absolutely_____
somewhat_____
not at all_____

10. My wife is smart enough to use the legal system to the letter or hire a good lawyer.

10. absolutely_____
somewhat_____
not at all_____

11. The state in which we were married has divorce laws which discriminate against men.

11. absolutely_____
somewhat_____
not at all_____

12. My wife has a tendency to air our dirty laundry to others, characterizing me as the villain.

12. absolutely_____
somewhat_____
not at all_____

13. My wife has made threats of what she would do to me if I divorced her or had an affair or something of that nature.

13. absolutely_____
somewhat_____
not at all_____

14. My reputation is an important aspect of my career and she is aware of my vulnerability.

14. absolutely_____
somewhat_____
not at all_____

15. My wife has a quick temper and is passionate not logical.

15. absolutely_____
somewhat_____
not at all_____

Scoring:
For each "absolutely" answer give yourself 10 points. For each "somewhat" answer give yourself 5 points. For each "not at

all" answer give yourself 0 points. Total your score and write your answer here_____.

Evaluation:

100–150 Points: Tidal Wave Victim. If you scored here in the highest range, you had better be very careful if you are planning a divorce. Your wife's capacity for spite is very high. She could act like a tidal wave and wash away your assets, your fatherhood, your good name, and even your job before her vengeance subsided. You had better go back to all those "absolutely" answers and reread them carefully. They determine the areas of your vulnerabilities, whether they be financial, professional, or your access to your children. The test suggests ways your wife could get even; for instance taking the children to a distant state or ruining your business standing. The test taps her spite potential—and if she has made threats, harangued your extended family, or remarked about taking you to the cleaners, watch out! Depending on the state you live in—and her state of discontentment at divorce time—you could be in for a flood of personal woes. You had better learn to safeguard your fate where you can.

50–95 Points: Rough Waters. If you scored here, and if you are contemplating divorce, there are some rough waters ahead. You had better learn just how rough and where in your life the dangerous shoals lie. Read those "absolutely" answers carefully. Give those "somewhat" answers a great deal more thought. If your wife has some pride, some temper; if she's made threats, you must assess her attitude if you ask for a divorce. If she doesn't particularly value her own dad or your parenthood, that is a meter of what you can expect if she became the single custodial parent. Her motherhood might take over, leaving you virtually childless. Finances are always worth looking at. Remember—be fair but not beyond the point of your own well-being. Divorce has a way of bringing out the worst in people. Keep that in mind in judging your wife's capacity for spite and your own vulnerability. It may be the most important judgment you ever make for yourself as well as the children!

0–45 Points: Good Sailing. If your scored low and you are thinking about divorce, spite isn't necessarily going to be your biggest problem. Your wife isn't geared in that direction. She may react with anger or fury, but those are natural in the rocky road of separation. However, she seems to be logical about her passions and what's best for the children in terms of access to both parental roles. You and your wife apparently have structured your life so that financially you are not particularly in dangerous waters. She can't take everything away from you, nor is she so inclined. Maturity is an admirable quality that your wife possesses. It is to be hoped you would treat her with equal consideration if the tables turn. However, don't think because she doesn't feel the spite urge that you don't have vulnerabilities when it comes to opting for divorce. Spite may not be an Achilles' heel, but there's always guilt, inertia, etc. Divorce is never painless.

In Conclusion:
When your wife exercises her right to spite, you are victimized and lose some of your rights. It's not a pleasant thing to ponder, but if you are contemplating divorce, it is one capacity of hers you should scrutinize. Any mistress reading this, save this test for your married man. A married man facing the American form of justice in divorce court had better know his points of weakness well in advance, for considerable vengeance is wreaked there even without supernatural intervention. If your wife is spite-oriented, learn to safeguard yourself. It may be the lesson of a lifetime. Taking this test could ensure your survival; ignoring it could mean your drowning in the future—broke, childless, jobless, and devastated. Michael should indeed write that book to help married men survive and choose between their marriage or a divorce. Perhaps if you nag him too, he'll become more prolific. It's crucial to know your rights and her right to spite!

PART FOUR

Old Wives Tales

CHAPTER THIRTEEN

The Contenders

Ladies and gentlemen, welcome to the Triangle Championships. You are about to see the greatest fight of the century. The Triangle Championships are a national event. The contest is the battle of the ages, the wife versus the mistress. The tension here in the ring is furious. The anxiety out in the audience is even more furious. What a fight this is going to be!

The contenders—the wife and the mistress—are in their corners waiting for their introductions. The crowd is churning impatiently.

In the white corner is the incumbent, the wife. The incumbent is wearing a frayed quilted robe, with the meaningful stains of coffee, infant dribble, and some kind of food. Once that robe was white, but now it bears the honorable tattoos of wifely duty. She takes off the robe and reveals a gray sweatsuit. Good choice because it camouflages the bulges here and the veins or stretch marks there. Bearing children has a way of scarring the body, but don't forget she bore those children for him. She's already in her boxing gloves, thank heaven. Those dishpan hands are a disgrace. The camera isn't permitted to pan in too close on the incumbent—wrinkles, you know. Close-ups wouldn't be fair. As the wife comes to the center of the ring, the crowd roars. Clothes don't make this contender. It's clear that the wife is the favorite here tonight. In spite of her outward appearance, she possesses added intangibles like virtue and respectability. Even God is on her side.

In the red corner is the challenger, the mistress. She slithers out of her red satin robe. The hisses in the crowd turn involuntarily into wolf whistles. What a body on that mistress! Underneath that red satin robe are matching satin gym shorts that highlight perfect sleek legs. The challenger is energetically sprinting about. She's had plenty of time to work out, not like her busy, harried contender. She looks it, all youth and all beauty. Her trainer is putting the gloves on her. What a shame to cover up those beautifully manicured, coordinated red long fingernails! As she comes to the center of the ring the crowd hisses in unison. The mistress may not have the crowd, but with that vibrancy and those measurements who needs them!

Now the referee steps to the center of the ring. He looks more rattled than either of the contenders. Why? He's the incumbent's husband and the challenger's middle man. That's enough to age anyone. It's a shock to see both of these sections of his life together, staring at him. He is about to announce the beginning of the fight.

Then, wait a minute! Someone's just raced into the ring and grabbed the microphone. *What?* "The Triangle Championships are a fraud! It's fixed. This is not a fair fight." What does all that mean?

That's correct. The Triangle Championships are not fair. What you just saw in the ring is a fantasy. The contest between the wife and the mistress is real enough. However, that characterization is ludicrous in spite of how many people believe it. In real life the contestants aren't like that. Competition is a real enough factor. In the following chapter we are going to analyze the real competition and the real enemies. We are going to portray the actual nature of the contest, and in the process throw out a few surprise punches. Wives may not like some of what they are going to hear, but if they stand up and take it like a person, they'll be better off.

In my travels during the last several years, and through their letters, I have met countless wives. Their major concern can be summed up in their common question: "How can I compete with a younger woman?" They view their husbands as a competition with unfair odds. They all say it's not fair because there are too many young women parading around the offices making suggestive advances to their husbands. And of course we all know that men, poor devils, are weak. Husbands aren't designed to resist temptation, especially when it comes from a young voluptuous tigress. Wives are certain that a young woman is too great a threat to them, their husbands, and their marriage.

Once and for all I would like to address this widespread American misconception and fear. I've implied it throughout the book by reporting mistresses' varying statuses and ages. Now I'm going to present the age statistics of the mistresses. And I'm going to review the relevant ramifications. The contest between the wife and the mistress is not any battle of the ages.

Approximately 37% of the mistress population are young, ranging from between twenty to twenty-nine. Approximately 27% are between thirty and thirty-nine. Approximately 13% are in their forties—between forty and forty-nine years. Roughly 16% are in a young grouping of seventeen years of age to twenty-one. 6% are in their golden fifties, between fifty and fifty-nine. Mistresses sixty years and older account for only about 2%. Mistresses under seventeen account for some 1%.

By looking at this statistical breakdown you can see that peak vulnerabilities for mistresses occur in the twenties and thirties. That accounts for more than half. However, we cannot assess these age-related statistics without adding that the married men associated with these mistresses were within the same relative age bracket. The wives, too, are peers. And therefore it is reasonable to conclude that in the triangle wives and mistresses tend to be rivals of the same age, give or take a few years. There is no standard pairing of a forty-five-year-old wife with a twenty-one-year-old mistress. The competition may be a battle, but not a battle of the ages.

It is only in our imagination that the contest between the wife and the mistress is an impossible match with a younger woman. It is a fraction of the true cases. I would like to say it a thousand times, and I have actually, and in a thousand different ways: THERE IS NO MAGICAL AGE FOR A MISTRESS. No wife is being railroaded into a fixed fight with a Bo Derek look-alike. The battle of the wife and mistress is not middle-age versus youth. Pardon my redundancy, but I am sick and tired of hearing indignant wives whining about ingenues. Complaining about not being able to avoid the aging process or losing their husband's attentions to a lithe, glowing, youthful body. Harping on the younger woman theme is a cop-out.

Wives who go on believing the old battle of the ages myth do so to avoid taking any responsibility for marital fidelity. Blaming it on age and youth, you see, makes them helpless and not in the least responsible for their husband's affair. Aging is a reinforcement of the martyr stance. You know—poor, aging, victimized wife, victimized by nature, younger seductresses, men's animal appetites, etc. *Triangles involve peers in the majority of cases.*

If it is not a battle of the ages, then is there a competition of another sort? What is the battle of the wife versus the mistress? Is it really a contest between the wife and the mistress at all?

Of course, you might say at first, any triangle is a contest between the wife and the mistress. Aren't they both in competition for the same man? Doesn't he have to choose one or the other, either permanently or in the course of delegating his time? In analyzing the opposition in triangles between wife and mistress, it is useful to look at different stages of the triangle.

Let's look at the outset, the beginning of the triangle. When a husband initially launches his liaison, his mistress' strengths are not formed yet. Her role as a mistress is defined only with time. On the other hand his needs as a married man with a void are very much defined. By the time you've reached this point in the book, you realize that affairs aren't sexual orgies. You know, too, that married men do not have a menopause that instinctually drives them toward a mistress. What married men do have is a need that they seek to fulfill outside the home with an extramarital friend. That says something about the wife's responsibility for the affair in the first place.

As I type this I can almost hear the hisses go up across America. Feminist-oriented women will scream that women are always blamed for men's animal roaming. Wives will seize upon the right not to "tap dance," a term that has been introduced by Phil Donahue. Tap dancing means wives are expected to jump and dance in order to satisfy their man, the implication being that this is one-way and degrading. Innumerable arguments will arise aimed at freeing the wife of any blame for the origins of a triangle. *Triangles take three people and each one of the players has some responsibility*. Wives have some responsibility for the making of the triangle and the making of the American mistress. Like it or not.

Some of the wives' responsibility and blame is owing to neglect; some is owing to a conflict in value structures. This makes some wives villainesses and others nonvillains. This will become clearer as we go along.

At the outset of a triangle, some of the wives are their own worst enemies. The competition is not always with the mistress, but it is a competition between the wife as she is now and the woman her husband married years ago. People change and those changes aren't always conducive to good, stable marriages. And what's a "good wife" anyway these days? The answer varies, and studying that answer can shed some light on triangles.

I have been a mistress and I am now a wife. I am very attuned to the differences of each. I am very aware of the advantages and the disadvantages of each. Each role has assets and liabilities. As I have made the transition recently, I am acutely aware of the wife's possibilities and influences in affecting her husband's behavior. Also I am steeped in mistresses' observations on the subject.

Therefore, drop your defenses of the wife for a moment. Let's be openminded. The mistress does not let her hair down and belly-dance across your husband's desk or work bench during the coffee break. The mistress doesn't lure your husband away from his sublimely blissful marriage. Mistresses don't have the power to destroy happy homes; if they did there would be no mistresses in the first place. We have looked at the real mistress—now let's look at the real wife in several cases.

These cases have been chosen because they highlight a wife's responsibility in priming her marriage for a mistress. You will see some of these women in many, many wives.

Too Good to Be True

To Joan, motherhood is sacred. Nothing has, or ever will, eclipse that incredible rush she alone experienced when she pushed her infant out into the world during natural childbirth. The experience was physical, and supernatural, and sheer joy.

Joan tries and succeeds in living up to that maternal trust. She is a domestic engineer of the first order. Her renovated farmhouse in South Carolina is magazine material. Most of the home improvements she did herself. She should receive a gold seal of approval from Mother Nature, but Mother Nature doesn't give out gold seals. Joan bakes her own bread, with unbleached flour. No artificial additives or preservatives ever touch the lips of her child or her husband. She gardens with organic fertilizer, cans all her own produce in the fall, and tends her own compost. Joan believes in nutrition, conservation, home baked apple pie, motherhood, and the American way. Her child is the light of her life and her husband basks in that glow. He felt lucky to have a wife like Joan until recently.

Joan is completely organized. Laundry on Monday. Baking on Saturday. She never fails to send a Hallmark card for anniversaries, birthdays, and even grandparents' and mother-in-law's day. She makes sure that her child spends a portion of each day with Daddy and some time each week with one set of grandparents. Only the best of everything for her child.

Everyone loves coming to Joan's. Hot phyllo hors d'oeuvres, home brewed wine. The table always has crisp linen, a fresh seasonal handmade centerpiece. Joan even manages little gifts for her guests—an afghan they admired some time ago, a jar of her best preserves, or a crocheted potholder. Everyone marvels at Joan and her domestic excellence. Everyone says how lucky her husband is and that Joan is part of a dying breed, one in a million.

You can imagine the scandal that reverberated throughout the family when Joan's husband's affair hit the fan. What had she done to deserve this humiliation, this betrayal? It was hard for her husband to explain. He always wound up sounding childish, immature, jealous, or just plain small. What ingratitude! Did he not benefit from Joan's peace through an organized household, from Joan's nutritional expertise, from Joan's family coordination and enviable social image? The answer is yes and no.

The best way to see it from her husband's point of view is to excerpt his mistress' letter. Therein lies the explanation.

"My married man told me he had brought his wife chrysanthemums. Her delight was only because they were exactly what she needed for tonight's centerpiece. He was crushed. She rarely thought of him or them as a couple except in a way that suited her. He lamented at the state of their relationship. He feels like a cog in a family machine. He told me he, as a person, is really dispensable. He describes his wife as one of those Stepford Wives in that science fiction movie of a few years ago. He feels like he's another item on her list of things to do to be the perfect family engineer. He says, 'She gets all the strokes, I don't get any.' My married man doesn't feel grateful, peaceful or satisfied with his marriage. He feels resentful, neglected and in turmoil, mostly guilt. I know he doesn't want a divorce. Sometimes I feel like calling Joan and telling her to be a little less perfect and a little more human. I know his needs; she doesn't."

Joan's profile is one of those stories about priorities. Her neglect isn't willful or malicious. Yet she is still partially to blame for her husband's affair. Her values as a good wife, mother, homemaker, come first in the definitions she designs of all these. What's lacking is communication between them; and intimacy. Her husband feels guilty asking for these in the light of her expertise. She's oblivious to him. So as not to feel smaller, he goes to another woman to explain things to. In between making crewel masterpieces in miniature and banana whole wheat cakes, Joan is making an American mistress. Her part in the marriage was too good to ensure her husband's being true.

Letting Go

The following came from a questionnaire that was penned in a "small city—58,000 people." It came from a mistress who explained her existence the way she saw and heard it.

"Their home is a disaster. They own a farm, too, also a disaster, so he tells me. His life at home is total chaos and clutter. His wife studied Home Economics in her school days, but you'd never know it. The bed isn't made for months at a time. Several days' stinking dishes stack on the table and are pushed aside from one meal to the next. Laundry all over the place undone, ironing still crammed in the dryer—and she is home all day. When my married man goes home meals are never ready. She usually sends him back out to pick up something for a meal. He is embarrassed to have anyone in the house, but she watches soap operas, goes bowling three times a week, sleeps a lot, and does her duty sexually if he asks once every ten days. Why he'd want her is a miracle in itself. I've known them for eleven years and she's never looked worse, although she could be attractive if she cared. She's twenty-five pounds overweight, doesn't care how she looks, and has let herself go beyond belief. It's no wonder our friendship turned into an affair two years ago.

"My home is always neat. I can rustle up a meal that he enjoys. I have a fire in the fireplace, a hot shower ready, fresh towels, scrub him and fuss over him when he's tired, encourage him when he's down. I entertain his guests in my home and do all sorts of jobs for him; typing, mailouts, etc. He takes me on an occasional business trip and introduces me by my first name. Most assume I am his wife. I don't do his laundry or feed him daily, but I do many things for him. I'm no spring chicken, I'm forty-four and he's forty-seven. I work myself as I am divorced. I like doing for him and he needs to be fussed over. We fuss over each other. I'm a refuge away from the total confusion of his life at home. I will marry him if ever I get the chance."

Perhaps the wife's slovenliness is exaggerated by this mistress. Letting the house go, letting oneself go, are hot issues in the wake of women's liberation. However, if the man goes out to work and the woman stays home to work at running the home, each should keep up his or her end of the bargain. Many husbands today complain because wives' feel that household duties are nobody's job. Especially when the wife doesn't work outside the home.

Letting the appearance go is perhaps the touchiest issue of all. Should a woman be a slave to magazine photographs and their cosmetics? Should a woman diet herself to death in order to compete with Charlie's Angels? Should a woman memorize Marabel Morgan's paperback to be appealing? Of course, the answer to all these is no. Letting oneself go is usually seen as a physical description of things. Letting oneself go is more than giving up on hair coloring or what's in and out in the fashion world. Letting oneself go is an attitude. It is an attitude that takes a marriage for granted. It is an outlook that takes a husband for granted. Letting oneself go in attitude applies to the household as well. Underneath it the wife seems to be saying to the husband, "I don't have to impress you anymore." "I don't have to go out of my way to please you or to be pleasing."

Letting oneself go is judged by mistresses to be one of the greatest mistakes that wives are making in droves. Wives do it themselves and they deserve all the credit. The only way that a mistress adds to this is that her fussing over him and herself serves to highlight the wife's neglect of the little things that can mean a lot to marriage. Letting go of oneself, one's home, can lead to letting yourself in for a triangle.

Charity Begins at Home

Religion is a wonderful thing. However, overzealousness can lead to marital problems as one mistress explained.

"My married man told me that his wife's whole life is the Church. I know that she ropes him into many activities that he would rather avoid. He comes home after a ten-hour-long workday and she gets him involved in driving a truck to pick up items for rummage sales. How thoughtless! They go to church-related family outings and he does all the cooking and cleaning up afterwards. She teaches Sunday school, heads the Ladies Club, runs Sunday breakfasts. Then there are the activities that involve a lot of time planning, cooking, decorating, collecting funds while he's left alone at home with nothing but things to heat for himself for dinner. I'm not knocking the Church mind you, but if I were married to this wonderful guy, he'd come first."

What this mistress is saying is that charity begins at home. Her married man's wife doesn't see it that way. Not only her busy schedule comes between her and her husband, there's more.

"He says even when she's home she's not much company. Whenever he tries to tell her something important, either she cuts him short or she interrupts and changes the subject. There's been union trouble on the job and he worries. His wife never listens to him. He never get his fears across. How can he get anything across when she is always rushing around wrapped up in her own holier-than-thou little world?"

Here is another example of a wife who would probably be surprised to learn of her husband's four-year affair. She would probably go off to her friends and blame the harlot who tempted her husband. That would not be entirely fair. The wife, here, made her charitable commitments and her priorities. She made her own rules about conversation and communication. She made her own marital weaknesses. She made her own triangle.

Ultimate Liberation

Jeannette didn't go to work outside the home to satisfy any aesthetic desires for growth. She and her husband needed the extra income. Finding a job was infuriating and taught Jeanette all about women's being second-class citizens. Finally she got a job in a factory.

Working at the factory changed Jeannette. She decided she'd been a doting mother long enough. It was high time the children and her husband learned about home management. Being one of the only women on the assembly line turned Jeannette into an instant feminist. She grew furious at the male opinion of her as an inferior worker, especially when her performance surpassed many male co-workers. She fumed at the constant sexual innuendos that subtly harassed her daily. Yet in spite of all her newfound rage she worked hard, often overtime, and toward a foreperson opening that was coming up.

Her husband was an easygoing sort of guy with a Southern pace. He wasn't wild about his wife's working, but the money really helped. He pitched in at home once he got adjusted to the necessity of it. He wasn't terribly angry about Jeannette's new feminist rhetoric either. In fact he was proud of her. He was changing as fast as he could.

Jeannette, however, was consumed by her new working life. Her rage at men included her husband. Nothing he did around the house was right. Most of his remarks were chalked off by her loudly as male chauvinism. Jeannette's revolution had no room at all for her husband's camaraderie. Liberation for Jeannette had not been an easy road. She was filled with frustration, ambition, rage, but more alive than she'd been in years.

Her husband was becoming liberated too. He became adept at household chores, aware of job discrimination that women like his wife endured, conscious of treating his fellow employees with respect and equality. All this liberation of hers and his didn't bring them together, but only farther apart. It didn't make sense, but that's how it went. So her husband tried the ultimate liberation from his marriage, an affair.

Going out of the home to work is stress-provoking on a marriage. Feminism is too. However, these new forces can make or break a lifestyle. In Jeannette's case they made a mistress and broke the bond of fidelity in her marriage.

All of these profiles pointed up activities of wives that made their marriages prone to triangles. Now of course you can blame it all on husbands or blame it all on mistresses, but in reality the wives deserve blame too, at least a third of the blame. *Every triangle has three sides.* At each angle there is a story. Oftentimes we don't believe the stories that point a finger at the wife.

Wives can ruin their marriages without any help from anybody. A wife can be her own worst enemy, deliberately or by default. When a wife adopts new concerns, new priorities, new philosophies, or new demands, she changes her marital balance. Sometimes in that process of change she ignores her husband, forgets about her relationship with him. Feminism, career, children, volunteer work, all of these are worthwhile exercises to be sure. However, overmothering, workaholism, letting go, can affect your marriage. There are times in a marriage when your priorities and those of your husband may not be the same. Coordinating one's life and one's relationships is the key. Change is a constant in marriage as it is in life. Change can transform a marriage into a triangle. When this happens it is overly simplistic to shove blame onto the husband or the mistress.

It's so easy to blame the other woman. After all she has been the perfect scapegoat for years. It's so difficult to admit a certain degree of responsibility for the way a marriage goes, especially when it goes downhill.

It's so easy to blame husbands, after all they are men. It is high time we took all the sexism out of the issue of adultery and triangles. Adultery isn't a male norm anymore if you look at the extramarital statistics. Fifty % of spouses stray without regard to gender. Culpability isn't for the man alone or for his mistress. Wives are not martyrs blameless for their misfortunes. All three should shoulder blame and responsibility in some measure.

While we are on the subject of sexism and a wife's neglect of her marital relationship, let me add this. A wife doesn't have to tap dance, but she does have to remember that her relationship with her husband is the foundation of the marriage. This obligation is a two-way street. A husband, too, must not forget that his relationship with his wife must be worked at continually or it will stagnate. What I said throughout this chapter about how wives ruin their marriages can go both ways. Husbands must counter the temptation to take their wives for granted. They must resist letting themselves go in attitude as well as the rest. When either half of a marriage gives up and lets the union slide, the marriage becomes ripe for a mistress or a lover. No one wants to tap dance, but how many husbands and wives are sleep-walking through life in a marital coma? No highs and no lows, but really fertile for the passion that an affair can suddenly bring. The truth about wives is that when a wife ignores the marital relationship, a certain emptiness sets in. In that void the other woman enters. A wife must set the standards for the kind of marriage she will have. Close marriages are not totally affair-proof, but they are seldom mistress-prone.

Next up is a test that will help a wife take a new look at her marriage. Is your marriage moving toward the making of a mistress?

Is There a Love Affair in Your Marriage?

Every mistress will tell you that her relationship with her married man is a love affair. It's more than a friendship, more than a sexual liaison; it's love. A mistress has to stress the romantic aspect. She has to have a *love affair*, because there can be nothing else. There is no room for a life together, a lifestyle, or a life plan. Many a mistress wishes with regret there were more. A marriage, unlike an affair, is a relationship that has many aspects. There is the household, the care and feeding of the family, the budget, the rearing of children, the goals, etc., etc. In the frenzy of jobs, schedules, bills, relatives, sometimes the love affair gets lost.

The following test analyzes your marriage. Be honest, or taking the test is useless. Before you can balance out the demands of marriage, you must understand how yours is functioning.

Directions: Choose one answer from the multiple choices and put the letter of your answer in the space provided. Then proceed to the scoring and evaluation.

1. My husband and I communicate best
   (a) after a crisis (b) after making love (c) after a few cocktails   1. _____
2. My husband would consider my greatest asset to be
   (a) warmth (b) maternal instinct (c) efficiency   2. _____
3. When my husband talks to me I'm usually
   (a) preoccupied (b) surprised (c) understanding   3. _____
4. I believe that children
   (a) come first (b) come second in importance to my husband (c) are our responsibility   4. _____
5. In our daily conversations on the telephone we usually discuss
   (a) family logistics—who's picking up whom, what's for dinner, things like that (b) how our day is going—miserably, happily, how we are feeling (c) the latest bills, payments due, social invitations   5. _____
6. Time for making love
   (a) is a must, come hell or high water (b) just happens regularly (c) is juxtaposed in between family crises and hectic demands   6. _____
7. If my husband had a real problem
   (a) he might tell me and then again he might not (b) I'd be the first to know (c) I'd be the last to know because he wouldn't want to burden me.   7. _____
8. A husband's most important role is that of
   (a) a father (b) a companion (c) a provider   8. _____
9. When I try to talk to my husband, he most often
   (a) is apathetic (b) listens patiently (c) responds.   9. _____
10. Our day off (Saturday, Sunday, or whatever) is for

(a) mutual fun, frustration, or frivolity
(b) the free pursuit of our hobbies or
independent interests (c) us, but we
usually get sidetracked by chores,
children, or relatives   10. _____

11. If I learned that my husband was having
an affair I'd be
(a) humiliated (b) furious (c) devastated
(You must choose *only one* answer
here.)   11. _____

12. Our typical night out would best be
characterized as
(a) a social obligation (b) family
expectation (c) a date   12. _____

13. What I would find most frightening
about the thought of divorce is
(a) poverty (b) independence (c)
loneliness   13. _____

14. If I had to do it all again, I'd
(a) do it all the same way (b) have fewer
children (c) have pursued a career as
well as a family   14. _____

15. A society without marriage would have
no
(a) backbone (b) security (c) order   15. _____

Scoring:

Each answer that you have chosen is equal to a certain number of points. Below is a scoring table. First list all your answers from 1 to 15 in the spaces provided below. Then write the number of points based on the table next to each answer. Total your score. Compare your total with the categories and see if there is still a love affair in your marriage. And if not, what's taking its place.

Scoring Table

		Answer	Points
1.	(a) 5 (b) 10 (c) 1	1. _____	_____
2.	(a) 10 (b) 5 (c) 1	2. _____	_____
3.	(a) 5 (b) 1 (c) 10	3. _____	_____
4.	(a) 5 (b) 10 (c) 1	4. _____	_____
5.	(a) 5 (b) 10 (c) 1	5. _____	_____

6.	(a) 10	(b) 1	(c) 5	6. _____	_____
7.	(a) 1	(b) 10	(c) 5	7. _____	_____
8.	(a) 5	(b) 10	(c) 1	8. _____	_____
9.	(a) 1	(b) 5	(c) 10	9. _____	_____
10.	(a) 10	(b) 1	(c) 5	10. _____	_____
11.	(a) 1	(b) 5	(c) 10	11. _____	_____
12.	(a) 1	(b) 5	(c) 10	12. _____	_____
13.	(a) 1	(b) 5	(c) 10	13. _____	_____
14.	(a) 10	(b) 5	(c) 1	14. _____	_____
15.	(a) 10	(b) 1	(c) 5	15. _____	_____

Total_____points

Evaluation:

15–55 Points: The Laissez-faire Marriage. Your marriage has become too much of an economic contract. Laissez-faire is a term that describes an economic policy; a policy of non-interference. Your relationship with your husband has become very much like that policy. You have your interests and hobbies and he has his. Free time is likely spent separately. Your mutual efforts are probably spent maintaining your standard of living and managing your lifestyle. For instance, phone conversations probably revolve around bills, shopping lists, social invitations. You tend to view your husband as a provider. He probably admires your efficiency. Your pattern of communication lacks depth unless a few cocktails loosen your tongues. Talking occurs in an atmosphere of apathy or surprise. Your sexual communication may be habitually good, but you could use work in the before and after intimacies. Words like poverty, security—these are your concerns. It's time you realized that a marriage that is too heavily weighted in economics gets lonely. Too much independence can make you both vulnerable to having an affair. A love affair is an important part of life. If it's gone from your marriage, it may pop up outside your marriage!

60–100 Points: The Family Affair Marriage. Your marriage has become too much of a domestic arrangement. The romantic arrangement you started out with has become sidetracked by hectic family life. The children come first and come they do. They come into all your conversations, they come in between you both in the bedroom and on your days off. Running the family, meeting filial expectations, is what you and your husband do most of the time. You view each other too much as parents and not enough as companions. He loves your maternal instinct and you think he's a terrific father. Keeping the family life orderly and smoothe is fine, but a marriage needs more. You probably communicate best after some family crisis. If you don't both work to increase your romance, the next crisis may be infidelity. Don't lose sight of how you and he created that family!

105–150 Points: The Affair of the Heart Marriage. Your marriage may be harrowed by domestic demands and plagued with economic strategies, but you have not lost sight of love and romance. You and your husband still relate to each other as companions. Vibrations of warmth and questions about feelings are a part of your usual communication. You tend to share fun, frustrations, and problems with each other first and foremost. You feel that taking care of each other's sexual as well as emotional and romantic needs is an important part of any family life. You look at marriage as the backbone of society, the pattern that people choose to avoid loneliness. No marriage is problem-free, but you'd do it all over again with the same man. The responsiveness and understanding natures of both of you have kept your love affair current. If you found out that your husband was having an affair you would be devastated. Chances are you won't have to go through that so long as you are both coming home to a love affair every night.

In Conclusion:

Now that you have taken an outside look at the path your marriage is taking, don't despair if there's not enough romance and don't relax if there still is enough. If you've been submerging yourselves in economics or domestics, it's not too late. The love affair factor in marriages often fluctuates. Times when you're beginning that family, or forging that lifestyle, can take precedence. All it takes is a little awareness. Then you can work on that love affair, and that's not really work now is it?

If a wife works at having a close friendship and a love affair with her husband, in all likelihood she is not going to contribute to the making of a mistress.

Let's go back to the Triangle Championships. Let's adjust the picture. In the white corner is the wife, the incumbent. In the red corner is the mistress, the challenger. They are about the same age. The husband stands in the middle to referee, but he's hardly objective the way a referee should be. He's prejudiced toward the wife. She bore the children, she's intertwined in his lifestyle; his past and his future; how can he be above prejudice? The wife has the crowd, respectability, family, all on her side and the referee in her pocket. The mistress doesn't necessarily have beauty, certainly not contrasting youth, and really no one in her corner.

There are no dishpan hands; today we have dishwashing machines. There are no wolf whistles for the mistress; leers perhaps. Comments like "You knew what you were getting into!" There is little sympathy for the mistress and much sympathy for the wife. In reality the wife deserves less sympathy than she usually gets; the wife deserves more blame than she usually gets.

The contenders may be real. The contest may be real. It is only our images that are false. There is only one more fallacy. In the Triangle Championships there are no winners. Everyone loses something. The difference between the contenders is this: The wife loses but usually keeps the husband; the mistress loses alone.

CHAPTER 14

The Triangle Conspiracy

What's it like to be a wife trapped in the perpetual motion of the triangle? What role has she when her husband shares himself and their marriage with a mistress? What's a wife to do when she finds herself starring in a Triangle Conspiracy? Is she a co-conspirator or a victim of the Conspiracy?

Many people out there in America clearly see the wife as a victim of the Triangle Conspiracy. I'm going to share a letter with you, actually a facsimile of many I've received, on this point of view.

"Dear Ms. Sands,

I won't condemn you for your book about mistresses or say that you're terrible for what you have done, I know it happens. All I can do is speak from experience.

I had the experience of being the oldest daughter in a family of five children. I sat back and watched while my poor mother suffered pain and hurt while my father had an affair with a woman who called herself a friend. My mother went through six years of living in hell. My dad played around hiding in corners, making excuses for his many nights out when my mother knew the truth. He even had the gall to take off for weekends with this other woman. He wasn't kind enough to get a divorce and let my mother's wounds rest. He wouldn't let Mom start a new life or let things settle. He let it drag on and on for six long years until...my mother died.

I'm sorry, Ms. Sands, but whether it's because people, times, generations, whatever, are changing, I don't know. All I know is that I can't accept that change. My mother was hurt and her life torn to shreds and there was nothing any of us could do for her. What those two did to my mother was not right no matter what color you try to paint it."

The letter goes on, but we'll get back to it later in the chapter. What you have read so far is the essence. According to the daughter her mother was (1) victimized, (2) helpless, and (3) killed by a triangle. Her death was a rather extreme dénouement, but many many women feel almost murdered emotionally by their husband's infidelity. This case in point is dramatic maybe, but it exemplified a viewpoint that is fairly widespread—that the wife is the undisputed victim in a triangle with a cheating husband.

There is something very wrong with that letter. In between its pathos and its tragedy, there is a major fallacy. This chapter will be dedicated to that fallacy. No wife is totally helpless, nor is she victimized unless we say she is in part victimized by her own choosing. In the Triangle Conspiracy a wife is a co-conspirator.

In the preceding chapter we looked at the wife's angle of the triangle at its inception. We looked at the issue of blame with regard to the wife. Now, everybody hates the concept of blame. However, the issue of blame and its byproduct, guilt, is more eternal than the eternal triangle itself. The wife, like the other two players in the triangle, has her alliance with blame. The wife, like the other two players in the triangle, has her responsibility in keeping the triangle in motion.

That letter implied that the betrayed wife had no choices but to stay and take all the insults, neglects, lies, and demeaning behaviors that the husband dished out. It was the man who wouldn't ask for a divorce, let Mom start a new life, etc. It was the man who let this mess drag on and on. It was the man who was ultimately responsible for "killing" poor Mom.

I'd like to know why didn't poor Mom (1) throw the man out, (2) file for a divorce, (3) start a new life and, (4) find something else to live for? (That is if you buy the fact that his betrayal indeed killed her literally.) Most wives have choices in a triangle. Most wives have power that goes often untapped. A wife has the power to end a triangle immediately as does the mistress. If a wife has that power, why do so many endure triangles rather than explode them?

The Triangle Conspiracy is rarely understood. We hold on to our myths instead so as to avoid any responsibility. In the remaining pages, we are going to explore the nature of the Triangle Conspiracy. We are going to look at the wife's role in it. We are going to address ourselves to questions such as,

"Are wives aware of their husband's mistresses?" We are going to see how wives react to that knowledge. We are going to examine the choices that wives have in the triangle. We are going to look at the Silent Conspiracy that pervades so many lives. We are going to see just how much wives and mistresses have in common. They have an alliance. Finally we are going to see how much power the wife actually has—from the mistresses' mouths. Once the truth is out about the Triangle Conspiracy, many affairs are going to be doomed. Yes, that means Triangle Conspiracies make and break mistresses.

Do wives usually learn about their husband's relationship with his mistress? In most cases, the answer is unequivocally YES! The mistress/married man liaison is, after all, not a one-night stand. It goes on for years at high intensities. Any wife who knows her husband well and intimately can divine when another woman lives within his life.

How can I be so sure, you might ask.

On my questionnaire I asked a number of pertinent questions. "Do you think his wife knew about your affair? If so, how; what makes you think she knew?" "Did you ever have contact with his wife? How, a coincidence, business, a confrontation?" "If his wife found out, did it end the affair? Did it change the affair and how?" On the basis of the responses mistresses made to these questions, a picture emerges of the wife as, yes, co-conspirator.

A wife knows either subconsciously or consciously if her husband is having an affair with a mistress. It is something she senses by instinct or whatever. Admitting it to herself is another matter. Listen to what the mistresses say.

"Yes, his wife knew about our affair. My mother told her. I had contact with his wife. A telephone conversation and a confrontation." *(Mt. Clemens, Michigan)*

"If his wife didn't know she would have to be pretty dumb. He was with me almost every day. He was the type of person that went home all the time prior to our affair. So if you add two and two, it is easy to figure." *(Lake Zurich, Illinois)*

"I believe his wife knows but since I represent no threat to her I believe she just ignores it. She knows because he has, unwisely, thrown hints around. You know what they say about wanting to be caught. She has picked up things when he brings home little presents I gave him. Hell, I must have stacked his clothes closet with leather gloves, herringbone scarves, among other things." *(Smithtown, New York)*

"I know his wife knows about us. The courtesy was extended by my ex-husband in a jealous rage. Here's how it went. My ex-husband interrogated my daughter and found out my married man's name. My ex looked up the number in the telephone book and called it. My married man's wife answered and my ex-husband told her she should know that her husband was having an affair with his ex-wife. His wife gives him the phone, in the middle of Sunday dinner with relatives and all. My ex then tells my married man he knows what's been going on and he wants to come over to his house and have a little talk. Of course my married man denies it all. My ex comes to my house and tells me all this including how my married man behaved like a scared rabbit. The sad thing is I know it is the truth, all of it." *(Russell, Kansas)*

"I did the quiz in the end of your book for the wives, *Is Your Husband Having an Affair?* Only I answered as his wife would have answered from what I know as facts in our case. His wife has to be stupid too if she doesn't realize that he is most likely having an affair!!!!" *(Seattle, Washington)*

"His wife knows; I know she knows, she knows that I know she knows, he knows she knows and I know; we all know all and so what! This mess just keeps on going. I may not be making too much sense here as I just reread my letter, but what I'm trying to say is that your book helps me see things clearer. All women should read this book, not just present mistresses and their lovers. I hope and pray every female, young and old, single and married, will get a copy and read it. I'm giving a brand new copy to our library. If every mistress did the same, the contribution to all women would be great. What we all know won't be able to hurt us as much." *(Clemson, South Carolina)*

The point made here by the mistresses is that most wives know that their husbands are involved with a mistress. Secrets have a way of exploding, especially so volatile a secret as an affair. Gossip has a way of spreading among friends as well as enemies. Husbands confess in a bout of guilt. Ex-spouses tell in a fit of jealousy or concern. Angry parents tell wives, hoping to save their daughters. The secret is exploded in any number of ways. Even mistresses will tell, hoping it will bring the affair to a head in some way and bring about a solution.

Then wives, too, can tell. The quiz to which that one mistress referred was in the epilogue of *The Mistress' Survival Manual*. "Is Your Husband Having an Affair?" was an exercise intended to help wives see the telltale signs, take action, and in so doing save mistresses from more years of triangular tortures. I'll summarize the test to illustrate how obvious it really is to see an affair, once you know where to look.

A husband who has a mistress is recognizable. Being a middle man leaves tracks and evidence, no matter how careful one is. Let me be a bit more specific. The test zeroed in on a husband's patterns, behaviors, and moods. Change is the key word and the theme to be examined.

First there were questions about a husband's patterns. By patterns I mean his schedule, his routines. If a husband suddenly has a new hobby that takes up time, or if he has new blocks of unexplained time, his hobby could be a mistress. If his routine with regard to his appearance is changing, perhaps he is dieting or taking up weight-lifting, is his new pride in his appearance to please himself or another? If his schedule planning suddenly means he's preoccupied with your schedule, could that mean he's looking for time for a rendezvous? Every husband has habits, and when his habits change suddenly that could spell an affair.

Behaviors can also be saying a variety of things about the marital relationship and the husband's extramarital relationship. For instance, has he been bringing home new sexual techniques and a new enthusiasm for them? If so where did he get all this sudden new expertise? Possibly from the innovativeness of a new partner. What about communication? Is your husband taking less time to tell you things about work or whatever? Is he treating you more like a mother, a domestic, and less like a social partner and wife? Is he encouraging you to get out without him, make new friends, or take up new interests solo? If so, he may be trying to make you less dependent on him so he can feel less guilty about his new dependent, his mistress. He may be looking for more time for more double living. If a wife feels isolated, ignored, neglected by her husband's actions of late, that behavior is saying something loud and clear.

Lastly, there were a number of questions about a husband's moods. Mistresses tend to think that no one knows the middle man like they do. However, a wife lives with her husband day in and day out for years usually. That simple fact makes her an expert in her husband's moods. Maybe not his soul, but she knows his moods by his gestures, remarks, and his attitudes. If a husband is increasingly hostile, or evasive, or irritable, it can spell trouble. If he is very harried, and preoccupied, or overanxious and ready to blow at the drop of a hat, that indicates something is brewing in his mind. Double living is a strain and that strain shows up in a husband's moods. Even the most adept conniver can't cover all his tracks and all his close calls all of the time. Hints and signs surface.

Change may be a natural in marriage. However, when the changes all point to a disconcerted air in the marital atmosphere, it's time for a closer look at the telltale signs. Change is the barometer, and behaviors, patterns, and moods are a way of measuring the changes. A mistress is not as simple to spot as lipstick on a collar, but the signs can be just as visible and just as hard to miss.

Once a wife knows where to look, she knows whether or not her husband has a mistress. Having the knowledge that one's husband is involved with another woman is quite a mammoth discovery. What does a wife do with a hypothesis such as that? What do most wives do? What are the choices and the decisions? Once a wife knows that her husband has a mistress she is in the Triangle Conspiracy. What she does with her knowledge can make her a co-conspirator or not.

Whan a wife realizes that she lives in a triangle, it is her move. She has three possibilities. The first is to ignore her husband's extramarital behavior. The second is to react passionately without definitive demands. The third is to issue an ultimatum. According to the mistresses, the first two choices are the more popular. There is a logical reason, which you will see in a few paragraphs.

The wife who discovers that her husband has a mistress feels like she has just opened Pandora's box. If she demands his return to fidelity, what possible ills will fly out at her? He can withdraw financial support, leave her alone, abandon all responsibility, and worst of all move in with the mistress. Therefore a majority of wives just close up the Pandora's box, hoping that all the human ills will not escape out of the box and into their lives. They turn their cheeks, close their eyes, stick their heads in the sand, or whatever euphemism applies. When they ignore the triangle, they become strategists of the Silent Conspiracy.

"His wife confronted him about his affair several years ago. He didn't deny it so he tells me. He says she just pouts. I'm sure she doesn't bring it up as she fears it might cause a split." *(Minneapolis, Missouri)*

"His wife says she doesn't give a damn what he does. She even called me once and told me right out, 'If you want him, take him.' I wish it were that simple." *(Bridgewater, New Jersey)*

"A mutual friend told his wife everything. To make a long story short, my married man convinced his wife that that guy was a madman lately, under stress from his own divorce. He'd seen us having coffee at a community college which we both attended, and jumped to conclusions because of his own wife's cheating. She believed him! We continued for two years after that. Last year out of heaven knows what, I sent him a Christmas card and signed my name. Pardon the expression, but the shit hit the fan again. Again she believed whatever baloney he fast-talked her with. I don't know who is crazier after six years of this, her or me." *(Millville, New Jersey)*

"I often felt that I was being squeezed by some invisible vise. I couldn't take being alone at midnight knowing he was in bed sleeping soundly next to his wife. Every weekend he practically lived at my house. How could she stand it? Yet she didn't do anything to stop us. It was as if she just couldn't care less." *(Morgan Hill, California)*

"If a wife insists on living with a man when she knows the problem and doesn't do anything to correct it, she must pay the price. I know. I've been on both sides of the triangle. I had an unfaithful husband. I stayed for security reasons, knowing full well what was going on. Now the shoe is on the other foot. His wife has no right to interfere. She has her summer home and her winter home, her car, her friends, and the rest. She does what she likes and refuses to be a wife in the intimate sense. She thinks he owes her everything. What does she owe him? She knows about us, and resents it, but pretty much looks the other way when he says he's going out." *(Tampa, Florida)*

"His wife knew he was seeing me but she quit worrying about it, me in his life anyway, about the time I bore his child. The only thing that changed our affair was when his new mistress called the house. He said we had to cool it, but I know it was a front for seeing his new gal." *(Reedsburg, Wisconsin)*

All of the wives referred to here, and thousands more, have chosen to ignore the affair and therefore chosen to partake in the Silent Conspiracy. Their silence, the omission of pressure, and the implied tolerance makes them silent co-conspirators. Their behavior or lack of it, whichever way you interpret it, keeps the triangle in motion.

Wives choose the Silent Conspiracy for a variety of reasons. Fear is a common one. They fear that an ultimatum will unleash horrors. They fear raising the children alone, making it out in the world alone, spending the night in the house alone. The fears can range from serious pragmatic ones to superfluous ones. Like fears of what in-laws will mutter behind their backs or what the neighbors will say. Judgments aside about the reality or the validity of these fears, they immobilize many a wife and make her prefer a Silent Conspiracy. Learning of the triangle, opening and closing the Pandora's box, doesn't prevent the human ills from escaping. In fact it's ironic that what remains in the bottom of the box, according to Greek mythology, is hope. Many wives choose the Silent Conspiracy, hide Pandora's box, and savor the hope that husbands will "come around".

The wife who chooses the Silent Conspiracy is so much like many a mistress. She feeds on hope that their love will triumph. She settles for half a man, half of the time. She adjusts to the pains of triangle living. She ignores any power she might have if she would assert her feelings, fears and demands. A triangle works most effectively when the wife and mistress behave in this silent conspiratorial way.

Silent conspirators tend to accept the theory that infidelity is the nature of the male beast. Extra-sex may be a phenomenon that men have inflicted, but it is a theory that mothers have taught their daughters. It is a painful legacy that women have passed down from generation to generation, saying that is what happens and it must be accepted no matter how unpleasant. So countless wives learn of the triangle secret and do nothing but suffer in silence. However, doing nothing is still a choice, and one that makes mistressing easier.

The second move is to react but without a clear direction. This is also quite common. In this strategy the wife screams, rages, cries, but never actually puts her foot down with an ultimatum. This passionate directionless tirade usually makes the husband "cool it" with his mistress for a while and then resume the affair as things at home calm down. A wife who chooses to let off steam yet not risk exploding the marriage and the triangle sets herself up for the Revolving Door Marriage. Again this is her choice and her part in the conspiracy. Typically the Revolving Door Syndrome goes like the following profile. (It was written from the mistress' viewpoint, but the role of the wife is very clear.)

Hurricane Celeste

Celeste began her letter with a whirlwind question: "Why would a reasonably intelligent twenty-nine-year-old woman with a respectable well-paying job get herself into this situation not once, but four times and worse yet with the *same* man?" As for the situation, it goes somewhat like this.

Celeste met Aaron during one of his short-lived separations from his wife of thirteen years and his three children. Shortly after, he went back home for a reunion with his family. Celeste said that she was not too upset because at this point they were not heavily involved.

Six weeks later, Aaron called and asked to see Celeste. Celeste said, "I thought I could handle the situation." Famous last words of many a mistress—

"Needless to say after our reunion Aaron and I became very involved. We separated for a while, but we could never stay away from each other for long. Over the summer and fall, Aaron made plans to separate again from his wife. I never pushed him. I never asked him to divorce. I knew Aaron was deeply in love with me, and no amount of anger, hurt, or misgivings will ever make me doubt this.

"Around November, Aaron appeared at my doorstep at three in the morning with a suitcase. I had never seen a more welcome sight in my life! He had told his wife about us and said this was our Someday. He said his wife was calling her lawyer first thing in the morning. I must admit I was surprised, but the best is yet to come."

Aaron and Celeste had a few idyllic days, but middle man morning sickness began to circulate through Aaron's bloodstream.

"Aaron started having doubts. We talked, and talked, and talked and I knew that there was nothing I could say to resolve his doubts. I couldn't give him any guarantees. Next morning Aaron awoke me with the glad tidings that he was returning home. I accepted it as I accepted everything else and watched him move his things out and leave. I said nothing. I was immobilized. All of my concentration centered on keeping whatever was in my stomach down."

This was not the end of Aaron and Celeste.

"A week later, Aaron and I agreed to meet and talk. He cried. I cried. Already he was unhappy at home again. He wanted to see me again. I agreed, again. We have been through the same thing again and again in the last few months. We've always managed to return to square one. As I said before, I do not doubt Aaron's love, in fact that is the only certainty in this stormy mess."

Celeste was writing to me looking for answers to her questions. Her life was like a hurricane. Occasionally she would slip into a peaceful period with Aaron, but that was only the deceiving eye of the hurricane. After she caught her breath, she'd be back once again, swirling in the high velocity of passions and indecision.

"This past week he left his wife and then returned again. I never in my life want to go through the panic and torture of this. Yet I keep going back with him. I realize full well that it will happen again. I realize that Aaron may never change, he could possibly go through life swaying back and forth forever. So do I stay in there pitching? Do I sit back and hope for the best? Do I make demands which I don't think Aaron will like? My question to you is, is it worth it? I don't think I can survive this much longer."

I think that Celeste has just answered her own questions. Hurricanes can be brutal. This hurricane will go on unless Celeste battens down her hatches and goes underground alone.

Although this profile traced Celeste in her experiences of what I call the Eternal Crisis, Aaron's wife played a similar role. The Eternal Crisis for the mistress is living on the verge of the end while the married man bounces back and forth from wife to mistress, giving you a future one day and changing his mind the next. This bouncing back and forth is the married man's reaction to the Gemini Bind, not ever being satisfied with whatever choice he makes from moment to moment. For the wife this situation is the Revolving Door Marriage.

When a wife allows the husband to come and go time and again, she becomes the doormat for a revolving door, as does the mistress. So long as this wife doesn't lock the door, it will keep on revolving. Screaming, crying, reuniting, harassing the mistress; these reactions just make the Revolving Door marriage more melodramatic. In the Revolving Door marriage the wife, and every one else actually, loses their credibility, self-respect, and presence of mind. Yet the Revolving Door marriage is very common. It has the magnetism of a soap opera. It continues as long as the wife allows it to do so.

In the Revolving Door marriage the wife is a co-conspirator in the triangle's revolving repeating motions.

The third and last choice the wife has is the ultimatum. This is not usually reported by mistresses for a simple reason. Once the wife chooses this third option, the ultimatum, the triangle explodes. Therefore the mistress leaves the picture and has nothing to report. Most mistresses who answered my questionnaire were still in triangles. Most wives were reacting as co-conspirators, continuing the triangle. The wives who refused to conspire left the mistress with no triangle on which to report. Those mistresses only reported their demise.

"If his wife found out, did it end the affair?" That was the question that separated the conspirators from the non-conspirators.

"His wife found out. That brought him crashing back to earth. She turned on the guilt or whatever. It bothered him that she wasn't so dumb after all. I'll say, she wasn't dumb. Her finding out stopped our affair." *(Grove City, Pennsylvania)*

"His wife found out and at first it didn't end our affair. It did strain things though. He came over less. Things got uncomfortable for him at home. Then I guess she must have laid down the law or he made his choice. He called to say it was over." *(Lockwood, Missouri)*

"While I was in the hospital, Stan told his wife about us. That's when the real hell started for me. If I thought the first three years were bad, they were nothing compared to what came next. His wife went on a self-improvement kick. She started taking care of herself and taking better care of the house, and the kids. She began planning family outings, family camping trips, trying to make Stan see how nice their life really could be. She began to go to a marriage counselor, so did he, I later found out. He started taking her out to dinner, to the movies, and making love to her. He admitted all this to me, explaining that it was for the sake of the fifteen years he had invested in it all. He said he would understand if I didn't want to see him anymore. What I understood was he was looking for a way to get out without being the cad to break up with me." *(Manhattan Beach, California.)*

"He told me it was over because his wife found out and told him he had better say goodbye to one of us. I guess the only consolation I feel is that I know his household can't be all peace and love with his affair on her mind. They're not living happily ever after; this affair has got to drive her crazy for a while. Although he told me, 'You can't believe how good she is to me now.' Maybe their marriage will be better and stronger because of me. I told him he should send me a thank you card. I feel like a walking sympathy card. He has put two women through hell. I don't even think he bleeds." *(Sodus, New York)*

Wives, like mistresses, often underestimate their power and overestimate their helplessness. I've heard it from more than one unhappy mistress—how she actually made her married man's marriage better. After the explosion that an affair can trigger in a marriage, the husband and wife have the option of sorting out why it happened and where to go from here. Most mistresses have no such option.

The ultimatum is the most effective move to make after learning of a husband's infidelity. It is the move whereby you have the most to lose or the most to gain. Most wives are too scared to venture the risks. That is why countless wives settle for a sham of a marriage and the shadow of a husband. In that one question, "Did his wife's knowing end the affair?", the answer is yes or no. A wife's power is that simple to exert.

It is the wife, and not the mistress, who can make or break a marriage. A wife can have her marriage improve as a result of an affair. It can become a better relationship or a second honeymoon. A wife can have her marriage deteriorate, too. For better or for worse is the wife's decision. Most of them choose to remain in the Triangle Conspiracy. Most choose to hold on to the myths that blame all on the mistress. If only wives would acknowledge their alliance with blame and responsibility, they would realize the power that is involved too. Those wives who courageously choose the ultimatum gain a better marriage, a more concerned husband, or a new life. Those who silently go along or hysterically shout token threats live out the tortures of the triangle as co-conspirators.

As I discussed in the preceding chapter, wives are often their own worst enemy. This tends to be true at the outset and into the turning of the triangle. As contenders wives have many advantages. Yet rather than acting on their strengths, many react timidly and ally themselves with the mistress. A triangle conspiracy is rarely in anyone's best interests. This goes for the wife, the husband, and the mistress.

Now I want to get back to the letter that introduced us to the theme of this chapter. Is the wife a victim or a co-conspirator? Has the question other implications?

"I feel to keep a marriage together you have to have a determination in your heart. My children were too young to see what happened to my mother, thank God. My children love me and they love their father. Who would I be to make them choose between us? They are only children and they learn by watching their parents live their lives. If they don't see their parents together how will they ever know what marriage means? What I saw in the life of my father has made me hate the ground he walks on. I've spent years trying to forget it all and the toll it took on my mother. It's knowing Jesus Christ that has given me peace and helped me through things.

Sincerely,"
(Decatur, Georgia)

I sincerely hope that the author of this letter gets a copy of this book and reads it. She places an unfair burden on her father and not enough of a burden on her mother for the course of their marriage. As for the children, what she learned as a child was not a lesson that encouraged marriage. A divorce could have possibly saved them all from the scars of living inside a Triangle Conspiracy. As for her comments about making children choose between one parent or the other, she chose. Choosing is wrong and it will take an entire chapter to broach this sensitive subject.

Being a wife trapped in the perpetual motion of the triangle is torturous. Pleading helpless victim to the designs of a mistress is not the solution. Owning up to the co-conspiracy in the triangle is the first step in breaking loose. A wife has to choose a new alliance; an alliance with blame, an alliance with responsibility, an alliance with power, and an alliance with integrity. Nothing less—unless she wants to go on turning in the eternal triangle forever.

I've included a test which is a sort of review. Take it yourself; save it for a wife who needs it. Knowledge is the best weapon to combat ignorance and the Triangle Conspiracy.

How High Is Your Adultery Quotient?

We are all born with an I.Q.—an Intelligence Quotient—but our A.Q.—Adultery Quotient—is another matter. How much do you know about affairs? Do you really understand triangles? Why is it that some marriages navigate through life calmly, while others hit rocky territory? Here is a test designed to chart your Adultery Quotient.

Directions: Read each of the statements carefully. In the space provided at the end of each statement write True or False. Then proceed to the evaluation of your score.

1. Some husbands are born to cheat; some are not. 1. ____
2. My husband can't afford a mistress. 2. ____
3. Husbands use the other woman for sex, that's all. 3. ____
4. If I keep my husband satisfied sexually, he'll never stray. 4. ____
5. A good wife stays on her toes and off the feminist bandwagon. 5. ____
6. Men don't talk about their feelings. 6. ____
7. A wife can spot the other woman a mile away. 7. ____
8. In bed mistresses are willing to do things that wives aren't. 8. ____
9. If I'm patient, he'll outgrow this infatuation and stop seeing her. 9. ____
10. A wife just can't compete with a younger woman. 10. ____

Total _____

Evaluation:

In the space provided give yourself 0 points for every True and 10 points for every False answer. Then total up your score.

Now for the meaning of your score... All the statements in this test are myths. By that I mean they are commonly held beliefs about affairs, triangles, mistresses, and husbands. I know that these myths are held because I have spent three years meeting wives all around the country and listening to their comments about mistresses and married men. These myths are not only widespread but held steadfastly. And yet believing in them is dangerous. *The higher your score on this test, the more dangerous your beliefs are to you, your marriage, and your husband.* That old adage "Ignorance is bliss" just doesn't apply when we are speaking of our Adultery Quotient. The better informed you are about your needs, your husband's needs, and the challenges of marriage, the higher your chances of marital bliss.

If you think that mistresses are expensive to keep or that they are purely for sexual exploitation, you are wrong. If you think they are always younger women and you can't compete, you're wrong there too. Mistresses can't always be spotted; they don't glow with an incandescent scarlet A. They could be your neighbor, that frumpy secretary that takes calls at the office, or anyone. Mistresses will not cost your husband any money, but they will cost you quite a price in anxiety and pain.

Will it happen to you? Never say never. There is no foolproof adultery insurance. Routinely "servicing" your husband won't guarantee his faithfulness. Nor is tap dancing always going to work. Wrapping yourself in cellophane or perfuming yourself with whipped cream are also absurd tips even though they are guaranteed by famous female media stars. Sex cannot be frosted, processed, or quick-fried to ensure quality. Nor can husbands be labeled.

Men most surely have feelings. Furthermore they talk about them endlessly. Ask any mistress. If your husband doesn't talk to you about his fears, his feelings, his problems, that doesn't mean he doesn't talk at all. That flat statement that "men can't talk about their feelings" just couldn't be further from the truth. I don't care if Marilyn French swears by it or not. Being in touch with mistresses has put me in touch with an outpouring of male confidences. Mistresses have reported to me all that husbands say about their lives, their jobs, their children, their marriages. If you think that all a married man ever tells his mistress is "My wife doesn't understand me," you are in for an education in intimacy. Verbal communication in marriage is not easy. Conversations are always interrupted by demanding children, overflowing sinks, pressing deadlines of this or that. The right atmosphere has to be created for verbal ease. You are never too old to learn about communication or your husband.

None of this means that you can't be yourself or grow on your own. In fact the awareness that feminists have helped us achieve can only help your insights and your relationship if you put them to use positively. Knowing what is important to you is just as important as knowing what is important to him, your husband.

If your marriage is sucked into a triangle it's not because your husband was born to cheat or because you were a bad wife. It's not because some Freudian neurotic set her malevolent sights on wrecking your happy home either. Affairs are the biggest danger to marriage these days. They happen even to the most unexpected husband or wife. Adultery is a very complex happening. Pointing a finger at a sure-fire villain is as meaningless as sitting by passively and hoping that the whole mess will blow over. Triangles couldn't go on for years and years—and they do—if wives didn't cooperate. Patience, looking the other way, are not the best options in this difficult situation. There are better ways to cope.

Your I.Q.—your Intelligence Quotient—is something that you were born with, for better or for worse. Your A.Q.—your Adultery Quotient—was born the day you said "for better or worse." The good thing about the A.Q. is that it can be upgraded. And as you upgrade your insights into adultery, you are upgrading your odds for happiness as a wife and as a person. The improvement will surely be reflected in your life. You owe thanks to the mistress for helping you with this.

PART FIVE

The Children of Affairs

CHAPTER 15

Do Mistressing and Mothering Mix?

If you are a mother in the grips of a triangle, you know it is affecting your life. And you—the mistress—are probably concerned about what you are getting from this affair, be it passionate peaks or dispassionate injustices. But what about the children? What are the children getting out of your affair? Do mistressing and mothering mix?

I didn't spend a great deal of time exploring the subject of children in either section on the married mistress or the divorcée-mistress. The reason is that married mistresses and divorcée-mistresses didn't say all that much about the children. Oh, there were profound types of remarks like "I couldn't live without them" or "They are the air I breathe," but not much about how mothering was affected by mistressing. Now and then a mother would say, "I'm not there for my kids these days," but those kinds of remarks were rare.

Fathers, on the other hand, were acutely aware of the potential effects, mainly because for them there is usually a choice. Choosing a mistress means losing their children. Mothers rarely have to contemplate that choice. Nine out of ten mothers are awarded custody of the children in divorces. So mothers don't have to ponder what the affair may mean to their maternal future. Fathers do, and they do in myriads.

It is important for a mistress who is a mother, married, or divorced, to see if the affair is jeopardizing her children. It may be jeopardizing her motherhood and the children in ways she is too preoccupied to see. If you are a mistress, the triangle is affecting your children. The following test will explore how your mistressing and your mothering are mixing. By its conclusion you will see what the children in your family are getting out of your affair.

Directions: This is a True and False test. The statements are simple. However, they demand scrupulous honesty if your answers are to be valid. You must really think and compare how you are acting and if it is different from your pre-mistress days of motherhood. If you are divorced, some of your answers may be because of the divorce and not necessarily because of the affair. Either way it's important to your motherhood and more important for the children. Don't think of yourself or your image of motherhood before you answer. Think of the children. This is for them.

Answer True or False to all the statements. Then proceed to the scoring and evaluation.

1. Mealtimes are different now; there are more TV dinners, can openings, and hot dogs. 1. ____
2. Arguments and scenes erupt spontaneously and the children often get a front row seat before I realize they're listening. 2. ____
3. I'm encouraging more television-watching for the children than I used to. 3. ____
4. The household isn't running as smoothly as it once did; dishes and dirty laundry and dust seem to be breeding on me. 4. ____
5. I'm too preoccupied with my current problems to know what problems are currently upsetting the children. 5. ____
6. I can't hide my tears and my anxieties from the children anymore. 6. ____
7. I arranged hasty child-care at least once, leaving a questionable sitter or an older sibling. 7. ____
8. I don't have the presence of mind to read stories, go over homework, or listen to the children's tales like I once did. 8. ____
9. I've lost track of how the children are doing in school; all I know is if I were in school now I'd be failing. 9. ____
10. There is more screaming, less patience, and more anger in my mothering these days. 10. ____

THE CHILDREN OF AFFAIRS

Scoring:
Each True answer is worth 10 points. False answers are worth no points. Add up the number of True answers and multiply by 10. Don't be aghast at a high score.

Evaluation:
10–30 Points. If you scored in this range your mistresshood and motherhood are mixing like oil and water. You can see the elements separately. The mix isn't very harmful or volatile. Mothering isn't easy even when there is no stress in your private life. Everyone goes through periods of maternal malaise when the children aren't number one in your mind or your attention span. Quick dinners, a boycott on housework, capitalizing on the TV as a crutch: these could be a function of your mood, a new job, or the ordinary cycles of living. While mistressing may be the prime cause for you it hasn't taken over your life yet. The children are getting a bit neglected, but it's not drastic. They should learn that mother has a life too, but you should also know in what ways your life is affecting theirs. So note your True answers and see exactly how your mistressing is affecting your motherhood and the children.

40–60 Points. If you scored in this range, your mistresshood and your motherhood are mixing like bleach and ammonia. You know that mix yields fumes and isn't workable. Your mistressing at this point isn't conducive to your mothering. Your children are very much aware of your state of mind. They can sense it even if they are young by your preoccupation and your lack of time for them. If they're older chances are they've seen you in tears, arguing, glued to the telephone, or pouring your heart out to a confidante. You do have a life, but the children don't deserve to suffer at the expense of a triangle. It's not that TV dinners are so heinous or that dust is unconscionable. However, these represent a trend that is bordering on neglect. If you aren't aware of the children's problems, grades, insecurities, you can't be influencing them or guiding them properly. They need you, and their needs shouldn't be put off because of your needs. They are children; you are an adult. Go back and assess the impact on your mothering of this affair. They need you even more than that married man does!

70–100 Points. If you scored in this range, your mistresshood and your motherhood are mixing like gasoline and matches. Watch out, because you are playing with fire. Mistressing is thriving at the expense of your mothering. Your end result is that the children are suffering. Children are self-centered and they may even think they are the cause of the hysterical bouts, screaming, and loud arguments they are witnessing frequently. Hasty child-care even once is too much. You may have lost your presence of mind, patience, and maternal interest in the strains of triangular living. Mistress often is equal to my-stress. You are losing your maternal talents and may wind up losing your children. If you express no interest in their lives, no guidance, they will have to turn elsewhere for attention and advice. Where will they go? Perhaps to Father, to peers, or to shoulders that could be harmful. Right now you are losing; more importantly, those children are losing. They are getting an overdose of neglect, tension, and anxiety. You had better forget about mistressing long enough to see how your affair is hurting the children. They didn't do anything to deserve this.

In Conclusion:

Don't panic. If you are a mistress there is enough panic and anxiety in your schedule already. The good thing about this test is that if your motherhood isn't mixing with mistresshood, *at least now you know*. You are aware enough to change things and give the children a little more of you, of order, and of care. Mistressing has a way of taking over with its intense passions and pains. Your maternal lapses are standard, but they should be adjusted. Children of affairs suffer. To what degree varies. Only you can tell how your affair is affecting the children and just how much. Now you have a gauge.

Whenever motherhood comes up I tend to hear a lot about "birth" and "rights." Things like "I gave birth to my children" and therefore "I have some kinds of rights." These things are more shouted about prior to divorce. The consensus seems to be that mothers have "rights" over children. What happens is that we often lose sight of the children. They have a birthright to love from both parents, to security in or out of marriage, and to order. An affair, a divorce, affects the children. Their rights must always take precedence over yours—isn't that what parenthood means? Be wary of the mix created by mistressing and mothering. More than your life and your happiness are at stake. The children may be getting more suffering out of the affair than even you!

CHAPTER 16

Someday's Child

I didn't start out looking for Someday's Child. In fact she never crossed my mind in the beginning. Then little by little, a tale about her here and a story about him there kept repeating itself. I started by recording facts and figures about the mistress. In that process, Someday's Child was born. She and he were facts that figured in the lives of many mistresses and married men. Someday's children were sufficient in numbers to deserve a chapter all to themselves. Their population was much higher than I anticipated. Discovering the community of Someday's children was a surprise, a mystery, and a tragedy.

Someday's child is the name I have given to any child born out of the union of the mistress and the married man. Society defines them as illegitimate offspring. I didn't wish to call them that because they have problems enough without that additional stigma.

What do the statistics say about Someday's children? The rate of these births is 7%. 7% of mistresses bear the child of the married man with whom they are involved. In a manner of speaking, Someday's child adds a new triangle within a triangle. Without asking, Someday's child becomes a player in the triangle.

Given the difficulties of triangles in general, and given the turmoils of the mistress in particular, why are there so many of Someday's children? There is no singular answer just as there is no simple answer.

The only way to learn more about Someday's children is to look at the mistresses and the married men who bore them. Motivations varied. However, after getting to know a significant number of mistress/mothers and married men/fathers, motivations fell into several categories.

First we are going to look at the different forces that led to the births of Someday's children. Some were conceived out of different needs. Others were conceived out of different designs. Then we are going to look at the similarities shared by the community of Someday children.

All of the mistresses reported to me that their children were born out of love. Although that may have been true for all, it is a purely romantic explanation. Some of the births represented more than the natural fruition of a loving union. But not all. In fact that explanation aptly describes the story of Dolores.

Dolores and Bart's Child: An Accident of Love

Dolores's blindness was not an accident. She was born that way. Yet that blindness didn't prevent her from doing many many normal things. In twenty-eight years Dolores had a BS in Education, her first counseling position, a new apartment on her own in Miami, an avid sports life, and a married man. The married man had come into her life by way of her job. He was her boss's husband. Her boss suggested that Bart guide and teach Dolores to waterski. Being a new woman in town and needing assistance, Dolores accepted. In time the offer included more than ski lessons.

It had something to do with holidays. Bart's wife was an atheist. One Christmas eve, Dolores invited him over for a bit of holiday cheer and to receive a gift. His Vermont upbringing had glorified holidays. He hadn't realized how much he missed the tradition until he smelled the Christmas tree and saw the lights. It was that night that Bart realized how much holidays and his newfound friendship meant to him. He told Dolores, "I don't go chasing after women, I want you to know that." He also told her that his marriage was sort of dead and had been these last seven years. It was just a habit, devoid of companionship and lovemaking.

Dolores had no reason not to believe him. She loved the sound of his Southern accent, which he put on for fun. She couldn't believe that this fantastic man loved her. His wife went about her life, and didn't seem to care about all the time Bart spent with Dolores. In time Bart promised divorce. He didn't anticipate any problems. There were no children.

Then suddenly quite unexpectedly there was a child and a

lot of problems. Dolores knew that she was pregnant even before the doctor verified it. She was overjoyed as were her parents who knew Bart and knew that things would work out. Bart was initially delighted. He got a lawyer, an apartment, and a tandem bicycle. He bought a rocker that he spent hours refinishing for his first child.

Dolores went shopping one day for maternity clothes and came home with nothing except a sick premonition. She called Bart for reassurance and got no answer. That was the beginning of the end. The answers she started getting after that were sad. Even their psychologist was surprised at Bart. Yes, they had gone to counseling to make sure that Bart could handle her blindness, his divorce, and their baby.

It seemed as though Bart had changed overnight. What happened to the man who had agreed "no abortion"? Dolores couldn't even think of that. What happened to the man who wanted Dolores to stay and be his wife? She had wanted to move to New York with her family so as not to pressure him. What happened to that man? He was gone once and for all. This new Bart was bent on staying with his wife. He couldn't leave her without a profession, with nothing but loneliness. Oh, he'd support the baby. And he told Dolores he was sorry for hurting her so much. She couldn't even remember those last few conversations. She was in some kind of shock that only subsided when she felt their baby kick.

Dolores moved North. She was blind, pregnant, and according to popular opinion dumb. Nothing made her smile until she smelled that new baby coming into the hospital room and right into her arms. She felt a little frightened but the baby felt wonderful. She kissed Someday's child, an accident of love.

In another state, Bart and his wife of 11 years toasted their reunion. They were unaware of the birth of Someday's child, aware only of the rebirth of their marriage, which was no accident.

Dolores' story is quite common in that it typifies the accidental pregnancy. In spite of our birth control technology, in spite of the complicated risks, many mistresses and married men gamble in the bedroom. They are so busy dealing out affection, sympathy, hopelessness, and pathos that they forget the cards can come up with a new life. The unplanned pregnancy is a shock. That kind of child enters the world out of love and into a unique set of problems.

The next several categories of motivation are different in that the pregnancies were preplanned. The first of these I have decided to call "the Souvenir Syndrome." That label will become a great deal more meaningful after you've traveled with me to Richfield, Minnesota, and met Gloria and John.

Gloria and John's Child: A Memento of Love

Richfield is a suburb of Minneapolis and looks like many suburbs. It has green lawns, recessed tract houses, and neat little families all in a row. As in many neighborhood communities, the neighbors are friendly and socialize regularly. That all-American fabric is what led to this complicated pattern woven by Gloria and John. Gloria was married to a salesperson and had two beautiful children. She lived next door to John. John was an industrial illustrator, married, with three beautiful children of his own. The families were friends; the children played together. John and Gloria's husband even looked alike.

Gloria vaguely felt that something was missing in her American dream. So did John. One night they filled that gap together and began a four-year affair. Guilt caused them to halt their affair as frequently as passion caused them to resume it. Then finally they decided to end it once and for all. John planned to take a new job which would relocate him to Dallas. Neither Gloria nor John wished to hurt their spouses or disrupt their family units.

If only they had met years before, they could have been happy. They were so compatible, sharing similar backgrounds, interests, and outlooks. Neither regretted their affair. They retained their respect for each other. To make their parting easier, they decided to conceive a child. John assured Gloria he wanted more than anything to sire this baby. Gloria told me, "My husband wanted this marriage more than I. He wants me to be happy. This secret child would afford me great happiness within the marriage structure. I'm not mentally ill and somehow I do not feel that what I'm doing is immoral."

Together John and Gloria calculated the peak of her fertility. Gloria figured that the baby wouldn't arouse suspicion because John bore a striking physical resemblance to her husband. The fact that John was moving wouldn't complicate the paternity issue either. Her husband need never know the truth about the real father of the baby. The child need never know either. Only she would know. She would know that, although she couldn't have John, she would always have a part of him.

After Gloria knew that she was pregnant with John's child, they switched to a strictly platonic relationship. The day Gloria delivered, Richfield Memorial Hospital was like Grand Central Station. All her friends, relatives, and neighbors crowded in with their congratulations. This was her first son. Only Gloria noticed that John and his wife were missing. Neighbors conveyed their excuses. It seemed that John decided to push the move up a month and they were swamped with last minute packing and arrangements.

Gloria's husband was so proud. He loved his daughters, but oh how he loved his new son! Of course the child would bear his name with a junior attached to the end. Secretly Gloria wanted to name the baby John. To her he would always be John. It was too bad that John couldn't see how healthy and lovely the baby was. It wasn't like him not to come.

The day Gloria took their son home, her husband was still green from all the cigar smoke he'd been inhaling. Cigars were everywhere, jumping out of ashtrays, desk drawers, his pockets. She thanked God his greenness was only from cigars.

John dived into his new job, landscaping his new home, fencing in his property, and took up racquetball. He was trying to get away from the nagging thought that back in Richfield their was a little baby who was a part of him and would never know him. John hadn't bargained for the feeling, the weight of that legacy.

Gloria and John's separate lives would always look the same. John's new suburban setup looked very much like the old one he had left behind in Richfield. Green lawns, recessed tract houses, and neat little families all in a row. A nice house with big closets and skeletons just like those in Richfield and how many other suburban communities.

Let's hope that skeletons stay content with only coming out for Halloween! Otherwise Someday's child will have to learn how to spell memento.

Having a child to retain some part of the married man is the Souvenir Syndrome. Breaking up an affair is not easy, but letting go is even harder. Mistresses and married men who can't handle the concept of letting go forever are the prime candidates for memento parenthood. They conceive a baby out of love, illusions, and romanticism. The conception is deliberate. It is no surprise. The surprises only come afterward. The fantasy of having that wonderful child of their union is soon complicated by some unnerving realities. Those realities we will look at a bit later in this chapter.

Right now, let's look at another story. This, too, represents a premeditated pregnancy. This one seems more logical because of our times. As single parenthood becomes more common and more acceptable, more mistresses use it as a rationale for bearing another of Someday's children.

Leah and Nick's Story: The Single Parent Love Child

Leah first met Nick ten years ago. She was then twenty-two years old, as was he. Nick worked for his father's fruit company in Fresno, California. Leah worked for a food cooperative and regularly picked up orders from Nick. In between veggie runs Leah had a brief fling with Nick. She was crazy about him but he had a girlfriend. And anyway Leah wasn't looking for a husband. She was looking for peace in Vietnam, justice for Bobbie Seale and Angela Davis, inner harmony and all the rest of those things that hippies were looking for in Southern California in the late sixties.

Times changed; addresses changed. Then seven years later Leah ran into Nick in the parking lot of a local university. Leah told me that it was like in the commercials. In slow motion they ran into each others arms. Leah hadn't changed in that she still had this magical love for him. Nick was now married, about to leave for Hawaii with his wife. That didn't stop them from reminiscing and making love for old time's sake.

The next time Leah saw him she was pregnant. It was his; she'd had no other lovers of late. She was ecstatic. Long-term relationships never worked for her. She had given up birth control and was waiting for this to happen. She was looking forward to single parenthood and had been for quite some time. Leah didn't believe in multiple parents; too many conflicts. This was even better than what she had planned. Instead of bearing an anonymous man's child, Nick would be the father.

Nick hadn't planned on resuming their affair until he heard the news. He incorporated Leah into his schedule. He loved to feel the baby kicking in her womb. It seemed that his wife was having difficulty conceiving. They were trying all sorts of gimmicks to get her pregnant. Part of the problem was a low sperm count. Nick's extramarital sexual indulgences weren't helping in that area.

Leah and Nick's little girl is two years old now. Leah says that Harmony still looks like the pictures Nick took those first few months. She recalls vividly, too vividly, the day Harmony was born. "I hated that he wasn't with me when she was born. He was home in bed with his wife."

Now Nick is seriously considering divorce. He was just about to leave his wife when suddenly she turned up pregnant. With each day Nick moves closer to his wife and their new embryo and further away from Leah and Harmony.

Nick's photo reproduction business isn't too lucrative so he can't help Leah out too much. Leah says that she doesn't resent the financial part as much as knowing that Nick will be supporting his other child physically and emotionally. Not that Leah is having it easy financially. "Trying to exist on welfare, trying to get through the university as a full-time student and a full-time mother. Having to sell blood once in a while to be able to feed the little child. Being careful not to eat too much, so that Harmony will have enough." That reality is something that she never bargained for while patiently planning her single parenthood.

Leah said that she still isn't sure that she'd marry Nick anyway. She'd rather live with him for a while. She would like the choice, though. At first his marriage wasn't a barricade, only a separate part of him that they didn't share. It didn't matter then. Now it does. So much so that Leah admitted that she has continual headaches, cries a lot, is impatient with Harmony, and goes to bed with a brandy bottle or a jug of wine.

Leah says she knows that Nick is never going to divorce. She's trying to adjust and worrying how Harmony is going to adjust to seeing less and less of Nick. His family ties are too strong. At least the ties to his wife and extended Italian family. His family ties to them aren't strong enough.

Leah would like the same consideration, the same future for Harmony and herself. But when all is said and done Nick will have his wife and family and Leah will have Harmony.

Harmony, Someday's child will have a single parent who loves her more than two parents put together. Will it be enough?

There is an increasing number of women who are in favor of single parenthood. They feel that just because you don't have a husband and a marriage, you shouldn't be prevented from having the joys of motherhood. Especially when women are equipped with all the apparatus they need. Many men, too, favor single parenthood but they have different perspectives. Usually they are divorced men who desperately want the child-rearing experience with their own children. Slowly but steadily society is becoming accustomed to the single parent experience. As society indulges the concept, it is also simultaneously providing the rationale that many mistresses are looking for. The right of single parenthood is a cause behind many of Someday's children. This trend is on the rise.

The rights of the single parent even become more vocal and more poignant when they are espoused by an older woman. A woman who is at the turning point in her childbearing career. A woman who is on the threshold of middle age. For her, it's now or never. This next story is about the Last Chance Child. It was now or never for Joanne with a little help from Jim.

Joanne and Jim's Child: The Last Chance Child

Joanne had never married. It was a mystery because she was warm, fairly attractive, accomplished careerwise, and bright. Perhaps it's true what they say about not finding the right person. Well, that isn't entirely true for Joanne. She found the right person. She found him thirteen years ago when she was twenty-seven years old. Now Joanne is forty and still single, because her friend, Jim, is already married.

Joanne and Jim met at a high school in Arlington, Virginia. She was in Library Science. He was in Chemistry. Chemistry won out over her virginity. Although they were discreet, in time Joanne had to leave her job. Jim's wife was an alcoholic, everyone knew that. However, neither Joanne nor Jim were regarded with any sympathy. In fact the story of their triangle was rewritten so as to make Joanne the villain who drove Jim's poor wife to the bottle.

Joanne found a new job with a Christian mail order firm as a creative development editor. The firm had a catalogue of greeting cards, posters, children's activity items, and religious articles. She brought sophistication and liberation to their line.

The first thing that went were the Old Maid playing cards. Since Joanne was thirty-five when this battle was won, her subordinates got quite a charge out of it. "The old maid doth protest too much," was one variation of the theme that hummed furtively through the office behind her back.

Joanne knew about all this but had long since armored herself against public opinion. She really didn't care what anyone said or thought, except Jim. Time had proven all of them cruel, crude, and insincere. That old academic community back at Arlington had taught her well a stab-in-the-back routine that she would always remember.

Joanne's fortieth birthday was a gala affair, no pun intended really. It was just she, and Jim, and the child that was brewing inside her. Jim had to cut the celebration short. His wife was having dinner guests. Joanne didn't mind. She had accepted the limits of their life together. And the limits she couldn't accept, she transcended.

Yes, the limit she couldn't accept was not being able to bear a child. She just refused to let society or convention dictate to her. In her thirty-ninth year she graciously said farewell to youth and to the hopes that Jim would divorce. She couldn't say goodbye to the promise of motherhood.

Joanne never had white gown or a piece of wedding cake. She never had a honeymoon or a ride over the threshold. So what, she told herself. She had Jim's love and she wanted a baby. The only frightening aspect of middle age according to Joanne was the end of her childbearing years. She knew Jim would always be there. His marriage was a pickled sham. Only his inertia and guilt were real. He, too, had little respect for the world because all of his respect was for Joanne.

When Joanne asked him about having a baby, he couldn't say no. His whole life was one big no to Joanne and almost all her dreams and desires. This was her last chance at parenthood, her only chance. She was too old to find a new man, nurture a relationship, marry, and wait for the stork. Besides, she was too in love to do that. So it was now or never for Joanne. They gave up birth control and studied rhythm. The end result was their pregnancy, that's how Joanne looked at it.

Joanne was ecstatic. Her life was far from normal but that was just the way it was. She had studied hard, worked hard, and loved generously like other people but had somehow wound up very differently. Joanne knew in her heart she was a good person despite what society said about her affair, her lifestyle, and now the baby. She knew that this Someday's child was her last chance. And someday the child would know, too, that she was a good person. Hopefully, after not too much ridicule.

Joanne's age, her profile, and her parenthood drive is very much shared by a segment of women who wrote to me. They were all women who had become extricated in affairs in those years when other women were planning marriages and families. Somehow a decade or two whizzed by and suddenly they stood on the brink of middle age childless.

Too many years had been spent waiting. Too many years had been spent hoping. Too many years had been spent thinking about his problems, his children, his marriage, and his future. Now on the verge of middle age, the concept of their future hits home. The event or the passing of their motherhood was on the line and couldn't be put off another year. The Last Chance Child of the mistress and the married man is the easiest one to justify. If only that would make it easier for Someday's child. The now or never mother isn't looking for anything except that feminine fulfillment that has been ingrained in us since even before Gerber baby food and Johnson and Johnson.

The next and final category of mistress/mothers is looking for fulfillment of a different sort. She is aiming for the fulfillment of all her dreams, her hopes and her needs. She is aiming for a happy ending with her married man and taking out a little insurance that it will happen. That insurance is getting pregnant with his child. It's love, of course, but it's also strategy. Before you assume that it is all callousness and deceit, let's meet Pamela.

Pamela and David's Child: The Strategy Child

The jukebox was playing "Stand by Your Man." Pamela sat there at the bar of this Country and Western Club and wondered how many battered wives went home to miserable marriages humming that tune. Oh the power of Tammy Wynette. Those days were over for her. She was only nineteen years old and she was tired of feeling thirty. She had suffered enough. The decision to separate wasn't easy, but now every day seemed to get easier. Even her baby seemed to be gurgling more. Her husband would be better off too. She'd always let him be a father. And here she was, actually enjoying this scene.

Across the room she saw a familiar face. At first she couldn't place it, but then she recognized her husband's barber. Trying to dodge loneliness, she walked over and said hello. David didn't really recall ever meeting her, but he was anxious to now.

Pamela and David generated an electric current that probably was visible to all the pilots flying over Shreveport, Louisiana, that night. That electricity continued through Pamela's divorce. David was separated too, at least half of the time anyway. He bounced in and out of marriage. Pamela couldn't really understand. He spoke about his wife with a loathing and hatred that was too violent to be summed up in a punch or a slap. He seemed a gentle man and said he never hit her. Pamela knew it had something to do with his father-in-law owning half of the barbershop. He had two small children too.

This merry-go-round went on for eight years. Pamela got a good paying job waitressing and even started a secret bank account for David. Then he could start his own shop. Then on the night of her twenty-seventh birthday she gave him a bank book with $423 in it. Instead of being elated as she assumed he would be, he seemed embarrassed. Pamela was crushed. She had struggled with all her hope and desperation to save that money. That was the way to win him once and for all. But it didn't work.

Pamela was no genius. She settled for just never understanding the nature of his marriage or what kept him with his wife. Still she knew in her heart that the marriage was wrong. Too much hatred and sickness. Their relationship had none of that.

Pamela's desperation and hope started to get the better of her logic. She spent hours trying to figure out what would make David happy to live with only her. It didn't hit her like a bolt of lightning. It was more like a gradual awakening. What would be more appealing and binding for them than a child of their own. Pamela had always wanted a large family. She and David had certainly had enough discussions about what their child would look like and be like. So she went ahead and retired her diaphragm. She told David when she was in her third month.

He was happy enough about it. He was there the day Jessica was born. She looked exactly like her father. He was there the day she took their baby home. He was there a lot in fact, but not all the time. They baby had no effect on his indecision. David's wife didn't care. She had made a career out of looking the other way. Pamela couldn't believe it. She had been sure than this would finally do it. That this baby would bring all her dreams of marrying David to the real stage.

Now that her expectations fell by the wayside, she got very depressed. Even her ex-husband felt sorry for her. He was ready to beat up the son of a bitch if she gave the word. That wouldn't solve anything. Her dreams were shattered. Life was taking on the hue of a new nightmare. She hardly even enjoyed the baby. She didn't even enjoy going to their favorite place anymore.

There she was again. Listening to that same "Stand by Your Man" song, at the same Country and Western Club. Only this time she was figuring how far that little bank account could take her. Someday's child had failed her in the strategy arena. David had failed her. Or—oh God, was it the other way around?

Designing a child to ultimately create a foolproof strategy rarely works. In the end the mistress winds up playing the fool. A married man who already has children by his wife isn't likely to value the child by his mistress any higher. The logic of this strategy is faulty. Usually the mistress' mind is clouded with desperation and depression. In this frame of mind the plan seems right. It's not right especially for Someday's child who begins life as some kind of failure. And although the failure is not the infant's fault, she or he will bear the consequences.

That brings us around to the consequences. What are they for Someday's child? Whether the child was initially unwanted, desperately wanted, or wanted for the wrong reasons eventually becomes irrelevant. Someday's children share a different prenatal history, but their postnatal history is similar in many respects.

Procreation, maternity, reproduction, immortality—these concepts are bigger than the mistress, bigger than all of us. Unfortunately they are not big enough to stamp out the smallness of human beings at times. They are not big enough to temper our prejudices or to eradicate our pettiness when the gossip urge bites. What I'm trying to say is that these concepts are not big enough to protect each and every Someday's child from that first introduction to the concept "bastard." Every child born out of the union between the mistress and the married man is illegitimate in the eyes of the world. My reluctance to use the term doesn't eradicate the stigma. It is there as if it were tattooed on the child's forehead just like that legendary scarlet A on the mistress/mother.

If the stigma were the only consequence inherited by the children born out of wedlock, it would be difficult enough. However, the children born to the mistress/mother and married man/father aren't like the typical wedlock offspring. Being born out of a triangle is different. It's not that your parents didn't marry; they couldn't. It's not as though your parents didn't both want to rear you together. It's that your father wants to rear you some of the time but not all of the time. How does a mother explain that to a child?

Every mistress/mother who continues her relationship with the married man/father has to explain oddities to their child: Why can't Daddy live with us? Why can't he be here on Christmas or when I need him? How can mistresses who are mothers explain this to their children when they don't even understand it themselves! *Why isn't he with us all the time?* sounds like a living epitaph.

When you have a child, you naturally want that child to have more, better, the best. Someday's children have more— more shame. More confusion. More hardship. Yet they have less too—less of Daddy.

Leah thought that multiple parents meant problems. That is naive. Single parents have problems too. One problem that they can't overcome when they are mistresses is making up for the daddy that is missing. Bringing a child into the world knowing that there will be no father to parent is giving your child only half of what every child has automatically. It doesn't matter how much mother love you can muster. It's not the same as father love. Children know the difference. Someday's children learn that the hard way.

Mistress/mothers who are sure why they want their child and motherhood will learn some very sad lessons. Naming a child after Lara, *Doctor Zhivago*'s heroine, or naming one after me is pure fantasy. Reality sets in soon enough. Having a souvenir baby or a strategy baby has another cruel reality that some mistresses don't realize. Planning a child is not a one-parent right. Mothers who figure, like Gloria, that no one need ever know the paternity, that the real father will be absent and therefore not complicate things, mothers like these have a frightful disregard for their men. What about the feelings of the fathers? Men who know that they have children, living parts of them, and yet will be exiled from contact. Men who know the responsibility of parenting and yet are not consulted in the decision to parent. So what if married men aren't all fair or always fair in their affairs. That doesn't justify a mistress slipping in a child. Two wrongs don't make a right—not for the mistress/mother, not for the married man/father and most importantly not for Someday's child.

If I'm being hard on parents in triangles, it's because I have heard from so many. I hope this discourages another mistress from seizing a foolproof strategy, opting for a souvenir, or single parenthood. The Last Chance Child is the one exception that it is difficult to pass judgment upon. Surely the drawbacks have to be exemplified.

At the start of this chapter I estimated the percentage of Someday's children at 7%. That was a very modest statistic. For, in one of my studies, involving in-depth case histories of approximately 500 mistresses, the rate of illegitimate births was 11%. I set 7% as a sort of national average. How many mistresses and married men have borne children outside the purview of my research? We haven't any way to answer that question.

I didn't start out looking for Someday's child. But once I found her, once I met him, I couldn't wipe them out of my mind. My heart goes out to them all, each and every one with their own individual mysteries and their collective tragedies. I hope that by stimulating your understanding of the mistress/mother and the married man/father, things may be a trifle easier for Someday's child. Because somedays rarely come.

CHAPTER 17

The Unmaking of the American Parent

For fathers, divorce is a killer. Many married men in the middle know that a divorce will cost them their parenthood. Therefore they remain in the middle. Mistresses know full well about this price. Therefore they remain in triangles, martyring themselves for his children and his fatherhood. Mistresshood will be an institution so long as divorce means the unmaking of the American parent. The unmaking of fatherhood is responsible for the making of many mistresses.

The following "tour" will help you see the correlation and the ramifications of the issue. There is a morbid landmark, but a landmark nevertheless, deep in the heart of America. It is a morgue for fathers. You won't find this unusual morgue on any tourist map, but it's there. It's corpses are an elite assemblage of victims of patricide. Each death certificate is ordered by our hallowed judges, verified by our pragmatic lawyers, and signed by triumphant ex-wives. The witnesses are the fatherless children. You say that you've never heard of this place? That's entirely possible. By the time the fathers reach the morgue, their corpses don't bother talking much. Although the ex-wives harbor great glee and purpose, it's not something they brag about. Lawyers go on preparing the next candidate for entry. Judges, well, they render us speechless with their contempt-citation powers.

How could such a landmark exist without incurring some publicity? Children know about it, but they should be seen and not heard. Besides, the morgue, we are told, is a byproduct of the best interests of the children. Some of the children remember to pray for their fathers. Often their prayers dissipate in a stream of brainwashing.

A few courageous souls have written about the victims of

patricide. Their books are awfully depressing, though. No one reviews them. No one buys them. No one reads them. There's no real market for these books. Women aren't too interested in so depressing a subject—especially the women who conspired to populate the morgue.

Talk show hosts as a rule don't like to host this subject. Phil Donahue is an exception to the rule. My husband, Michael, and I appeared on *The Phil Donahue Show* to speak out for the children being deprived of their fathers after divorce. Following that appearance we were deluged with tales of patricide.

The morgue for fathers is a great piece for an investigative reporter. The story behind the morgue is a real chiller. It's full of matricide, patricide; high finance, and low blows. The cast is teeming with Perry Masons, Sherlock Holmeses, and a Marquis de Sade or two. The weaponry is dynamic—victimized children. The story is black comedy, high tragedy, a real thriller. It is what we call the Unmaking of the American Parent.

Although fathers don't talk much in the final states of patricide, we were able to get the story. Ninety-five % of our information came from second wives, who witnessed, or were told of, the patricide firsthand. The rest of the file was filled in by fathers and children of divorce.

Nineteen seventy-nine was designated as the International Year of the Child. We think every year should be a year for the child. Perhaps this legacy in print will save some of the children by saving some of their fathers. It is our contribution to the children of divorce.

For Michael, the last stop before the morgue was John F. Kennedy International Airport. Mourning had already begun. He and his two children were in tears. Soon the children would be airborne for their new life in California. Putting 3000 miles between a father and children was killing Michael's fatherhood. There was little room in their new life for a little of the old life—their father. Geography stood in the way, not to mention the other obstacles which we will see throughout this chapter.

Not to diminish Michael's particular patricide, but there was another man bidding farewell to a daughter in the same tormented, tearful state. What was ahead for him and for Michael?

Those answers are in the future, but for some of the morgue dwellers the answers are at hand. Let's pull out a few of those metal drawers and see what histories these corpses bear.

Here Lies Peter

Peter's crime was falling in love with another woman. He amicably divorced his wife—amicably at first. The marriage has gone loveless. It was as if the conception of their daughter had drained them of all their love. The other woman was branded as a scapegoat. Peter was scarred until his fatherhood was bled dry.

The actual patricide occurred over the state line, but the FBI waived jurisdiction. Peter died a slow death in Georgia. You see, his ex-wife took their three-year-old daughter to Massachusetts for a new life. Peter paid child support for the privilege of not seeing his daughter, and alimony to his ex-wife for not cooperating with the visitation agreement.

Visitation agreements are clauses in the divorce that state when, how often, for how long, and where the father and child will meet. Peter's visitation agreement was meaningless now that the child was in Massachusetts. In his spare time, of which he had plenty, Peter bounced in and out of court trying to salvage his fatherhood. After thirteen months he succeeded in getting a Georgia state court order to go to Massachusetts and pick up his daughter for a two-week visit. Two weeks may not seem like a lot to you, but to Peter it was worth all the money it cost him for both sets of lawyers.

Peter planned the trip with all the efficiency and zeal characteristic of a *Mission Impossible* agent. He asked his father to accompany him on the long drive from Georgia all the way to Massachusetts. The grandfather had not seen his grandchild in so long, of course, that he was delighted. Both arranged time off from work. The Georgia court notified the ex-wife of the order and when the two-week visitation would be. All systems seemed Go on the morning Peter and his dad revved out onto the highway, heading north.

Unfortunately, Peter's paternity was dead on arrival. When he and his dad arrived at the address, no one was there. The doorbell rang unanswered. How could his ex-wife do this to the child? He wanted to report her, but to whom? After all, it was no one's jurisdiction. There are no laws to enforce visitation except in a few states—but not for Peter's crisis.

Peter took his fancy legal court order home, by way of the

morgue for fathers. It was buried along with his paternity. Last thing we heard about the remains of Peter was that he mailed a letter to Massachusetts. Along with his monthly check he politely asked for a snapshot or two of his daughter, now six years old. He hadn't seen her in three years and he wondered how she looked. The problem with a corpse like Peter is that his fatherhood never quite rests in peace.

Next up is Jonathan's story. He was dealt a double blow. First patricide, and if that wasn't enough, thirteen years later a few nails were hammered into his paternal coffin.

Here Lies Jonathan

Jonathan's marriage collapsed in its eighth year. There was another man in his wife's life, but if the marriage hadn't been bad to begin with, it wouldn't have totally fallen to pieces. Jonathan's wife divorced him and soon married the other man, who was in the military. Immediately they moved from their Wyoming address to Texas. They took with them the two daughters and the son; respectively ages three, four, and seven. Jonathan remained in Wyoming, childless.

In time Jonathan remarried, too. Seeing the kids summers went okay for the first two years. Then the letters began. The first informed Jonathan that the children preferred to spend summers in Texas, their new home. The second announced the children's last name was being changed to that of their stepfather. Jonathan hired a lawyer to stop that name change legally. He lost the case. However, the judge did say that Jonathan did not lose the legal responsibility to continue paying child support.

Jonathan felt like a wallet. He told his new wife that he'd be damned if he'd pay support for children he would never see. Children who didn't even want him in their lives. Children who didn't even want his name. Naturally he never saw the children again. His ex told him, "Just stay out of our lives. We don't want you or your money."

Jonathan had a new baby. That helped. He got a dog. That helped too. But those three children were always vaguely in the back of his mind. It wasn't their fault they were brainwashed. That incantation was as constant as his shadow.

Then, out of the clear blue sky, one summer his son appeared at the door. After thirteen years Jonathan didn't even recognize him. He wondered if they had discovered a scientific breakthrough to bleed the kid of his genes too! His son presented Jonathan with a typed accounting of his college expenses. He was billing his father for some $12,000. It seems he lost out on a government grant because his stepfather was not his legal father. And there was something about an insurance policy in the ancient divorce decree that implied college support.

Jonathan discussed it for hours with his wife. No, his son didn't want to come for dinner, but said he would telephone in the morning. Jonathan was a telephone repairperson and didn't really have much money put away. However, he thought maybe he could contribute something. It wasn't his son's fault that things turned out this way.

Promptly at 9:00 A.M. the next day his son called. Jonathan was still perplexed and began thinking out loud. He couldn't believe his ears when his son interrupted with, "My attorney said to have your answer in writing before I leave town today."

Jonathan flipped. "If you need an attorney to deal with your own father the answer is no!"

His son didn't say goodbye. Instead he sued Jonathan. Jonathan lost that case too. But by this time he expected the worst from the judicial system. He decided to appeal the case. Either way he would be ruined financially. What about emotionally? Wasn't losing his family enough? Did he have to be subjected to a second slaughter?

Aside from Jonathan's tragedy, which is obvious, this story illuminates two concepts of importance. The first is brainwashing. There's nothing foreign or clandestine about this activity. There's nothing bizarre about it either. It happens frequently. All it takes is a mother's removing the children from access to the father. Moving often eliminates paternal proximity and influence. Mix a little absence with a host of degrading remarks for a decade or so, and it's done. Children become what they learn. Jonathan's son was a mere pawn used to extract a pound of flesh and a pile of money from his father.

The second concept is father deprivation. It is a term that applies to the child being denied a relationship with his/her father. It's a new term because society doesn't acknowledge the loss much. The courts don't do much either to ensure the father/child relationship. There is no one and nothing in our system to protect a child's right to the noncustodial parent, usually the father. Children have no rights on this score. Only they know and care about father deprivation and they are too young to often do anything about it except fantasize about Daddy.

We have received a barrage of letters about these concepts from fathers and children, too. Peter and Jonathan are only two accounts. We could fill a book. How can this happen? Where is justice for fathers? Where are the rights of children? Don't they have a birthright to the two parents who bore them? Where is justice?

Lincoln's story is about justice. It's about how justice categorizes fathers. It's about how justice venerates motherhood. It's about how lawyers navigate the courts. It's about Lincoln's patricide.

Here Lies Lincoln

Lincoln was a fighter. "If I don't fight for my son, how will he know I care?" he often said. He had wanted to sue for custody at the time of divorce, but his lawyer said he'd never win. His wife had the house. He worked. Right up front his lawyer told Lincoln, "In this game if you are a man you are the screwee. Remember that—*screwee*." In time Lincoln learned that was an understatement.

Lincoln got a good visitation agreement. There was only one problem. Every weekend when he went to pick up his son, his ex-wife wouldn't let the child out the door. Lincoln had legal papers but the police didn't want to get involved. It was a domestic dispute as far as they were concerned. They told him to go back to court.

Lincoln went back to court. The judge reread his ex-wife the visitation agreement. Not one word did the judge utter about a father's or a child's right to each other. Not one word did the judge utter to admonish the ex-wife for interfering with the visitation.

Next week after court. Same thing. Scene. No son.

At this point the ex-wife hired a psychologist, with Lincoln's financial support checks to be sure, to prove the visits were harming the child's emotional welfare. That was a joke, considering there were no visits, only preliminary scenes and attempts. The psychologist ploy backfired, as he recommended counseling for all at $40 an hour. Once again the same judge told the ex-wife that the father was paying alimony and support and therefore entitled to visitation. No one ever mentioned all the legal expenses Lincoln was incurring. The worst of it was after every day in court, his ex-wife exited laughing. And why not—she was never never held accountable for breaking the law! In fact the judicial system was encouraging her to break the law by default, by letting her get away with her illegal behavior. Breaking her son's heart was never mentioned by anyone.

All this fighting and never getting anywhere was taking its toll on Lincoln's fighting spirit. He felt like a criminal after each encounter. On the way out of the court building, Lincoln was stopped by his ex's lawyer.

He told Lincoln that his ex-wife was still in love with him, in a twisted way of course. She was thriving on these battles, living for them, doing it all in the name of motherhood. Her child had to be protected from his "bum" father. The child was a tortured, withdrawn little wreck. The lawyer confessed that for the next eight years, he or some other lawyer could continue to help her get away with this behavior. He knew this to be a fact because his ex-wife was doing it to him!

Lincoln was a fighter. However, after this little talk and a review of the past year and a half, he knew he was beaten. There was nothing he could do for the child. If he surrendered at least the child could have some peace. He knew that his son would hear how his father deserted him. Every weekend he heard that speech and a lot worse. The poor kid must have heard it for breakfast.

Lincoln's lawyer agreed with the decision to give up. He told him once again, "Remember—screwee." We met Lincoln's wife on one of her visits to the morgue to lay flowers on the gravesight of Lincoln's paternity. "Lincoln," she said, "was not lying down and taking it forever, but this was not his time."

When is it going to be the right time for fathers and for their children? Lincoln's profile illuminates another crucial concept, psychological child abuse. In this day and age, physical child abuse is a great cause. Everyone's concerned about it. What about psychological child abuse? No one even mentions it. Psychological child abuse is the torture that children suffer when mothers make scenes to restrict visits with fathers; when mothers make constant remarks about a father's character or intentions with regard to the child. A child's self-image is a combination of both his feelings about mother and father. Destroying his concept of a parent is partially destroying his self-esteem and security. Psychological child abuse is cruel, brutal, and epidemic in America.

The ultimate test of parenthood comes after a divorce. Countless mothers fail the test. They opt for patricide and the courts allow it all in "the best interests of the children." When a woman destroys the father-child rapport and their relationship, she is murdering the fatherhood of her ex-husband. In doing so she is not acting in the best interests of the child. In that way she is betraying her own maternal instincts. As she destroys her own mothering responsibility, that is the unmaking of one American parent, the mother. Her mommist actions destroy the impact of the other parent, the father. That doesn't leave much for the child, now does it?

In fairness to the few mothers who are in the morgue, we must mention parent deprivation by either parent is wrong. Ninety % of custody cases go to mothers. The 10% that go to fathers should not follow the trends of psychological child abuse, parent deprivation, or brainwashing. *Motherhood, fatherhood, parenthood—it's childhood that's most important!*

We hear so much about how fathers fail their children after divorce. Always in monetary terms, like the loudest statistic that "80% of men don't pay child support." The father as wallet syndrome. We hear about the poor divorced woman left alone to single parenthood, jobless, deserted, at the mercy of the singles bar. The implicit theme is that the divorced man is living it up free and fancy.

We have never read one single statistic about the number of patricides. We have never read about the number of innocent victims of brainwashing or psychological child abuse. We have never read about the number of women—they don't deserve the title mother—who are guilty of visitation interference. The number who will not allow their children to spend time with their father. If we knew about these statistics, would it shed some light on why 80% of fathers don't pay support? How many cases go like this:

"It is this mother who actually keeps the children's father away. In spite of the legal document that says he has visiting rights. She becomes like a vicious tigress, coming on slowly with low-tone remarks, every time her ex-husband comes to pick up the children. Quickly she escalates to jeers and insults and screams until a really unpleasant situation takes over. The best outlet for the father is to leave. When he doesn't show on visiting days she beams, telling the kids he doesn't care, calling her lawyer and demanding a restraining order because the visits depress the children. This kind of thing is standard. I've seen it in my own sisters. Little does the mother consider the children who love and need their father, and love and need their mother. The children stay torn, and silent, complying with the parent they have to live with. This is wrong. I've seen these children cry privately because of their deep yearning for their father." *(suburb, New Mexico)*

If we treat men like fathers, perhaps they will feel like fathers and meet their emotional and fiscal responsibilities. We don't wish to disregard the plight of the sincere divorcée who is in need of financial help and sympathy. Not all divorced mothers use their children as weaponry, but a significant number do. When will that injustice be recognized?

History is partly responsible for our disregard of fatherhood and the bad reputation that divorced fathers have. In the last generation divorce was the exception. It was rare. It was standard behavior for the father to fade out of the life of the child. That's what happened in the case of Stuart. He was one of the original corpses in the morgue for fathers.

Here Lies Stuart

Stuart had a mathematical orientation. He taught Mathematics to junior high school students. You know what they say about mathematicians—eggheads, repressed, and quiet. Stuart was a bit of these. His marriage failed and he divorced. It was a real scandal back then. He was the only divorced man on the faculty. No one knew why or how Stuart felt about it all. No one even knew whose idea the divorce had been. It wasn't anything that anyone talked about, certainly not Stuart.

Every Sunday morning, Stuart drove 100 miles to pick up his son and daughter. They had to be back home at 5:30. Therefore they had to stay around their locale. There was no Disneyland around, but Stuart took them to parks and zoos, and movies on rainy days. The children never saw much of how Daddy lived. There wasn't much to see. After the settlement all Stuart could afford was a studio apartment, garage-sale furniture and alimony and support payments. His wife kept the house, its contents, etc. Stuart had wanted continuity for the kids.

Stuart felt more like a social director than a father. He was a "Disneyland Dad" before the term came into vogue. He tried hard on Sunday to ensure a fun time because that was the only time he had with the children. The kids always greeted him with, "Where are we going today?" He didn't like that much, but it wasn't their faults or his. He was a fun dad, but in time that really began to bother him.

As the months went by, Stuart watched the distance grow between him and his son and daughter. They never seemed to talk about much. All the kids seemed to care about was popcorn and cotton candy. One day of the week, on-location escapades, wasn't the way to build a solid relationship. It didn't take a genius to make that calculation. Soon he felt his fatherhood was a joke. He felt like a buffoon, a chauffeur, an unknown in an impossible equation. He made the Sunday trips less.

One Sunday Stuart decided not seeing them anymore was best. After all, they were like strangers thrown together for a few hours to kill time. It was all too absurd, too lonely, too painful. That's not what being a father was. Stuart was a mathematician. He believed in absolutes. Either you were a father or you weren't. What he was wasn't a father.

Stuart tried to erase his fatherhood like he erased the blackboard at school. He never talked about his loss; no one inquired. All those children he taught every day were a constant reminder of his own, but he couldn't escape his fate. He wondered if perhaps he deserved this. If so, he never solved the problem and found out why.

Nowadays we would say that Stuart was wrong to give up on the children. He shouldn't have let the endless driving, the distance, the pressure of finding entertainment, get to him. He should have hung in there. Fathers are forever. No matter what, children need their fathers even under less than perfect circumstances. Back then did anyone ever tell Stuart his fatherhood was important? Back then no one ever said that.

Men like Stuart thought they were doing what was best for the children. They thought they were bowing out to avoid confusion for the kids, or poor examples. For themselves they were doing what was the least painful. It's not easy to be a father one day and forget it all the next. Yet that is exactly the reputation the men have had historically. There are many grown-up children running around feeling they were unloved because their fathers bowed out.

We have a feeling that there is an unknown story for every unknown father. There are few unloved children and many fathers who didn't know how to convey or communicate their love or their loss after the family break-up.

Today there are enough men who won't let go of their fatherhood to make us doubt the old reputation of fathers. Today men are fighting for their fatherhood and for their children. Society is beginning to realize the important role of fathering in parenting. If you doubt that fathers care, ask a second wife or a mistress.

Choosing divorce oftentimes means sacrificing fatherhood. There is no protection against patricide in divorce decrees. There are not enough laws to ensure the rights of children and fathers to each other. Second wives have written to us in droves. All over America fathers are fighting. Their intentions are honorable even though the courts are not. Right now it seems the only right fathers have is to pay. The only ones who have fewer rights are the children of divorce. They have fewer rights, less power, and less of fathers.

In this depressing tale there is one redeeming aspect. Sometimes the redemption takes a lifetime. Sometimes it only takes a decade or two. Raymond's story can explain this better than I.

Raymond's Easter Marathon

Raymond is fifteen years old now. He's celebrating Easter every day of the week. That's the way he explains it. All those years in Bible school have finally hit home, in an unusual new interpretation. You see, Raymond has had a hand in raising his father up from the dead. Like the Resurrection. Now they are finally together and it is heaven on earth.

Raymond's whole story is a miracle of sorts. It's not easy to get all the background because Raymond doesn't recall all that much. We therefore had to fill in the blanks by talking to Ray's dad.

Raymond was five years old at the time of the separation. His mother went to church every morning to pray. Somehow her Christian spirit never encompassed Ray's dad. Everything was his fault. The marital problems, the fights, the separation—everything. He "deserted" them and didn't deserve to see the child. Ray's father did move out of the house and file for divorce. But he never deserted them. He paid all the bills until the court stipulated a settlement. He came around three times a week to see their son. That was hardly the behavior of a deserter. He simply couldn't live with his wife anymore. That cost him his fatherhood.

Ray's father got tired of playing judicial roulette. This court, that court, meaningless court orders, the constant drain. By the time his paternity arrived on the doorstep of the morgue, it was a kind of relief. This morgue was better than the hell his ex-wife was satanically creating. Sometimes he really thought she was the devil reincarnate. Ray's fatherhood was laid to rest along with all the transcripts of the judicial travesty that put him there.

Ray's father eventually found another lady and remarried. He moved to another town. He was never allowed to see his son. Then, almost a decade later, he came home from work one summer day and found a houseguest. His long-lost son. Ray was a beautiful adolescent, and rebelling as adolescents do. Thank God for adolescent rebellion! Who would ever think that someone would be grateful for that! Ray's father was, because that is what brought his son home at last.

Ray had lots of unpleasant questions. "Why did you desert us?" "Where were you when I needed you?" The questions were charged with an agony and an anger that had been brewing a lifetime for Ray. He confessed to his father, "I don't know why but I love you. I don't understand, but I had to come here and see why..." Tears ended the sentence.

Ray's dad knew that a foundation of love had been laid in those first few years when he had nurtured his son, changed diapers, worn upchuck casually and all that. The best way he could explain things was just to put Ray to bed with a bit of reading—all the court transcripts.

After that lesson in judicial procedure, Ray moved in permanently. He called his mom, called her a sick liar, and hung up. That was the beginning of a beautiful relationship. The miracle of Easter had visited Ray and his father in a resurrection of their bond.

This tale is a harbinger for the ex-wives who feel patricide is a fait accompli. It is a ray of hope for fathers who feel that they have lost their children forever. The next tale is music to the ear if you are a victim of patricide.

Tiffany's Symphony

Tiffany was an unusual child. She was gifted musically. By the time she reached sixth grade, her talent was far beyond her years. She was playing the flute, the clarinet, and toying with the saxophone in addition to her main instrument, the piano.

She was a continual source of amazement to her piano teacher. She was an occasional source of joy to her father because he was only allowed to see Tiffany on Sunday. No source of amazement musically because he was never permitted to hear her play.

It sounds idiotic but Tiffany's mother and stepfather felt that they raised the child, they bought and paid for the instruments and lessons and, therefore, the music was for their house, period. Tiffany never understood this. Music was so much a part of her identity. It was natural to share it with everyone. Why was it right to share her talent with audiences, students, and not her own father? That was the way it was in her household. Her mother told her, "With the measly amount your father sends me, he's lucky I let you spend Sunday with him!" Tiffany felt lucky, too. She loved her father and felt awful on the Sundays when her stepfather and mother made plans that canceled out her visits with her father.

In the seventh grade, Tiffany really started to become troublesome. She took to smoking cigarettes, pot, and hanging out on street corners. Her piano teacher, also divorced, sensed the problem from dribs and drabs he was privy to from Tiffany and the household. It wasn't really his place to butt in, but Tiffany's musical potential was at stake. Her only problem should be not devoting enough time to her practicing. When he heard that her lessons were being canceled until she shaped up, he knew he had to speak his mind. Tiffany's mother and stepfather were basically good people. He couldn't believe that rigid rule about no music for Tiffany's father. He called Tiffany's mother and plainly told her that the child needed more freedom at this point. He suggested that she be allowed to spend more time with her father and share her musical ability with him. Tiffany's mother was rather terse and obviously not interested in his insight or his advice.

When September rolled around, Tiffany wasn't in school. It seemed she had moved in with her father. It was a blow to her mother. The last thing Tiffany told her stepfather was to take the instruments and . . . you know the rest. It was Tiffany's time to play a symphony with her father.

Those stories are true. Fatherhood has a certain resilience. Any ex-wife who thinks that she can drum a parental birthright entirely out of a child is naive. In some cases brainwashing works, but it can wear off with the onset of curiosity or adolescence. In some cases it backfires. Each child is different. The attraction to a parent, however, is a constant that runs through us all.

The caretaker of the morgue for fathers is a Greek gentleman. That seems apropos given the preoccupation of the ancient Greeks with patricide and all. He's had enough of his job and wants to retire. We certainly want to help close down this morgue for fathers. We can't do it alone. We need the help of men, second wives, mistresses, and ex-wives. We need the help of women, many of whom misunderstand the subject and think it is antimotherhood or antifeminist. Of course, it is neither. Equality in parenting is better for everyone in the family; the mother, the father, and most important the child.

Right now there are no real rights for fathers. There are no rights for children who want to see their fathers and are told, no. However, the momentum of the issue is growing. Society's consciousness is slowly grasping the importance of fathering. There are more and more cases on the court calendar of fathers who are determined to fight for their children. As more and more fathers fight for their children, the old image of men as nonparents is dissolving. There are countless men who are martyrs to this cause. They have contributed thousands of dollars in court fees, and in the end their own paternity. What can you contribute?

This chapter is a call to arms to those mistresses who know how a man's fear of patricide continues their mistresshood. If you believe that fear of patricide is keeping your married man in an unhappy marriage, there are things you can do. Take a few minutes out of your day and write a letter to your Congressperson about fathers' and children's rights; asking for laws to enforce visitation rights throughout the nation. Advocate joint custody legislation. Spend one night a week working for the Equal Rights Amendment, which will ensure equality for parents. Take every opportunity to explain the ERA to people who don't understand it. Try and talk to local politicians and national leaders and make sure they know about your concerns. If you love your married man and his paternal sensitivity, fight to save it. That is an act of love which will not only benefit him, but the benefits will ripple like a stone tossed into a stream over a sea of children and fathers.

I would have given anything if I could have changed that scene I witnessed at the airport. All I could do was handle the ticketing. My husband was too choked up to talk to the ticket agent, trying to think of a way to say goodbye to the children. There was nothing for me to say as we drove home and I watched him solemnly parade all their toys into the basement. All I could do was drive to the morgue for fathers and deliver his paternity along with a few mementos and the lyrics to a song that he wrote. I've included his musical tribute.

California Split

The memory of my son
Will be forever young
'Cause it's been so long since he's been here;
He's growing with his sister
God knows how I miss her
Coast to coast I'll wonder all these years
    Must this California split
    Be the end of it
    Can't I be a father for forever.

Because a man chooses
To leave, he loses
A part of him he cannot forget
But if a man stays
He pays with a lifetime wasted
For some ex-wives compassion's not in yet.
    and the
Memory of my son
Will be forever young
'Cause it's been so long since he's been here;
He's growing with his sister
God knows how I miss her

Coast to coast I'll wonder all these years
Must this California split
Be the end of it
Can't I be a father for forever.

Time and time again
I've heard from other men
They fought for years and now they fight the tears;
Now I'm on my own
And I fill this childless home
With this song in hopes that someone hears...
    that the
Memory of my son
Will be forever young
'Cause it's been so long since he's been here
He's growing with his sister
God knows how I miss her
Coast to coast I'll wonder all these years...
    Must this California split
Be the end of it
Can't I be a father for forever.

People often tell us to have a child of our own. We hear that from friends, lawyers, judges, etc. Perhaps that will help my husband, but that proposal won't help the children he *has* much! For now, we bought a dog, who's become our family. We bought a piano to drown out the silence of a childless house. I took to gardening to ensure perennial flowers for Michael's paternal gravesite at the morgue.

Michael couldn't save his paternity or save his own children. Now he devotes as much time as he can to saving other children and other fathers. Late at night he plays the piano, and I hear him playing a song that is helping him. I'll offer it here for a mistress or a second wife to keep and show her man if he's suffering from patricide or the paranoia of it. Save it. Perhaps it will be of some consolation. Perhaps it will raise some consciousness. Perhaps it will unmake a mistress or make a real parent. Perhaps it will convince some ex-wife to allow her child a visit with his/her father. Perhaps it will convince some "fatherless" child that his/her father does indeed love him or her.

The Children's Waltz

When evening comes
And you close your eyes,
I pray that you know
How your Daddy tries
Every day to be part of your life again

But when

Mommy took you
From your Daddy's touch
She thought of herself
Just a little too much
Dropped out of sight, out of state, out of line
Of what's best for you
Kids need Daddy too

Become a father for all time
Stand up and fight for yours and mine
Father's life, Father's love, Father's rights.

EPILOGUE

From Mistress to Second-Wife: Marriage, Once Removed

Sometimes the mistress and the married man do extricate themselves from their respective dilemmas and marry. The mistress becomes the second wife. The affair becomes a marriage—once removed from the triangle. This union is collectively hexed, and uniformly jinxed, and rarely publicized. My marriage to my former married man fits that description except for the publicity element.

I am eternally quizzed about my marriage, once removed. I'll probably write about being a second wife with a scarlet past. Before I do, let's compare notes. If you married your married man how are you doing? Please answer the following questions and let's see what really happens in a marriage, once removed!

1. Do mistresses who become second wives have it tougher than ordinary second wives?
2. Does it affect your stepparenting?
3. Do you think the age of stepchildren figures in your relationship with them as far as your past history goes?
4. Does a mistress history ensure permanent hostility in your relationship with his first wife?
5. Does the former triangle ensure permanent conflict between your husband and his ex-wife, and if so in what way?
6. Does the tug-of-war tendency between you and his ex-wife still create more rivalry over say, finances?
7. If your husband is the noncustodial parent to the children from his former marriage has he been encouraged to continue seeing them by you? By his ex-wife?
8. Does the past have a way of reemerging in your arguments or in your grudges or in his?

9. Has the former triangle caused stilted relationships with your new in-laws?

10. Do you think mistresses who become second wives have better marriages, or marriages more prone to divorce because of additional troubles?

Can the mistress and the married man live together happily ever after? Or will the legacies of any triangle sour their future? Starting out as a mistress and finishing as his wife is dramatic ground, unique, and certainly never dull. When the mistress and married man cross the threshold it is a new kind of marriage. It's not exactly the second time around; it's more of a marriage, once removed, from a triangle. What does all that mean to you—once a mistress and now his wife?

Mistresses Anonymous Questionnaire

This questionnaire is designed to collect the real facts about women who are involved with married men. The myths will continue so long as mistresses are afraid to tell the truth about themselves. Please answer these questions and feel free to add anything you desire. I guarantee that you will remain anonymous, no signature is necessary. And I guarantee you will be helping women everywhere.
Thank you.

1. Where do you live?
2. How would you characterize your location? small town, big city, etc.
3. How old are you?
4. Are you single, married, separated, divorced, widowed?
5. What religion, if any, are you? If you practice one, how?
6. What is your occupation, if any?
7. Do you consider yourself liberated? In what way?
8. Do you consider yourself a mistress?
9. How old is your married man?
10. What is his occupation?
11. How did you meet him? (at work, socially, or whatever)

12. Was the first date your idea or his? _____
13. Was he the first married man you dated? _____
14. Why did you chose to date a married man? _____
15. Did you know he was married first off? _____
16. How long have you been seeing him? Or how long did the relationship last? _____
17. If he didn't tell you right from the start he was married, when did you find out? And how? _____
18. How did his being married make you feel? _____
19. How often did you meet? _____
20. In what kinds of places? _____
21. What did your meetings consist of? _____
22. Could you see him whenever you wanted? _____
23. When did sex enter into the relationship? From the start? If not, when? _____
24. How important was the sexual aspect? _____
25. Was your sex life with him rewarding? More rewarding than with other lovers before him? _____
26. If he was still sleeping with his wife, did his infidelity with her inhibit you? How? _____
27. Was he still having relations with his wife? _____
28. Did you have sexual relations each time you met? _____
29. Describe if you wish any aspect of your sex life that

MISTRESSES ANONYMOUS QUESTIONNAIRE

you think would shed light on this subject.

30. Did he complain that his sex life with his wife was unsatisfying?

31. Are you or were you in love with your married man? How do you know?

32. What do think is the main reason for your relationship? (sex, friendship, business or any other)

33. Did you ever ask him to get a divorce?

34. Or did he promise divorce?

35. After how long in the course of the relationship?

36. If you asked him to divorce, how did he respond?

37. Did divorce become an ongoing question, struggle, argument? (which or all)

38. Do you think his wife knew about your affair? If so, how; what makes you think she knew?

39. Did you ever have contact with his wife? How—a coincidence, business, a confrontation?

40. If his wife found out, did it end the affair? Did it change the affair and how?

41. Did your married man give you any money? For what? (rent, expenses, etc.)

42. Did you want him to give

you money or gifts?
43. Did you refuse to take money or gifts? Why?
44. Did he have children? How many?
45. Did you meet his children? How?
46. How do you feel about his children?
47. Would you marry your married man if he divorced?
48. Why do you think your married man hasn't divorced?
49. Do you think he will divorce? What makes you think so?
50. Did you date other men during your relationship?
51. Did you have sexual relations with other men?
52. How did you feel about this?
53. How did he feel about your dating or having relations with other men?
54. Whom did you tell about this affair?
55. Did you tell your mother?
56. Did you make new friends because of him?
57. Did you lose friends because of him?
58. How did he change your life? (your job or friendships, social life, emotional state, etc.)
59. Have you ended the relationship or has he? Why and How?
60. Is he or was he the first married man with whom

MISTRESSES ANONYMOUS QUESTIONNAIRE

you became involved?   _____

61. Are you glad you met him?   _____
62. Are you sorry you met him?   _____
63. Would you ever date a married man again?   _____
64. What did you like about being a mistress?   _____
65. What didn't you like about being a mistress?   _____

Thank you for answering this questionnaire. If you wish to add any comments, I would be most appreciative and interested.

Since the questionnaire is anonymous, may I quote you if the opportunity arises?

Let me conclude with my gratitude and the gratitude of all women who will at last be able to know the real story of the mistress and the married man—not the mythical one.

Return this questionnaire to

Melissa Sands
% Berkley Publishing Co.
200 Madison Avenue
New York, New York 10016

Helpful... Candid... Fascinating... Important... Shocking... Timely...

...And Bestselling!

___ **THE AMERICANS**   04681-8—$2.95
Alistair Cooke

___ **BRANDO FOR BREAKFAST**   04698-2—$2.75
Anna Kashfi Brando and E.P. Stein

___ **FAT IS A FEMINIST ISSUE**   05009-2—$2.75
Susie Orbach

___ **THE MS. GUIDE TO A WOMAN'S HEALTH**   04796-2—$3.95
Cynthia W. Cooke, M.D., and Susan Dworkin

___ **MOMMIE DEAREST**   04444-0—$2.75
Christina Crawford

___ **NURSE**   04685-0—$2.75
Peggy Anderson

___ **THE POSSIBLE DREAM**   04382-7—$2.50
Charles Paul Conn

___ **A TIME FOR ACTION**   04840-3—$2.75
William E. Simon

___ **A TIME FOR TRUTH**   05025-4—$2.95
William E. Simon

___ **WE ARE THE EARTHQUAKE GENERATION**   04991-4—$2.75
Jeffrey Goodman

___ **ORDEAL**   04749-0—$2.95
Linda Lovelace with Mike McGrady

___ **THE WINNER'S CIRCLE**   04500-5—$2.50
Charles Paul Conn

Berkley Book Mailing Service
P.O. Box 690
Rockville Centre, NY 11570

Please send me the above titles. I am enclosing $_____
(Please add 75¢ per copy to cover postage and handling). Send check or money order—no cash or C.O.D.'s. Allow six weeks for delivery.

NAME _____

ADDRESS _____

CITY _____ STATE/ZIP _____

More Bestsellers from Berkley
The books you've been hearing about and want to read

__	**THE AMERICANS** Alistair Cooke	04681-8—$2.95
__	**THE THIRD TIME AROUND** George Burns	04732-6—$2.75
__	**DUNE** Frank Herbert	04687-7—$2.75
__	**FAT IS A FEMINIST ISSUE** Susie Orbach	05009-2—$2.75
__	**THE LAST CONVERTIBLE** Anton Myrer	04034-8—$2.50
__	**LEAH'S JOURNEY** Gloria Goldreich	04690-7—$2.75
__	**THE NORTHERN GIRL** Elizabeth A. Lynn	04725-3—$2.25
__	**MAYDAY** Thomas H. Block	04729-6—$2.95
__	**WIZARD** John Varley	04828-4—$2.50
__	**THE SECOND DEADLY SIN** Lawrence Sanders	04806-3—$2.95
__	**THE SUNSET WARRIOR** Eric Van Lustbader	04452-1—$2.50
__	**WE ARE THE EARTHQUAKE GENERATION** Jeffrey Goodman	04991-4—$2.75

Available at your local bookstore or return this form to:

Berkley Book Mailing Service
P.O. Box 690
Rockville Centre, NY 11570

Please send me the above titles. I am enclosing $_____
(Please add 75¢ per copy to cover postage and handling). Send check or money order—no cash or C.O.D.'s. Allow six weeks for delivery.

NAME_____
ADDRESS_____
CITY_____ STATE/ZIP_____ 85A